ROYAL FAMILY
YEARBOOK
Volume III

First published in Great Britain 1984 by Colour Library Books Ltd.
© 1984 Illustrations and text: Colour Library Books Ltd.,
    Guildford, Surrey, England.
Display and text filmsetting by Acesetters Ltd.,
    Richmond, Surrey, England.
Colour separations by Llovet, S.A., Barcelona, Spain.
Printed and bound in Barcelona, Spain by Rieusset and Gráficas Estella.
ISBN 0 86283 250 0

ROYAL FAMILY
YEARBOOK
Volume III

FOREWORD BY
THE EARL OF LICHFIELD

TEXT BY
TREVOR HALL

FEATURING THE PHOTOGRAPHY OF
DAVID LEVENSON

PRODUCED BY
TED SMART & DAVID GIBBON

COLOUR LIBRARY BOOKS

FOREWORD

Perhaps, as you read this latest volume of THE ROYAL FAMILY YEAR BOOK, you will be struck, as I was, by a remark made by Princess Michael when reminded that at one public engagement she was on her feet for one and a half hours. "Well," she replied, almost dismissively, "there are worse things." She did not elaborate, but you will recognise the truth of her comment from the many examples mentioned here of occupational hazards suffered by the Royal Family during the past twelve months.

The criticisms and potential dangers of royal visits to Ulster and Jordan, and the furores raised by Prince Charles' deprecation of modern architecture or by Prince Philip's spirited defence of hunting, all spring most readily to mind as hot, public issues. Then the more private matters: premature speculation about a new baby for the Princess of Wales, unedifying stories about Prince Andrew or his female acquaintances, rumours about Princess Anne's marriage, a distinct hostility between Prince Edward and the Press and the constant battle to keep private royal holidays private. At best unpleasant, at worst ugly, these aspects of life make standing for one and a half hours a positive royal delight.

It is reassuring to see that, now and again, a more constructive light can be shed on the Royal Family's activities. Such is the appeal of a book like this. Its wide-ranging and well-produced photography illustrates not only the enormous scope of royal duties and private pursuits, but also the agreeable, generously-committed manner in which they are undertaken. You will find the occasional contrasts – a pensive Queen, a serious Princess of Wales, a tight-lipped Captain Phillips – but these only serve to heighten the overall impression of a family of individuals determined to bring pleasure and enjoyment to the people they meet, even on the days – sometimes weeks – when the fierce light of publicity makes the going really tough. The book's much expanded text will also help the reader to put the crises and criticisms, which are all too often over-dramatised, into proper perspective.

So I am delighted to welcome the appearance of the third volume of the Year Book. Such a complete record in words and pictures of yet another busy and varied royal year is more than just another book. It is an authoritative, serviceable reminder to us all of what we owe to a family who, in spite of the drawbacks of their position, continue to perform their sometimes unenviable work with a dedication for which they have long since become renowned.

RT. HON. THE EARL OF LICHFIELD F.I.I.P., F.R.P.S.

Like her grandfather King George V, the Queen has a retentive memory which lends a special sense of significance to royal anniversaries. So it was not surprising that, in a year which had already been marked by tributes to her on the thirtieth anniversary of her Coronation, the highlight of her State Visit to Kenya was a sentimental journey to the Aberdare game reserve, a small dot on the African map, where she became Queen in 1952. 'I still remember with gratitude the sympathy, support and encouragement which the people of Kenya gave me as I embarked so suddenly upon my new responsibilities,' she had told her host, President Arap Moi, at a State banquet on the first day of her tour in mid-November.

The reality of renewed acquaintance was less rewarding. Experience teaches us all that to return to the scene of affectionate or poignant memories is to invite disillusion. Like Thika, which the Queen also visited, and where a huge industrial complex has replaced the celebrated flame trees, Treetops Hotel, the snug, three-bedroomed tree-house affording the most unusual location for a Princess to become Queen, was burnt to the ground by Mau Mau terrorists in 1954, and has been replaced by a 38-room luxury tourist hotel on stilts. A plaque recalls the Queen's last, fateful visit, but she ignored it. Where there was once dense forest and a deep watering hole, there is now only a muddy pool on a large, treeless plot. The Duke's visible concern for the vanished forest was hardly placated by the information that the trees had been killed off by elephants stripping their foliage and bark, while the Queen seemed disappointed and nonplussed: 'So this is all that is left. I hardly recognise the place. Was this where we came before?' On the night she became Queen, she saw forty-seven elephants come to the water hole. Now there was none, though piles of elephant dung on the ground indicated that she may have arrived at the wrong time of day. However, the royal party saw plenty of warthogs, baboons, gazelles and water-buck, and spent a few minutes on the viewing platform of the hotel to film them. There was a brief alarm as, during her walk round the compound, a couple of buffalo came within twenty yards, but the Queen's safari guide, a 68-year-old Englishman with twenty years' experience in the bush, and a 400-calibre rifle to match, headed them off by the simple expedient of throwing stones at them. He admitted later that he was glad he didn't have to use his rifle: 'When I saw the buffalo standing so close to the Queen, I was really worried.'

The previous evening, the Queen had completed the more public part of her State Visit – her first to Kenya, though she had dropped by in 1972 on the way back from a tour of the Far East – with a journey to Sagana Lodge where she had first learned of her father's death. 'Thoughtful rather than sad,' was how one official described the Queen's reaction. The building, a wedding present from the people of Kenya, was given back by the Queen when Prince Philip came to Nairobi to give the country its independence in 1963. It is now the President's official country lodge, but on the day of the Queen's visit, the Royal Standard flew above it again, and the house was full of flowers. The Queen met the gardener who had helped her plant two trees when she came here as Princess, and she planted another one to mark this, her brief return.

High ceremonial had marked the Queen and Prince Philip's arrival in Kenya, an event which proved something of a surprise for the citizens of Nairobi, who had been kept in ignorance of the impending visit until the last moment. No bunting therefore decorated the streets through which the royal party drove on the twelve-mile journey from the airport to the city centre, yet the warmth of the welcome given by the half million strong crowds – 'stupendous' was the description given by one Buckingham Palace official – left the Queen in no doubt as to their feelings for her as she fulfilled her 31-year promise to 'come back one day.' Incessant cheering, the ululations of tribal dancers festooned in sea-shells, beads, bangles and strings of bottle-tops, and the pounding of snake-skin Mukanda drums by raffia-skirted Chuka tribesmen in their huge, feathered headdresses – all marked the brilliant beginning of a popular visit. 'She will not feel a stranger here,' commented Kenya's Foreign Minister Mwamunga, reflecting on the troubled history of relationships between Britain and Kenya from the the days of Mau Mau to the more recent suspicion that Britain was behind an attempted coup against President Moi in 1982. His sentiment was echoed by the ordinary people, as they yelled their approval of their visitors: children referred to her in awed tones as The Great Lady; their elders preferred the more blunt, but no less sincere description of 'Damn fine Queen.'

For the first time since 1968, when she was in the middle of a State Visit to Brazil, the Queen led the Commonwealth's annual Remembrance ceremonies in a foreign country. On the second day of her Kenyan tour she and Prince Philip laid their wreath at Nairobi's Commonwealth cemetery, where lie almost two thousand casualties of the '2,000-mile war' which drove the Axis powers from East Africa in 1942. The blistering heat compared strikingly with the dull, cool autumn climate back in Whitehall two days later, when Prince Charles was leading Britain's own tribute to the fallen.

It is tempting to imagine that State visits carry only superficial benefits. So perhaps the people of Bangladesh – the next country on the royal itinerary – could not believe their luck when, on the very day of the Queen's arrival, the military ruler, Lt-General Ershad announced a relaxation of the martial law which, imposed in 1975, he had inherited in a bloodless coup in March 1982. 'I hereby permit open politics from this moment,' he declared, less than two hours before the Queen landed, and he promised elections the following May to pave the way 'for a smooth transition to democracy.' The manoeuvre was widely seen as a ploy to head off opposition protesters who, fearing that the royal visit would lend undeserved respectability to the military ruler, were expected to stage demonstrations during the Queen's stay. The régime certainly went out of its way to present itself in a good light: a million pounds was said to have been spent renovating the State guest house, while roads were spruced up, public buildings whitewashed, and their gardens almost lit up by the vibrant colour of newly planted borders. Huge, vividly-coloured portraits of the Queen went up everywhere in the capital Dhaka, where several hundred wildly enthusiastic people saw her and Prince Philip welcomed by President Chowdhury. Up country in the village of Sreepur, which the Queen visited on her final day, the wattle walls of the school building were replaced by brick, a fish farm was stocked with carp, mud terrain was beaten flat, the bases of trees painted white, and young children taught to chant the words 'Long live the Queen.' Such are the inevitable preliminaries of a royal visit.

It was the Queen's first to Bangladesh since 1961, when it was still part of Pakistan. Independence in 1971 had been a bloody affair, and the three million who died in the cause were remembered on the second day of the royal stay as the Queen placed a wreath of marigolds and roses at the Savar War Memorial, a 150-foot-high brick pyramid set amid beautifully landscaped gardens. There were meetings both with General Ershad – a low-key occasion designed to prevent the Queen being seen to endorse the régime – and with President Chowdhury, who greeted his visitor beneath a rich crimson canopy embroidered with a huge lotus, the national flower of Bangladesh. But, as always, it was the crowds who set the visit alight with noise and colour. The Queen and Prince Philip toured the outskirts of Dhaka amid the deafening cheers of brightly dressed school children, hordes of villagers, women in colourful saris. Fifty thousand rickshaw cycles jammed the streets; everything stopped for the royal progress. Buses and lorries were overloaded with curious passengers, and even local fishermen left their day's work on the Ganges River to line the Queen's route.

'All the problems known to cities throughout the world have been magnified here in Dhaka,' said the Queen at a civic reception. Echoing Prince Philip's words during his previous month's visit to Bangkok – 'Unless people decide voluntarily not to have so many children, we're merely going to build up greater and greater problems,' he had said – the Queen went on, 'Progress in tackling these problems can only be made when people recognise the need to balance the number of their children with the means likely to be available to provide them with a worthwhile life.' She had just visited a child nutritional centre in the capital, and it was back to reality again. The one hundred million population of Bangladesh is increasing by almost three per cent yearly – a fact which would have scandalised Prince Philip, who was safely out of controversy's way inspecting tea plantations two hundred miles distant. The problem even of feeding the child population is not helped by what seems to be the custom by which parents abandon children to their fate in the city's gutters, an abuse particularly directed toward female progeny who are traditionally a burden rather than a source of wealth and status to their elders. The nutritional centre, established by the Save the Children Fund in 1975, acts as a rescue and rehabilitation service, and the Queen saw at first hand the swarm of children who, despite their swollen bellies and painfully thin limbs, might just count themselves lucky. Among them was a baby of ten weeks, a 3lb bundle of skin and bone, undergoing intensive feeding after being found half dead in the streets, and battling against tuberculosis as well as malnutrition. There, too, was a two-year-old boy, looking less than half his age, who reached out to the Queen and tried to take from her the single marigold she had received on her arrival. The Queen smiled her smile of indulgence, even of assurance and sympathy, asked to be kept in-formed of his progress, and said she would ask Princess Anne to visit the centre. The child survived, and through the Save the Children Fund, Princess Anne was able the following February to show the Queen an album of photographs proving it. Yet, for the moment, it was in the perverse nature of things that she still walked away one of the richest women in the world, forced by accepted priorities to leave the child to the hazardous fate typical of the vast majority of his compatriots.

The grim misfortunes of the poor presented themselves, though somewhat less graphically, to the Queen on her subsequent nine-day tour of India. Early on, she announced the award of the Order of Merit to Mother Theresa, who heads over two hundred Missions of Charity – the first was founded in 1949 – for the destitute all over the world. Towards the end of the tour, in a simple ceremony amid the grandeur of New Delhi's Presidential Palace, the 73-year-old Roman Catholic nun, one of five new appointees during the year, received the award – a red cross mounted on a turquoise and crimson ribbon – from the Queen, who told her, 'This is for the work you are doing.' Mother Theresa, in her familiar garb of white cotton sari and grey, darned cardigan – 'I hope the Queen doesn't mind but my habit is not very clean' – was her usual modest self. 'A great gift,' she called it. 'A beautiful gesture from a lovely lady, and a recognition of the problem of the poor. It makes the presence of the poor very real; people become more aware of them and it creates concern.' And she chatted awhile with the Queen, asking after Prince Charles, whom she had met in Calcutta in 1980, and assuring her she prayed every day for Prince William.

8

The prospect of the Queen's first visit to India in twenty-three years thrilled her hosts. Even a stridently left-wing Indian newspaper, *Blitz*, succumbed in anticipation of royal charm. 'Whatever she may be,' its editorial began, almost grudgingly, 'Queen Elizabeth II is undoubtedly the most popular monarch of our time. All we can say is, Hail the Queen and Prince Philip.' But their arrival at New Delhi on 17th November was an uncertain business. Security considerations, regrettably all too dominating a feature of royal visits these days, made it impracticable for details of the Queen's route from airport to city to be announced until the last moment, when welcoming arches of marigold and jasmine sprang up like mushrooms after rain, and Union Jacks were intermingled with the Indian tricolor at every crossroads. A march by tens of thousands of Hindu fundamentalists, part of a pilgrimage organised by the World Hindu Council, forced the Queen to postpone her own brief pilgrimage to Mahatma Gandhi's cremation altar. The astrologers made it no easier. By the same oracular advice which insisted that the grant of Indian independence in 1947 should take place in the middle of the night, the Queen's plane, due to touch down at noon precisely, was warned off for five minutes for fear of divine retribution.

Twenty thousand soldiers and police lined the ten-mile route which the royal visitors took in a bullet-proof Mercedes – another last-minute security measure – to the President's residence where, in the Dwarka Suite, the couple would be based for most of their stay. Especially for the occasion, the suite had been freshly redecorated in the style of the Raj, with valuable old furniture brought out of store, and fairy lights picking out the silhouette of the Palace at night. Tall Lancers in blue and gold turbans and long scarlet coats lined the corridors, while bearers in pristine white liveries emulated the splendour which had greeted King George V during his Durbar visit of 1911.

Though by no means as sumptuous and prolonged as her 1961 visit, the Queen's tour provided a well-blended menu of delights and interest. There was the inevitable State banquet, at which the Queen spoke of 'the shared history, and collective and personal ties embracing every sphere of human activity' upon which Anglo-Indian associations were based, and praised India's success in agriculture and in her space programme. She visited Gandhi's memorial, on ground so sacred that her shoes were removed (by a male assistant) and replaced by British Airways in-flight slippers, while Prince Philip was content to walk around in his socks. She toured St Thomas's – 'a progressive school for girls' according to its brochure – where she watched its pupils perform a play called *The Awakening of Indian Womanhood*, and then walked inside a palanquin, a sort of floorless sedan chair, carried by eight girls dressed as male bearers. At Hyderabad, she visited the ancient Golconda Tombs, minaretted memorials set in fragrant flower gardens dotted with banyan trees, while female descendants of the Nizam of Hyderabad danced before her, dressed in wedding saris of spun gold and silver thread, and with twists of pearls woven through their hair. And she visited the National Defence Academy at Pune – the legendary Poona of Empire days – where she watched a review and march-past of 1,500 cadets in a temperature of 100°F, before taking lunch and iced water in the Academy's marbled halls. 'It's a place I've always wanted to see,' she said, reflecting the reverence customarily accorded this one-time heart of the British colonial army, more British in its day, it was reckoned, than Aldershot. In a lesser way the tour was also notable for the thirty computers which the Queen gave to her hosts for use in schools and universities; for the discovery of the theft of jewellery and traveller's cheques suffered by a member of her entourage; for the tactful departure from the country, prior to the Queen's arrival, of Miss Koo Stark, who was anxious to avoid embarrassing the Queen by her presence; for the drama when the British High Commissioner was taken ill with severe stomach pains at the beginning of an official banquet; and for the letter written to the Queen, pleading the cause of 'a wretched and despised minority' – written by a spokesman for India's eunuchs. Some tours, it seems, have everything.

In mid-tour, the Queen and Prince Philip celebrated their 36th wedding anniversary – an occasion, said one British editorial, for congratulation, tinged with regret that, with Britain's divorce rate recently charted as the highest in Europe, so many people were failing to follow the royal example. On the previous day, the Queen had been presented with portraits of herself and her husband, as a gift from a nationalised firm she was visiting in Hyderabad. Perversely, the Duke wasn't with her: he was three hundred miles away, riding an elephant through a game reserve in the Gondia Forest, in search of mating tigers. It was all part of a ten-year-old project run by World Wildlife Fund India and which, having effectively rescued the country's tiger population from imminent extinction, the Duke described later as 'probably the most successful major conservation programme with which the Fund has ever been associated.' At the end of his brief safari – an episode contrasting starkly with the controversial tiger shoot in which he and the Queen were involved during their previous visit to India – he rejoined his wife for a wedding anniversary dinner at the Indian President's summer palace at Hyderabad – a colonial bungalow-style building cluttered with priceless antiques, and set in eighty-five acres of peaceful gardens.

The royal visit to India was timed to coincide with the Commonwealth Conference – the biennial meeting between Commonwealth heads of government – at which the Queen makes it her business to be, as it were, in attendance. She takes no political role in the formal proceedings by which the affairs of the conference are conducted, but it is a measure of the seriousness with which she takes her position as Head of the Commonwealth that she insists on being there when it happens. She is said to have helped in the past to reconcile argumentative delegates, to have cooled tempers – even, in 1979, to have helped build informal bridges between black leaders over the boiling question of Rhodesian independence. At New Delhi she was, according to a member of her staff, 'determined that the conference will work, and well aware of the difficulties: this is going to be a tough one for her.' Forty-two audiences filled her engagement book throughout the days of the conference, a total of fourteen hours spent meeting every one of the Commonwealth leaders, and discussing problems with the understanding, insight and tact which led her spokesman to describe her performance as 'one of the greatest feats of mental gymnastics.'

As on many previous occasions of this sort, the Queen had to tread gingerly in the political minefield which the meeting of heads of so many utterly disparate countries inevitably establishes. Mrs Thatcher and Mrs Gandhi were said to have clashed fearsomely over what the Indian Prime Minister saw as an Anglo-American venture into a new phase of the nuclear arms race; there was potential criticism of Britain's quiet reaction to the effective partition of Cyprus when the island's Turkish community declared UDI, and of her recent development of a rapid-response military unit designed to cope with unexpected dramas such as the Falkland Islands conflict of 1982. In all of these quarrels, the Queen had to play a listening, counselling part only. In one of them, however, she may have wished to add a few words of her own. Only a month before the conference began, the small Caribbean island of Grenada suffered a coup by a left-wing party called the New Jewel, headed by Mr Maurice Bishop. A few days later, a Revolutionary Military Council seized power, killing Mr Bishop and showing itself to be an extreme left-wing organisation, heavily tutored and sustained by the Marxist government in Cuba. America, whose support for Britain during the Falklands crisis had initially been only hesitant, immediately stormed Grenada with an invasion force of paratroopers, who found little difficulty in flushing out and dealing with the large Cuban contingent on the island.

How strong the Queen's concern would have been had she not been Grenada's head of state is arguable. As it was, she was evidently annoyed not only at having been taken by surprise by the speed of the American operation, but also at having been neither informed nor consulted about what action, if any, was considered desirable or indeed necessary. She was also concerned for the safety of the island's Governor-General, Sir Paul Scoon, who had disappeared in the course of the skirmish. The Queen's manner was reported to have been noticeably uneasy when she attended a dinner at the residence of the Indian High Commissioner to Britain in London as the crisis broke. She seemed withdrawn during the meal, and visibly upset while discussing the problem with the Commonwealth Secretary-General, Sir Sonny Ramphal. Prime Minister Thatcher's surprise at the turn of events was almost equal to the Queen's, and she had a rough passage in the Commons as Labour MPs went ostentatiously to the defence of the sovereign. 'It is no good the Government trying to pass the buck onto the Queen, pushing her into politics, and pretending it has nothing to do with them,' said one. Meanwhile, a report was afoot that the Governor-General had personally requested his nearby Caribbean neighbours to bring pressure to bear to overthrow the murderers of Maurice Bishop. All this, apparently, over the Queen's head.

The flurry of constitutional activity died down almost as quickly as it had arisen. Sir Paul Scoon turned up safe and well after the dust had settled, confirming that, while he was reluctantly resigned into accepting the first coup he took exception to the second, which was why he called for the assistance of neighbours. As the Queen's plenipotentiary in Grenada, he had every authority to do this, even without letting the Queen know of his intentions. The American invasion, executed as much in America's own interests as in answer to the Caribbean call for help, could thus not be construed as a move against the Queen's sovereignty, and the lesson was learnt that, by taking too seriously her role as head of states which are susceptible to political instability, the more vociferous supporters of the Queen's prerogatives might well jeopardise her relations with her more immediate ministers at home. At the height of the crisis, a cartoon in a British newspaper showed the Queen descending by parachute onto the island, radiating charm and calm with her sceptred wand and glittering crown. This piece of harmless whimsy unwittingly illustrated the hard fact that, as one American commentator put it, 'it was not the Queen who came symbolically to the rescue in a region with centuries of ties to London; it was Ronald Reagan in the guise of sweating paratroopers and marines.' But even this blunt reality had its funny side. Over two centuries after America's independence from Britain, the American marines, in order to give their actions in Grenada the proper degree of legitimacy, actually took the oath of allegiance to Her Majesty Queen Elizabeth II!

The Queen's seventeen-day tour of Kenya, Bangladesh and India effectively began her autumn round of duties, after a long holiday which had begun at the end of July with some pleasant family celebrations. The Queen Mother feted her 83rd birthday on 4th August, and proved that these successive anniversaries have become something of a national institution. Tributes normally reserved for use every ten years flooded out as the day approached. The *Daily Star* devoted a centre spread to details of a day of official duties which the Queen Mother had spent at the East of England Agricultural Show at Peterborough only a fortnight before. 'Eighty-three, and still flying,' proclaimed the headline, on the strength of the fact that she had travelled to Peterborough and back by helicopter. The following day, the paper concentrated on her 35-year-old patronage of National Hunt racing and contrasted disappointments such as Devon Loch's famous collapse in 1956 with the runaway success of Game Spirit, who won twenty-one races in the royal colours during a seven-year career ending in Jubilee Year. The birthday tribute from the *Daily Express* was a centrefold spread of five rich colour photographs under the title '83 Years Young Today', while the *Daily Mail* weighed in with 'Service with a Smile', a *résumé* of recollections of the Queen Mother's lifetime of service, from the days she played hostess, at the age of seven, to guests at Glamis whose sudden visits caught her mother unawares, to the period when Hitler called her 'the most dangerous woman in Europe'. The historian David Duff recalled that her celebrated love of charades was always forced upon unsuspecting guests, Sir Winston Churchill alone remaining the only person she could not persuade to dress up. London's Capital Radio went rather too far with an effusion of well-meant, but treacly tributes which, as one reviewer said afterwards, 'was like a meal consisting entirely of sugar mice'. Meanwhile, amateur artist George Dunn displayed his thirty-square-foot birthday card, featuring a full colour portrait of the Queen Mother, in the front garden of his Barking home. On a more earnest note, the Edinburgh National Portrait Gallery unveiled the latest commissioned portrait of Her Majesty, painted by the Israeli artist Avigdor Arikha.

On the day itself, flags flew from public buildings everywhere – for the 61st time in her honour – while forty-one guns were fired at noon in Hyde Park, and sixty-two at the Tower of London an hour later. That morning, a well-rehearsed ritual was repeated: two thousand people gathered in front of Clarence House to see the Queen Mother as she watched the Coldstream Guards march past to a pipe and drum version of *Happy Birthday to You*. Thirty children dodged the police in order to present flowers and gifts at the open gates of the Queen Mother's residence, while her two corgis, Blackie (sadly no longer with us) and Geordie, trotted about as if enjoying a new-found freedom. Three thousand cards and messages arrived in Post Office sacks, while van loads of huge bouquets were ferried from Fortnum and Mason. Watching all these goings-on with the Queen Mother were the Queen, the Prince and Princess of Wales, Princess Margaret and Lady Sarah Armstrong-Jones – just a few of the twenty-two guests whom the royal celebrant had asked to lunch. In the evening, the Queen Mother went to the National Theatre to see *Guys and Dolls* and, of course, the cast broke into another birthday song to her at the end of the show. And when she left for Scotland the next day, the aircraft which took her there looked, according to one of the crew, 'like a flying flower shop'.

The Queen Mother's was easily the most enthusiastically celebrated birthday of the year: indeed it is almost a tradition that it should be. But the public response to the event was in marked contrast to the reception the Queen experienced at the approach of her 58th birthday the following April. It came in an article by Prince Charles' unofficial biographer, Anthony Holden who claimed, 'Suddenly, she has begun to age more quickly. Her hair is clumsily dyed, her make-up too heavy.' Holden went on to compare the Queen to his previous vision of her as 'one of those fortunate women whose years have never showed', and attributed the change to the effect on her of successive crises like the security scares of 1982, the Falklands and Grenada episodes, and Prince Andrew's rather less proven affair with Koo Stark. Lacking nothing in boldness, Holden sparked off a thunder of rallying cries to the Queen's defence. Lady Longford, author the previous autumn of a best-selling biography of Her Majesty, stated simply, 'I would not agree with what Tony Holden has said', but it was a limp response by general standards. 'She's terrific!' trumpeted one columnist, adding, as if unconvinced that her assertion was absolute, '– despite that her face is a mass of laughter lines and wrinkles, her hair is dyed and she wears distinctly unfashionable clothes'. 'Do we really want our Queen to look like Joan Collins, who in turn is trying to look like a woman of 35?' barked one leader writer, while another called the Queen's critic 'a pipsqueak' who should be sent to the Tower 'if only for his own protection'. 'Queen Elizabeth I not only dyed her hair clumsily,' a man from Humberside pointed out, 'but also wore ill-fitting wigs. She is still the greatest monarch England ever had.' Holden wilted under the attack, but stuck manfully to his guns. 'She is perfectly entitled to grow old gracefully,' he said of the Queen, 'but I think anyone is entitled to say she is doing so.'

Perhaps after all that, the Princess of Wales was pleased to pass a relatively quiet birthday – her 23rd – on July 1st. Tributes were few and far between – inevitably so really, as most had been exhausted five weeks earlier when Princess Alexandra's 21st wedding anniversary coincided with Diana's thousandth day as a member of the Royal Family. 'Di of a Thousand Days' became a catch-phrase for a whole fortnight of eulogies. 'All by herself,' the managing director of Debrett's enthused, 'she has given the monarchy new magic and brought it much closer to the people.' Others went further, hailing her as the 'polished spearhead' of one of the most successful public relations firms in the world, an instant antidote to flagging magazine sales, the saviour of the British fashion industry, the boost to Prince Charles' new-found, or at least much more publicly apparent confidence, and the defender of monarchy against republicanism in Australia. Anti-feminists saw her, admiringly, as being unashamedly out of step with 'thrusting, ambitious career women,' inspiring the more domestically-minded by opting for family before career. The torrent of applause was as diverse as it was deafening, but you couldn't help agreeing with the opinion that 'it seems extraordinary that three years ago there was no Princess of Wales.'

The less spectacular watershed of Prince Charles' 35th birthday the previous November was marked by a glowing tribute from the historian A.L. Rowse who rejoiced in the Prince's literary talents and his zeal for collecting worthy books. 'We have not had an intellectual in the Royal Family since the Prince Consort', he added, thereby accidentally putting the noses of one or two of the heir apparent's relatives out of joint. Princess Michael of Kent, for instance, had only just been appointed a trustee of the Victoria and Albert Museum, and had gone off to Texas with her husband at the invitation of Lord Harewood to help raise money for the English National Opera. Other people pointed to the virtues which had made Prince Charles 'a credit to his country' – courtesy, concern for ordinary people and exemplary manners. (Choosing this last as an instance, however, someone had clearly missed his failure to hold an umbrella for his wife during their previous month's visit to Strathclyde Hospital.) His birthday was even remembered somewhere over the Indian Ocean that day, as the Queen made her way from Kenya to Bangladesh. A chocolate cake was presented to her in mid-flight – but she decided to hand it over to an orphanage in Dhaka when she landed. The most colourful commemoration came in a set of official photographs of Prince Charles, taken at Kensington Palace the previous January, and showing him in a few of the hundred or so uniforms which, as honorary head of several regiments, he is obliged on occasion to wear. Their issue was clouded by a behind-the-scenes row over the identity of the photographer: the pictures were originally credited to Colonel John Scott, a close and entrepreneurial friend of the Royal Family, but were later discovered to have been taken by a newcomer to the royal portrait scene, Paul Howard of Reading, who had been commissioned by Buckingham Palace on Colonel Scott's advice.

Both Prince Charles' birthday and that of the Queen presented the excuse for speculation on that old perennial – the question of the sovereign's abdication. Some saw the Queen's delegation of Prince Charles to head the Remembrance ceremony in November as evidence that an announcement was in the offing; others almost willed the prospect into life on grounds no more persuasive than that 'there comes a time in every family firm when the boss has to make way for the son and heir.' This line was taken by the *Sun* newspaper, so concerned that Prince Charles and Princess Diana – 'this stunning couple' – should have to wait a lifetime for their inheritance, that it took a poll of its readers on the issue. Sixty-one per cent of them thought the Queen should stay on. A few weeks later, the *Sunday Times* favoured a compromise – that the Prince of Wales should become Prince Regent on the Queen's sixtieth birthday. That at least had the advantage of good sense, unlike the following April's amazing allegation by the American paper *The Globe* that the Queen would abdicate within the next twelve months to 'stop Charles and Diana quarrelling.'

The matter was even said to have been the subject of discussion between the Queen and the Prime Minister during Mrs Thatcher's customary stay at Balmoral early in September, but it was an unlikely suggestion. The Queen's reason for being at Balmoral is to relax, and there is ample opportunity to talk business at the regular Prime Ministerial audiences in London. The Queen enjoyed a slightly longer Balmoral holiday than in 1982, if you count the leisurely passage along the south and west coasts of the country which she took in *Britannia*, picking up various members of the family along the way. Having stopped off to call on the Queen Mother, who had made her own way to Caithness for her annual holiday at the Castle of Mey, the Queen and Prince Philip, their three younger children and two elder grandchildren arrived at Aberdeen on Princess Anne's 33rd birthday, and drove to Balmoral for what initially looked like a two-month break. But the Duke left early in October to attend to official business in Switzerland and the Far East, Prince Edward broke his holiday for a fortnight's training with the Royal Marines at Lympstone, while Princess Anne began an extremely busy year with several public engagements carried out from the royal holiday headquarters. The Prince and Princess of Wales who, with Prince William, had arrived independently in mid-August, also paid several duty visits to London and to the Scottish provinces later that month, and in September and October. On one of these occasions – the opening of the World Petroleum Congress at the Royal Albert Hall – the Prince actually rebuked the delegates for interrupting his holiday, then promptly thanked everyone for 'clubbing together' to present him with a bouquet for his wife.

Only the Queen, joined later by Princess Margaret and her children, and the Queen Mother, remained at the ancestral home, venturing out in public only to attend morning service at Crathie Church each Sunday, and the Braemar Games – that annual Highland-dancing, caber-tossing, hammer-throwing beano attended by a large royal contingent early each September. That apart, it was a time for long rides into the forested Balmoral hillsides, joining in family barbecues – Prince Philip had in August taken delivery of a couple of £150 barbecue sets he had admired during an official visit to a Corby factory nine months earlier – and watching the rest of her family go off on deer-stalking and grouse-shooting expeditions. Though the Queen occasionally joins them in pursuit of game, she prefers a good, vigorous hike through the Balmoral estate. Because the land is shot through with public footpaths, it is always possible for members of the public to chance upon the Queen taking one of her constitutionals. Nevertheless, it came as a great surprise to a group of young pupils from Powis Academy at Aberdeen when, late in September, and completely without warning, they found themselves in conversation with Her Majesty, as well as with Prince Edward and Lady Sarah Armstrong-Jones, who happened to be using the same footpath!

The Queen likes to patronise local events while at Balmoral, and the Crathie Church jumble sale fete secured her attendance at the end of August. Those who think the Royal Family have no experience of handling money should see them in action at times like this. The Queen Mother had joined her daughter for the occasion, but was nowhere to be seen when the Queen was eventually ready to leave. 'I've lost the Queen Mother,' she announced, adding somewhat plaintively, 'I think she is buying up everything in the place.' Eventually, the prodigal reappeared, to face mocking indignation from the Queen: '*You* could spend a day in here!'

As usual on these delightfully domestic occasions, the Queen had brought her own contribution to the fete, in the shape of an iced chocolate cake which she gave as a prize for the correct guess at its weight. Barring the half Christmas cake, left over from the Sandringham festivities, which the Queen sent to a King's Lynn day centre for the lonely, it was probably the least significant of all the bounty bestowed by her and members of her family during the year in support of various charitable or other public causes. At the end of December, for instance, she had loaned three toy cars to the *Kids on Wheels* exhibition which took place at Beaulieu over Christmas and the New Year. They included a James Bond type Aston Martin given by that firm to Prince Andrew when he was six, and an electrically-powered version of a pre-war Daimler, which had been given to the Queen as a teenager, and passed on to Prince Charles in 1953, with its registration plate duly amended to read PC 1953. The previous August, the Queen gave an undisclosed sum of money to the Royal Academy as a contribution to its £1 million appeal for the restoration and repair of Burlington House, and when the Burlington House Fair was opened in mid-October by Princess Alexandra, visitors found a whole wealth of royal loans among its exhibits. They included a painting by Visentini of Burlington House as it was in 1746 – an item from the Queen's personal collection – an 18th-century Dresden gold hardstone box from Princess Alexandra, and two antiques from the Duke and Duchess of Gloucester's collection – a Siberian jade dish mounted with a silver snake, made by Fabergé for the Royal Family in London, and a personal seal made in silver for the future King Edward VII in 1855, in the form of a Viking warrior. But the most spectacular contribution came from the Queen Mother who loaned sixteen rolls of rare, indeed priceless, 18th-century Chinese wallpaper, the finest imitation of the hand-painted silk wallcovers used in wealthy Oriental homes over two hundred years ago.

In addition to this dazzling loan, the Queen Mother made several outright gifts to worthy causes, including a donation in October to a scheme, organised by the former Governor of Victoria, Australia, to send school children to an outward bound camp at Melbourne; a water-colour which was auctioned in November in aid of the Church of England Children's Society; and what was only described as 'a notable item,' accepted for auction to help the International League for the Protection of Horses at the end of 1983. In that connection she sent in February a set of hand-cut sherry glasses to be auctioned to raise funds for Downpatrick racecourse in Northern Ireland. It has been falling on hard times recently, and the Queen Mother has for two years supported its efforts to survive – in 1983 she sent a carriage clock for auction – in memory of her horse Laffy, which won the Ulster Grand National there in 1962. In April, the Queen Mother began to show interest in the restoration programme of the parish church of Llangurig, the mid-Wales village where, in 1917, her future husband Prince Albert had recuperated from an illness. She sent a bone china breakfast set – Royal Albert appropriately – to be raffled to raise funds for the repair of the church's spire. The following month, the Queen Mother replied immediately to an appeal for cash to establish a new hospice in Hastings, and sent a cheque 'with several noughts in it' to the director of the charity under which it was to be built.

Meanwhile, Prince Charles continued his support for the Royal Opera House development appeal by providing a foreword for a book published in January, about the building, in which he pointed out that behind 'the red and gold surroundings and the feeling of being somewhere special,' there is a lot of toil, sweat and aching effort; and for the Royal College of Music's centenary appeal by attending an auction in November at which he bought a double magnum of champagne for £120, while at the same time contributing a Victorian snuff box which ultimately fetched £800. In the same month he made a cash donation to the Plymouth and District Family Conciliation Service, and in February to the Farming and Wildlife Advisory Trust on the launching of its appeal. The Princess of Wales sent money in March to the International Centre for Child Studies, a cause for which her brother, Viscount Althorp, performed a parachute jump in May. And in April, both Prince Charles and his wife agreed to sponsor runners in the 1984 London Marathon. Prince Charles rooted for 37-year-old Bernard Wood, who ran to raise money for a cancer clinic in Morecambe – 'With the Prince behind me, I am determined to finish the 26 miles,' he said – while the Princess campaigned for Danny Maule, who ran in a *Daily Mirror* team to support the fight against muscular dystrophy. 'When I reach Buckingham Palace, I will give her a wave and blow her a kiss,' he promised.

But perhaps the most unusual helping hand given by the Prince and Princess to charity was that in September in favour of Mencap, the organisation which devotes its energies to assisting mentally handicapped children. This involved a couple of drawings – one, done on Highgrove notepaper, by Prince Charles of Sir Hugh Casson, the President of the Royal Academy; the other a portrait of Prince William by his mother. This picture brought praise from all quarters. 'The freehand work is marvellous,' said a representative from the Hamilton Galleries, where the pictures were exhibited. 'It has been done with great vigour and conviction – a sheer love of just drawing,' commented the artist Ruskin Spear, while a director of the auctioneers Sotheby's called it 'a highly professional work' and said that the Princess should draw more. Unofficial bids for the drawing reached £1,500, but the euphoria was dampened three weeks later when it was announced that the original would be kept locked away in the Royal Archives at Windsor. 'It's a great shame,' said the Hamilton Galleries representative. 'We were hoping it would go on display at the National Portrait Gallery.'

One painting which will doubtless find its way into several private galleries is that of the sinking of the *Atlantic Conveyor*, which Robert Taylor painted at the end of 1983. In January 1984, Prince Andrew signed a hundred prints of the picture in aid of King George's Fund for Sailors, who sold them for £150 each. Before doing so, the Prince had asked for two extra helicopters to be added to the painting, because with only his own helicopter shown above the sinking ship, 'he didn't want it to look like he was the John Wayne of the Navy. He was very modest about his role in the rescue of crewmen from the ship,' said the artist. 'He didn't want it to be a one man show.'

There were a few examples of more personal acts of royal benevolence. Two more of Prince Charles' forewords for books issued early in 1984 concerned personal friends of his. One was Tugg Wilson, the creator for many years of cartoons for *Navy News* – 'pungent and hilarious commentaries on Navy life,' said Prince Charles, who also spoke with affection of the evening when Wilson spent 'the entire duration of dinner drawing brilliantly funny cartoons on my napkin.' Another personal acquaintance was Bernard Aldrich, who published a book of reminiscences of his forty years as river-keeper at Broadlands, where Prince Charles has had many years' experience of salmon fishing as guest of both Lord Mountbatten and Lord Romsey. But perhaps the most touching gesture of this sort came from the Queen Mother. Back in 1963, she showed particular interest during a visit to St Mary's Hospital, Paddington, in a premature baby weighing less than 2lb, and fighting for life in an incubator. She asked to be kept informed of its progress. In March 1984 that baby, Karen Hammersley, was married. The Queen Mother heard of the forthcoming wedding, and sent along a set of silver spoons as her personal present.

Gifts and loans offer small, public illustrations of the vast spread of royal patronages which enable, and indeed oblige, members of the Queen's family to participate in the lives and work of her subjects, and to preside over a generous spectrum of national life. The year suffered no shortage of examples. In October, Prince Charles became Patron of the Atlantic Salmon Trust, while his sister Princess Anne was appointed Patron of the British School of Osteopathy. In November, the Anglo-Hellenic League secured the patronage of Prince Michael of Kent, whose mother Princess Marina was a Greek Princess, while Prince Andrew accepted the position of Patron of the British Schools Exploration Society, whose last royal supporter was the ill-fated Prince William of Gloucester. The Princess of Wales increased her tally of patronages, which now runs into double figures: in November she became Patron of the National Rubella Council as it launched a £2 million campaign to warn mothers-to-be of the dangers of German measles to the unborn child. 'Immunization is quick, easy and painless,' the Princess told an audience at Lancaster House, 'and the side effects are trivial.' She did, however, regret that there was no alternative to injections, and said she would prefer sugar-lump treatment because 'needles terrify me.' For some people, the royal boost came none too soon. 'One hopes,' said one woman who had encountered an alarming degree of medical indifference and even ignorance when she had asked to have tests, 'that this will have the effect of making doctors' practices and family planning clinics more aware of women's fears.'

Princess Diana had also become Patron of the City of London Ballet, though only after persistent applications – born presumably of public knowledge of her enthusiasm for ballet as a young girl – by its founder, Harold King. She was eventually persuaded to attend the company's rehearsals, and that seems to have settled matters. 'She was really interested in what makes dancers tick – what motivates them,' said Harold King. 'That showed how keen she was. She wants to help as much as possible.' And she did. She saw more rehearsals – then in February went off on a much publicised visit to Norway by herself, to watch them give a performance of *Carmen* in Oslo. Meanwhile the Princess of Wales' Charity Trust, which she launched in 1982, began to pay off when the Royal Marsden Hospital received a body scanner for the detection of cancer. The Princess also identified herself with her husband's patronage of the South Atlantic Fund when, at the Guards Chapel in London, she attended a Remembrance Week ceremony at which she laid a wreath on a new memorial to the Welsh Guards killed in the Falklands campaign. Prince Charles described them as 'dauntless men who knew their duty and did it. The dead man's abiding memorial is not graven on stone or in brass but on the living heart of humanity.' Three months earlier, the South Atlantic Fund had run into a controversy which threatened to embarrass its royal patron. Already, the widow of Lt-Col 'H' Jones – one of the Falklands heroes – had complained that 'the Fund has not told those who so generously donated the money, nor those it is intended to benefit, how the money is to be spent.' A prospective beneficiary asked the Prime Minister to look into delays and alleged discrepancies. The House of Commons was asked to debate the handling of the contributions on the ground that too much of the £1½ million of collected money went to existing Service charities which had little connection with the wounded or the bereaved. The *Sunday Mirror* claimed that it had put pressure on the Prime Minister to accelerate payments in time for Christmas, and demanded an immediate and complete breakdown of all payments so far made by the Fund. Prince Charles defended the Fund's operations and policies diplomatically, and with such a timely degree of conviction that the dispute blew over before it could sour an otherwise praiseworthy cause.

The culmination of another of the causes Prince Charles has made very much his own came in July, when he opened the new *Mary Rose* exhibition at the Naval Base at Portsmouth. It had cost some £800,000 to stage, and displayed over a thousand artefacts of war and peace retrieved from the sunken hull of Henry VIII's flagship, which Prince Charles himself dived into the Solent nine times to inspect before it was raised in 1982. The hull is now on show in an 18th-century boathouse within the naval dockyard, and lies not far from Nelson's *Victory*. The target of the *Mary Rose* Trust is to raise £½ million a year – a sum to which the American industrialist Armand Hammer, who has already contributed £300,000, promised to add £100,000 to fund running costs. The sense of achievement as Prince Charles finally opened the exhibition was somewhat damped a week later when the Ancient Monuments Board produced its annual report in which it criticised the lifting of the *Mary Rose* as premature, undertaken without adequate foresight, and in danger of becoming at best a liability, at worst a disaster because even now the trustees cannot be sure of securing either the technology or cash necessary to preserve the artefacts.

Rivetting as the story of Prince Charles' long involvement with the *Mary Rose* had been, it caused nothing like the stir provoked by his encouragement to the University of Wales, of which he is Chancellor, to establish a professional chair in the study of the paranormal, for which the recently-dead writer, Arthur Koestler, had left £½ million in his will to any university who would set up such a course. Prince Charles' interest in the subject came as something of a surprise, but in fact it is no sudden caprice. Years ago he read a book by Dr Winifred Rushforth, a world-famous authority in psychotherapy, called *Something Happening,* and this first encounter with the mysteries of occultism fascinated him. He formed a fruitful relationship with her, became engrossed by her life-long study of dreams, and when she died in August he sent another old friend, Laurens van der Post, to represent him at her memorial service. Perhaps it was her death which prompted him to take up his new public stance five months later, and although it was Edinburgh University rather than Wales which opted for the parapsychology chair in July, Prince Charles gave notice that he was in no mood to abandon his new pet subject. He revealed that month that he always tries to write down details of his dreams as soon as he wakes up each morning because 'I think we can learn a considerable amount from them.' He also condemned the prejudice against acknowledging the power of the subconscious. 'We are a left-brain society,' he said. 'We concentrate on organising the denial of the instinctive right half of the brain. Instinct, sensitivity – call it what you will – is enormously important.' Such public display of his new interest did nothing to play down talk that he was in the habit of using a ouija board in an attempt to contact the spirit of Earl Mountbatten. The allegation was made in May by the editor of the *Spiritualist Gazette* – and was repeated in the following month's *Psychic News* – on the strength of unattributable third-hand reports which, among other things, spoke of Prince Charles' consciousness of the presence of his great-uncle around him. In the light of the equally unsubstantiated stories that both Queen Victoria and the present Queen Mother used the occult in search of their deceased husbands, Buckingham Palace was under considerable pressure to comment. Predictably, the only response was that 'we have absolutely nothing to say on this matter.'

In spite of widening his range of interests, Prince Charles maintained his very personal supervision of the affairs of the Duchy of Cornwall. He paid several private visits to various parts of his sprawling lands – including a two-day tour of the Scillies in October, where he was seen riding from place to place on a bicycle, or tramping estates wearing a cheese-cutter and carrying a stick, or visiting the Countryside Commission in Tresco. This visit was probably preparatory to the report published the following April in which the Prince suggested that the Duchy should begin to relax its 600-year-old control of the islands, and allow the inhabitants greater opportunities for self-reliance. 'The Duchy will continue to help,' he proposed, 'but I personally hope that it will gradually become less prominent as the reins of leadership are handed over to the community itself.' In conservationist guise, he had already suggested other proposals, which Duchy staff had worked on that summer, to restrict the use made by the Ministry of Defence of parts of Dartmoor for shelling practice. A seven-year lease, with perpetual options for renewal, allows the Ministry almost unfettered licence, subject to a covenant not to crater the land or destroy monuments, and the thought of environment deterioration for many years to come clearly bothered the Prince. But, at the end of September, the proposals came to nothing: the Ministry insisted they needed to retain the firing ranges, and the Duchy had no alternative to renewing the lease when it expired in 1984. As if to add insult to injury, the Department of Transport confirmed that the Okehampton by-pass would cut through part of the Dartmoor National Park. The issues were aired by Prince Charles in a foreword to another report, published by the Duchy in December after three years of research involving some fifty-six bodies. He hoped to balance the conflicting claims of preservation and development, and the legitimate interests of farmers, tourists, conservationists, local people and the military – and he appreciated that future plans would accordingly not please everybody. This was a prudent reservation, as already some of the Duchy's actions were certainly not pleasing the tenantry. A large amount of Duchy land changed hands during the year – the most recent being an 85-acre farm near Wadebridge, sold privately in July for £1 million, and the most controversial being £100,000 worth of property auctioned off at Liskeard the previous October. The charity for the homeless, Shelter, accused the Prince of allowing the sale of 'everything in sight' while letting remaining properties fall into disrepair, when what ought to be concentrated on was the renting out of properly-maintained houses to local people genuinely in need. A Duchy spokesman protested that it was only selling off properties no longer required for agricultural tenancy, but the argument was in vain. Shelter continued to claim that 'Duchy policy was to reduce the amount of rented accommodation to local people.'

In November, a more specific case for criticism followed a complaint that the Duchy, having just benefitted by £93,000 from the intestacy of one of its tenants, had failed to supervise the erection of his gravestone, or even the tending of the grave. One of the deceased's cousins suspected that the Duchy was hoping that the whole thing would be forgotten, and a local Member of Parliament voiced his disgust. A Duchy spokesman swiftly explained that such matters were always the last things they attended to on winding up an estate, and promised that all would be put right by Christmas. But it was the sort of episode which gave one Labour MP the opportunity to condemn as 'absolutely obscene' the news in May that the Duchy's 1983 income had risen to almost £1 million, with Prince Charles retaining £734,000 after paying his voluntary 25% to the Government's Consolidated Fund. 'The existence of such wealth,' added a Liberal critic, rather too dramatically, 'is a direct provocation to those struggling to maintain their standards of living at the present time.' Neither critic made any mention of the fact that the Government benefitted by £¼ million from the Prince's voluntary payment, nor that any Civil List payments to him in the absence of a Duchy income would of necessity be an additional national burden.

In 1984, the centenary year of the NSPCC put Princess Margaret into a rare spotlight on the public stage. Her work as its President is comparatively unglamorous, but she suddenly found herself travelling the length and breadth of the country to grace or preside at its fund-raising events, from fashion shows to dinners, from balls to gala evenings in theatreland. Other members of the Royal Family were persuaded to join in – Princess Michael of Kent, for instance, went to Stratford-on-Avon in February for a variety performance, and her hosts were delighted that her presence had helped raise 60% of their target figure of £20,000 to be contributed to the national fund-raising effort; while in March Princess Anne attended the fourth Children's Royal Variety Performance, which is rapidly becoming a worthy rival to the adult version held each November. But Princess Margaret, always one for taking her own line, decided on something rather more original in May, when she visited the BBC to record an episode of *The Archers* – the long-running daily story of country folk, who on this occasion found their own local fashion show, staged in aid of the NSPCC, attended by its royal President. The script could hardly have been called original, but Princess Margaret took cheerful part in it, and the contrast between the hesitant, confused organisers, stumped for words at this surprise royal visit, and the mellifluous tones of the Princess as she tried to put them at their ease, had the ears of a whole nation glued to radios for those few brief moments at least. Only once did the NSPCC's luck run out, and that was when a ball to be held at Kentwell Hall at Long Melford, Suffolk in July had to be postponed because the local magistrates refused to grant a licence to serve drinks!

Prince Philip has often seemed to be Patron or President of just about everything, and it may well be that he is at times rather taken for granted. That appeared to be so when, in December, the International Equestrian Federation, of which he had intended to terminate his twenty-year presidency in 1984, announced that it had been unable to find a successor. While no doubt flattered by the implication that his services had become indispensable, he clearly baulked at the prospect of yet another four-year term in the presidential chair, when so many other and new causes were claiming his time. But at a meeting held in Amsterdam at the end of 1983, he confirmed that he would after all stay on in the hope that a new President-elect would be suggested and put forward to take over in January 1986.

One new preoccupation for Prince Philip was the Albert exhibition, a substantial and fascinating display, held at the Royal College of Art in Kensington, of the life and work of Queen Victoria's industrious and serious consort. Prince Philip consented to become Patron of the exhibition in mid-1983 though, as is his wont these days, he claimed no personal credit. 'I was asked and there was no reason for refusing. It is an exhibition about a royal consort; I am a royal consort, so I am the obvious person to ask to be Patron. I am the obvious choice – not the best choice, the obvious choice.' In actual fact it was Prince Philip himself who had suggested the exhibition in the first place, and he hoped that it would bring about a better understanding of the sort of person Prince Albert was, and of his immense contribution to British national life. It was indeed both comprehensive and instructive, with over seven hundred exhibits including mementos from many of the scores of industrial, scientific and philanthropic causes espoused by the Prince Consort during his lamentably short life, and a wealth of personal memorabilia – from his printed compositions of music to a slice of the cake, still in its own box, cut at Prince Albert's wedding to Queen Victoria in 1840. The centrepiece of the entire exhibition was a massive model of the Crystal Palace, whose inner walls were imaginatively faced with vast copies of the building's design blueprints, while a clever film projection simulated moving clouds over the top of the whole structure, to give the visitor the feeling of being outdoors. The exhibition was opened by Princess Alice, Duchess of Gloucester, accompanied by her son and daughter-in-law, and by Prince Andreas of Saxe-Coburg-Gotha, a grandson of Prince Charles Edward, who was the small German Duchy's last reigning Duke and a brother of our own late Princess Alice of Athlone.

It ran from early October until – appropriately enough – the 83rd anniversary of Queen Victoria's death in January, having by then received visits from Prince Philip, the Prince and Princess of Wales, and the Duke of Kent, who said he would bring his children to see it during the Christmas holidays. Princess Alice and her family also returned in mid-November to do some Christmas shopping in the Victorian shop attached to the exhibition. Indeed, the Gloucesters became strongly associated with this and the many other events organised in London to complement the exhibition. At the end of October, the Duke and Duchess brought their three children to Hyde Park for a 'Victorian Sunday' entertainment – it featured three thousand balloons in a Great Balloon Race; there was a display of Victorian transport which included carriages from the Royal Mews; there were Dickens readings, a Victorian costume competition, a penny-farthing bicycle race, and an exhibition of steam organs. In December, they attended a Christmas concert at the Albert Hall, the heart of what Victorians rather scornfully called Albertopolis. In the same month, the Duke made a rare television appearance in the BBC2 programme *A Modern Consort*, in which he was seen touring the Albert exhibition, and offering his comments both on it and on its subject.

Another fascinating period exhibition opened not very far from the Royal College of Art the following Spring. Towards the end of May, Princess Margaret opened a £500,000 display of Court dress from the 16th century onwards, exhibited in the State Apartments of Kensington Palace. Most of the exhibits were from private collections, though the more immediate royal contributons included a dress worn by Queen Victoria's mother, and the robes worn by Princess Alice, Duchess of Gloucester, at the Coronations of her brother-in-law, King George VI in 1937 and of her niece, the Queen in 1953. The entire exhibition justified in lavishness and creative precision the two long years of research, collation, preparation and design. Gorgeous gowns and resplendent uniforms glowed on no fewer than sixty models, complete with jewels, wigs and accessories. Some were arranged to form aristocratic groups, others were part and parcel of imaginative tableaux recreating the atmosphere of Court levees and drawing-rooms, and all, from footmen to ladies-in-waiting, symbolised the stiffly-ordered mentality that even today runs through the organisation of our royal courts. For the historically-minded, the restoration of two rooms in particular brought emotive evocations of the monarchy's great water-shed: the green silk room where Queen Victoria was born in 1819, and the Red Saloon where she held her first Privy Council in 1837 as a girl of barely eighteen.

The Albert and Court Dress exhibitions were the only ones devoted to royalty to open during the year, although the public still flocked into the Queen's Gallery at Buckingham Palace to see the magnificent display of portraits and sculptures of British Kings and Queens, which had opened back in January 1983. Meanwhile, at Windsor the hugely successful Madame Tussaud's exhibition devoted to Queen Victoria's Diamond Jubilee was extended in April to include a gallery of Victorian life in Windsor. The following month, a perennial exhibition, if it can fairly be called such, opened for its customary single day: the Royal Mausoleum at Frogmore. This monolithic structure, commissioned by Queen Victoria as a shrine to Prince Albert, and later containing her tomb as well as his, is open to the public on the Wednesday closest to the old Queen's birthday – 24th May. Poor weather kept the crowds away in 1983, but in 1984 a warm, sunny day brought out the reverent and the merely curious in droves. There, as always, was the huge sarcophagus bearing sculptures of the youthful royal couple, a dozen or more busts and statues of the closest members of Queen Victoria's vast family, the expansive and gloomy murals of Biblical scenes, and the gold-lettered Biblical texts set out in German as well as in English. The only splash of real colour in this lofty and sombre memorial to four generations of royal dead was the great wreath of carnations, orchids and lilies from the Queen and members of the Royal Family; the only unofficial tribute a cellophane-wrapped bunch of white chrysanthemums deposited by a visitor at the feet of Victoria's recumbent figure; the only unwitting touch of humour – at which even she might have smiled – the stuffed cat which, when the doors were finally closed for another year, was placed in the porch outside to frighten off the owls.

Queen Victoria might also have smiled on the contents of the *Time* magazine exhibition, previewed early the previous October by Princess Alexandra. Here, towards the end of a century which has seen the downfall of so many thrones once occupied by members of the old Queen's family, was a display of original *Time* magazine covers, spanning the last sixty years and betraying, if nothing else, America's barely-disguised obsession with British royalty. The present Queen has appeared on these distinctive and distinguished front covers most often among her compatriots: her first appearance – in 1929 at the age of three – was also the first by any Briton. Prince Charles has appeared no fewer than thirty-five times, one for every year of his life. Visiting the exhibition with Princess Alexandra was Countess Mountbatten, who obligingly stood on a chair to be photographed next to a cover bearing the portrait of her illustrious father, Earl Mountbatten of Burma.

As it happened, the following month was to see what might be called Mountbatten's supreme accolade from the people of Britain: the unveiling of his memorial statue in the presence of almost the entire Royal Family, a small army of royal and distinguished relatives, a total of thirteen crowned heads, and a galaxy of political and diplomatic worthies. The statue, which cost over £100,000, was paid for by public subscription and took its creator, the distinguished Czech-born sculptor Franta Belsky, two years to complete. Cast at the Meridien Bronze Foundry at Peckham, it weighs almost a ton, and contains a time capsule of artifacts from 1980 – the year following the late Earl's assassination. The Queen – Mountbatten's niece by marriage – had personally chosen the site on Foreign Office Green, from which the naval-uniformed Earl looks across his beloved Horse Guards Parade towards the Admiralty building where he was once First Lord. And it was the Queen who, in persistent autumnal drizzle and amid the most severe security since the Royal Wedding, performed the unveiling – the highlight of a ceremony delicately balanced between family intimacy and international formality.

She referred to him, for instance, as Dickie, while describing him as 'a first class professional naval officer who was equally at home with Burma Star veterans, Hollywood film stars, or world figures – a natural leader who managed to convey to those who worked with him his sense of enthusiasm and dedication.' She admired his 'vitality, force, astonishing range of abilities, and his never-flagging determination to get his own way,' adding, as if in justification of the immensity of the nine-foot bronze statue before her, 'The moment he came through a door, he seemed to fill the room.' 'I can't help thinking how much he would have enjoyed today,' said his elder daughter, Countess Mountbatten, gratified on her father's behalf that he had at last been 'placed finally in people's hearts and in his niche in history.' The Prime Minister called him 'one of the great men of his time – royal, bold, steeped in tradition, yet unconventional,' and quoted lines from Homer: 'Tell me of the man of many gifts who suffered many trials in the course of famous wars. He saw cities of a host of men, and knew their mind.' Amid such stentorian praise and gratitude, it was something of a travesty that a BBC pay dispute kept the live television presentation of the 90-minute ceremony off the air. The misfortune caused outrage to many, one of the Earl's admirers calling the offending strikers 'morons who have insulted the memory of a truly great man.'

The greatness of the man was evidenced by the continuing reputation which follows him even now, some five years after his death. In May, the new statue was adorned with a bouquet of flowers placed by members of the ex-Service CND in memory of his last great speech, the anti-nuclear statement he gave at Strasbourg in 1979. In March, his grandson Timothy Knatchbull, who had been badly hurt by the bomb attack which killed his twin brother Nicholas along with the Earl himself, named a new British Airways Boeing 767 after Lord Mountbatten, at Luton Airport. The previous February, the second annual two-day Mountbatten Memorial Concert had taken place at the Royal Albert Hall, attended by Princess Alexandra and Mr Angus Ogilvy, as well as by Mountbatten's grandson and eventual successor Lord Romsey, who was about to begin a twelve-day visit to Burma with his wife and the King and Queen of Greece. In June, Lord Romsey sold off a couple of pairs of shotguns made by Holland and Holland, and which commemorated, by delicately etched lock-plates, the history of Broadlands and scenes from Mountbatten's life. The guns fetched £260,000. And in July, work began on a six-hour film called *Mountbatten, The Last Viceroy*, which deals with the eighteen-month viceregency in India, and features Nicol Williamson and Janet Suzman as Louis and Edwina, the last viceroy and vicereine.

But it was also a year in which Mountbatten's reputation took a few knocks. Kenneth Rose's new biography of George V, published in June 1983, mentioned that one disservice which Lord Louis did to history was to encourage the myth that the Russian royal family – who were his close relatives – were doomed in 1918 because of a dilatory and indecisive British government, whereas the evidence in fact points to George V's vacillating courtiers at Buckingham Palace. A subsequent biography, this time of Edwina Mountbatten, by Richard Hough (who had already become *persona non grata* with the Mountbatten clan after his early attempts to pen an authorised biography of Lord Louis) cast new public light on the dubious love-lives of both partners of that sometimes tempestuous marriage, and indicated an almost unspoken arrangement between them which gave the Earl the financial security to enable him to pursue his own political and diplomatic ambitions. And in January, the circumstances of Mountbatten's death were momentarily resurrected when Enoch Powell claimed that the American CIA had been involved in it. Calling it 'a very high-level job, not unconnected with the nuclear strategy of the United States', Mr Powell sought to link the assassination with American attempts to accelerate the unification of Ireland, which might eventually be used as a nuclear base within NATO. Despite the successive controversies, however, the Mountbatten dynasty did not look back. When, in March, Edwina Hicks, daughter of the late Earl's younger child, married Jeremy Brudenell at Christ Church College Oxford, the Queen attended as godmother to the bride, along with Princess Margaret, the Duchess of Kent, and the Princess of Hesse-Darmstadt, the German duchy from which the Mountbattens spring. And in June, Joanna Knatchbull, a sister of Lord Romsey, became engaged to the French Baron Hubert de Breuil, whom she had met five years before in New York. They planned to marry in November.

The Northern Ireland problem – the background to Mountbatten's assassination – remained a recurrent feature of national life during the year, and the Royal Family was not immune from its effects. The horrendous pre-Christmas bomb attack at Harrods which killed six people and injured dozens of others brought a message of shock and condolence from the Queen, the scantily-concealed disgust of Princess Michael of Kent – 'A dreadful outrage,' she condemned at a ceremony in which she accepted part of the proceeds from the previous summer's Berkeley Square Ball which had been diverted to 'the police whose men and women suffered so dreadfully' – and a characteristic volley of righteous indignation from Prince Charles. 'It is extraordinary that people can cold-bloodedly plan an operation like this,' he said, 'knowing the effect it was going to have; that somebody should have the mentality to do such things.' His parting shot – 'Ultimately God is their judge,' fell on sympathetic ears, though when, during visits he and Princess Diana made to the injured at Westminster and St Thomas's Hospitals, he apologised to a wounded American 'on behalf of London', his well-meant gesture brought protest that it was the Americans who should apologise to Britain for failing to dissociate themselves sufficiently from organisations like Noraid, which supports the activities of the IRA.

The continuing Ulster troubles seemed to steel the Royal Family's resolve to play its part in keeping up the spirit of the province's beleaguered communities. Both the Duke and Duchess of Gloucester in November, the Duke and Duchess of Kent in early April, and Princess Margaret in June paid short one- or two-day visits as guests of the Northern Ireland Secretary of State, inspecting army units, factories, and social and charitable organisations. There were inevitable tensions, such as the barrage of heavy gun-fire which the Devon and Dorset Regiment came under, the day before the Duke of Kent was to visit, and the two bombs in Newry with which they had to deal on the same day. But there were also unrehearsed moments of laughter, of which the most amusing concerned Clodagh, a bitch who broke ranks at a dog-handling display at Lisburn. She fled from her kennel-mates, bounded up to the Duke of Gloucester, and promptly licked him all over the face. 'She's got to start her training all over again,' said an officer, with rueful resignation. For the most part, however, the royal schedules were carried out under the most serious secrecy. At one time, there was the possibility that the Prince and Princess of Wales would go – at least according to a claim by a satirical magazine in Eire. 'Operation Purple,' it alleged, was the code-name for the proposed visit in August, of which the Queen Mother's two-day tour the previous June was said to have been a dummy run. The allegations derived strength from Prince Charles' known concern for the problems of Northern Ireland – a concern which had led him only a fortnight earlier to send a gift for auction at a fund-raising fashion show organised by the wife of the Secretary of State in aid of the Northern Ireland Association of Youth Clubs – and they were taken seriously enough for MPs to bring the matter up at Westminster. But Ulster police maintained that they knew 'nothing of any proposed visit,' and Buckingham Palace refused either to confirm or deny the alleged leak.

One royal visit to the province was kept so secret that it provoked something of an international incident. In February, Prince Philip made his first journey to Northern Ireland for seven years – a six-hour trip to visit the Armagh Barracks of the 1st Battalion Grenadier Guards of which he is the Colonel. As it happened, the barracks were also a base for the 2nd County Armagh Battalion of the Ulster Defence Regiment, seven of whose members had recently been charged with the murder of Roman Catholics. Within Ulster, the Duke's visit caused the Social Democratic Party to protest at what its deputy leader called 'a calculated insult,' coming as it did shortly after a similar visit by Mrs Thatcher, and showing that 'the British Establishment are saying clearly to the Catholic population that their safety, fears and attitudes count for nothing. One cannot escape the conclusion,' he added, 'that this member of the British Royal Family has been used and manipulated in a way that is meant to be highly offensive to the Catholic community.' An Army spokesman countered that the visit was private and carried no political connotations, a view with which the Northern Ireland Office concurred, since the Duke had made the visit without prior consultation. Prince Philip similarly 'had no regrets. He was visiting a regiment,' explained his spokesman, 'which happened to share some land with the Ulster Defence Regiment, but he was not visiting them.' And when the Speaker of the Northern Ireland Assembly wrote to thank the Duke for his trip, he replied simply that he was 'glad to be able to visit a regiment with which I am closely connected, and to hear something of its experiences.'

This did not placate the Southern Ireland Government, which professed itself 'alarmed and dismayed' by this 'unacceptable' occurrence. Even the Irish Opposition called it insensitive, though it put the blame squarely on the British Government. The Northern Ireland Office dismissed an official protest from Dublin by asserting that 'a visit by a member of the Royal Family to a regiment of the United Kingdom of which he is Colonel is an internal matter for the United Kingdom.' Tory MPs rushed to the Duke's defence, while an Ulster Unionist fairly scorned the Irish for protesting merely because 'a member of the Royal Family dared to set foot in disputed territory.' Mrs Thatcher maintained a similarly strong attitude when questions were raised in the House of Commons, but in Dublin the British Ambassador was instructed to express his regret that the visit had caused such a controversy. The Southern

Irish government at last seemed placated by the more conciliatory tone, and the whole affair was cooled, though there was no doubt that Anglo-Irish relations had been seriously threatened by what had been conceived as essentially a private and legitimate visit of goodwill.

The security factors which led to such intense secrecy in Northern Ireland are never far from the public mind on the mainland, and the year witnessed one or two alarms on the subject of royal safety generally. In November, a 29-year-old unemployed man, who lived a hermit's life on a canal barge, was convicted at Aylesbury on two charges of threatening to murder members of the Royal Family – including the Queen Mother, the Prince and Princess of Wales and the Queen, to whom he addressed a threatening letter for the attention of 'Queen Elizabeth, degenerate.' Earlier the same month, the chatter of an unfamiliar helicopter above the Cenotaph during the Remembrance Day two-minute silence sent the eyes of Princess Anne, the Princess of Wales and the Queen Mother looking uncertainly skywards, scouring the heavens for an explanation. A BBC television commentator attributed its presence to a security operation, but it was found to be a West German military aircraft on a routine flight from Kent to Newcastle, apparently ignorant of the restriction on the day's flight paths over London.

In February, a 30-year-old man, Christopher Yeo attempted to force his way into a reception at the Royal Society of Arts, shortly before Prince Charles was due to attend. The man's green woollen tea-cosy hat rather gave him away as being other than *bona fide*, but he was not excluded without something of a struggle. He was dragged down the street, and eventually charged at Bow Street police station, found guilty the following day of causing a breach of the peace and £50 worth of damage to a police van and, despite his defiant shouts in court, was bound over for two years in the sum of £200. 'These things happen,' said Prince Charles when he was told of the incident, though he may have been less philosophical had he heard later that the man had a history of pestering the Royal Family, especially the Princess of Wales. Prince Andrew had his moment of apprehension when he learned in January that a couple of Navy ratings and a cook had been arrested for allegedly attempting to break into his quarters at Portland. Although disciplinary proceedings were immediately begun, it seemed to be little more than a prank committed after the consumption of rather too much alcohol.

Then in May came a batch of alarms of which the last – the rushing of the Queen Mother by an anti-nuclear demonstrator at Aberdeen, was also the least troublesome, as police were quick to restrain the protester before she reached her target. But a week earlier, two rather more worrying instances occurred. Princess Anne's helicopter had to take avoiding action on its way to Yorkshire, when a Cessna light aircraft began to circle it as it attempted to land. It failed to heed a warning to keep clear, and then disappeared after what a Civil Aviation Authority spokesman presumed was a mission of sheer curiosity. Meanwhile, Princess Alice was visiting Stowe School in Buckinghamshire, when a hoax incendiary bomb was discovered in a fireplace. The incident was condemned not only for the security fears it caused, but also because the Princess was being accompanied by Baroness Airey, the widow of Airey Neave, who was killed by a bomb at the House of Commons in 1979. She was to attend the royal opening of an art exhibition there in aid of the Airey Neave Trust. Sixth-formers at the school disowned the prank as 'an insensitive and sick joke,' while the headmaster cancelled the school's annual summer ball 'in mourning for what has happened.' Three boys confessed responsibility – two were expelled, and the other withdrawn by his parents – and in July were sent to remand homes.

These events apart, anxiety for royal security was sparked off by incidents no more worrying than the arrest of a man at Sandringham during the Royal Family's New Year holiday; a suspicious lorry – it turned out to be a delivery vehicle for audio equipment – parked outside the Albert Hall just before the Prince and Princess of Wales arrived to attend a rock concert in September; a television light which crashed down within feet of Princess Margaret during a ceremony of presentations to handicapped children at London's Savoy Hotel in November; and the gunshots heard one autumn evening in the grounds of Royal Lodge, the Queen Mother's Windsor retreat. That brought the police out in force, only to find Viscount Linley potting rabbits with an unlicensed .22 rifle. Thames Valley police confirmed that a complaint had been received, but the Viscount was not prosecuted, and escaped with a couple of rebukes – one from the police, and one from the RSPCA. 'No-one, whoever they are,' said one of its officials, 'should shoot aimlessly at wildlife.' Activity of this kind within the precincts of a royal residence recalled the notorious Fagan break-ins and trial of 1982, as a consequence of which moves were already afoot to change the law relating to trespass on residential premises. Despite the Home Office's reluctance to introduce changes which might put the Royal Family into an unenviably privileged position, a Conservative MP, Ivor Stanbrook successfully called for an end to the anomaly whereby Fagan had escaped conviction solely because, at the time of entering Buckingham Palace, he could not be shown to have harboured any intention to commit a criminal offence.

A rather more unusual slant on the dangers of being royal came with the publication in March of the memoirs of Alexander Haig, the former US Secretary of State. He alleged that the former Argentinian President Galtieri had told him of a Russian plot to sink Prince Andrew's ship *HMS Invincible* during the Falklands campaign, and to allow the Argentinians to take the credit. The Ministry of Defence dismissed this claim as 'speculation,' though it did tend to add credence to a report in an article in the *Sunday Times* in October, alleging that an Argentinian commando team had been sent out in October 1982 on a submarine mission to Mustique, to avenge the defeat in the Falklands by capturing Prince Andrew, who was then enjoying a well-deserved holiday with a party of friends. Buckingham Palace was vaguely amused at the story. 'If those intrepid explorers from *The Sun* and *The Star* couldn't get Prince Andrew,' said the Queen's Press Officer, Michael Shea, referring to the many press attempts to track down the Prince during his celebrated furlough, 'then I doubt if the Argentinians could.'

Mr Shea's genial aside was one of very few indulgent gestures the press received from royal circles during the year. True, the Queen had taken the unusual step of inviting a press corps onto the aircraft which took her on her three-week tour of Kenya, Bangladesh and India in October and November – a decision which appeared to owe much to her concern lest the difficulty of matching scheduled flights to keep up with the royal progress should involve the loss of valuable publicity. The Princess of Wales had also gently twitted photographers at a performance of *Hay Fever* in London in October, asking them not to photograph 'anything you shouldn't' as, in a low cut dress, she stooped to sign a visitors' book; and Prince Andrew had joked with David Frost during an interview the following month about the joys of life 'being pursued by hundreds of photographers.' But, by and large, royalty continued to be unamused by the efforts of the press to procure their stories and pictures. 'I simply treat the press like children,' was a typical quote, cited in Douglas Keay's book *Royal Pursuit*, as Princess Diana's. 'When they have nothing better to do, they just make up a story,' complained Princess Anne from Australia in October, reinforcing her decision to ban journalists from *The Sun* during the Gatcombe Park Horse Trials that August as a sign of her disapproval at being harassed by them in the past. 'I don't elude them on purpose,' said Prince Andrew, who has certainly been on the receiving end of press attention recently, 'but on a private run somewhere I take an extremely dim view of them.' Certainly his reference to the British newspapers as 'daily rags' and their contents as 'the latest rubbish', during a breakfast-time speech while on a visit to Beverly Hills in April, made him no friend of Fleet Street. While journalists present at the time indulged in some good-natured barracking – 'Do I detect a certain hissing from the back of the room?' the Prince had asked – the *Daily Express*, no stranger to royal criticism, marshalled all its indignation against him, and declared itself 'heartily sick of people who should know better, treating the press as the whipping boy of our sick and sorry society in exchange for cheap laughs.' Prince Andrew was in no mood to retract. Asked two days later what he thought of the American press, he replied crisply, 'Better than the British.'

The thought may have owed something of its expression to the annoyance of the Royal Family at the unwelcome attentions of the press during their Sandringham holiday, when the Queen had personally been driven, once again, to make a formal request for privacy. She was, according to a spokesman, 'very angry at the continued harassment,' though Ann Morrow, a journalist who had just completed a book about the Queen, claimed that the Royal Family were merely 'pretending to be cross. They always know exactly what they are doing. The day the media stops pestering would be a disappointing day at Buckingham Palace.' Prince Charles might once upon a time have echoed the sentiment, but with a skiing holiday coming up in the Swiss Alps, he was ready to come to a sensible arrangement with the press to avoid the unpleasantness and disruption of the previous year's fiasco. His proposal took the form of an understanding by which he and the Princess of Wales would pose for photographs on the first day of their stay as guests of the Liechtenstein Royal Family, while the press, having secured their photographs, would undertake to leave the area, allowing the royal couple a truly private holiday. At first, the British press was divided, two newspapers refusing to give immediate assurances. A Swiss magazine, which had hired a helicopter in 1983 to monitor the Prince and Princess' movements from the air, threatened their privacy again for 1984, though there was logic in its argument that 'there just cannot be restricted areas in public places.' When the day came, the Prince and Princess duly posed for five minutes on Hoch Eck, in front of eighty photographers who snapped eagerly away while Prince Charles jokingly offered to fall over for them. The Princess – who was so visibly less cheerful that one observer thought she really could have 'spared the time to look genuinely pleasant' – *did* fall over, quite accidentally, and the photographer who recorded the incident had his film confiscated. Eventually, the couple boarded a ski-lift and sailed away with a final message – 'Now a very good-bye' – from Prince Charles. The sentiment was formalised by his Press Officer, Victor Chapman, who announced that 'the Prince and Princess will expect the remainder of their holiday to be considered private, with no intrusive activity by any member of the media.' It worked. A few stragglers decided to stay on, but when a German photographer had his camera taken from him by the Prince's detective John McLean, even they called it a day and left the slopes to a peppering of determined yet eventually unsuccessful freelancers. And when they got back to Britain, the Prince and his wife made a point of expressing their appreciation. 'They had a very pleasant holiday,' said Mr Chapman. 'They had the privacy they wanted, and they appreciated that.'

Prince Edward achieved pretty much the same result with *his* skiing holiday, which took place in the Austrian Tyrol at the end of March. He merely told his journalist followers that his holiday was 'not for other people's entertainment. If I have to cancel this holiday because of your people, I will make sure that you never forget it.' Indeed, the Prince spent most of the year being less restrained with the Press than some of his family. 'You are the most boring people in the world,' he told a press crew at a Cambridge University Drama Society party at the end of November. The *Daily Star* newspaper was stung into a swift retort, insisting on an apology. 'He should know,' ran its editorial, 'that it certainly is boring, waiting all night for royals like himself to finish their champagne revels, and then to be greeted with pompous remarks.' Things were no better on the occasion of the Prince's twentieth birthday in March. Leaving a matinée performance of a University Rag review that day, he encountered fifteen photographers at the stage door. Enquiries after his health and plans for the day were ruthlessly crushed. 'I am trying to have a normal day like everybody else,' he snapped. 'If you don't lose yourselves before long, I shall lose my temper.' A day later, the Prince took ingenious advantage of an opportunity to grill the press when he began a sponsored crawl – one of the University's Rag Week stunts for charity. 'You have probably,' he announced to the good citizens of Cambridge, 'the most professional crawlers in the world standing in front of you.' The remark, probably inspired by a couple of syrupy birthday tributes in the papers that week, infuriated those sections of the press whose job it is to be infuriated by such jibes. Alix Palmer of the *Daily Star* called him a 'snooty, supercilious little princeling,' who should mind his manners, while her rival, Jean Rook of the *Daily Express* stated that 'stripped of his birth, Edward is an undistinguished lad with no obvious potential for being anything but the Duke of Something.' In this, she was supported by the majority of her readers, but Prince Edward was unabashed. Of the offending remark, he said, 'I've been wanting to say that all week.'

Much of Prince Edward's dismay with the press arose out of the circumstances of his early days at Jesus College, Cambridge. His admission to the college, in spite of indifferent 'A' level results had, early in 1983, provoked hostile and embittered complaints which were renewed as the Michaelmas term approached. It was found that, out of 126 students in the college's intake, nine had been offered places conditional on the minimum 'A' level passes – two at Grade E – and that Prince Edward's grades – a C and two D's – were only marginally above that. One newspaper reader protested at the college's readiness to 'prostitute its reputation by nurturing sub-standard material and cosseting a non-academic life,' while even the *Eton College Chronicle* branded the Prince's admission as 'a clear indication that the class system is flourishing.' Mrs Sheila Clements of South Shields wrote a letter of complaint direct to the Queen, but discovered that the Palace had washed its hands of the affair. 'No doubt there are others who achieved better 'A' level results and did not gain admission,' came the reply. 'It is, however, perhaps fair to point out that his admission to Jesus College was a matter entirely for the college authorities, and there was no question of any pressure being brought to bear on them to ensure his admission.' There was talk of Prince Edward being sent to Coventry by students whose own petition of protest had been rejected by the college, but Sir Alan Cottrell, the Master of Jesus, was adamant that most undergraduates supported his admission, while the senior tutor, Doctor Gavin Mackenzie insisted that 'he was evaluated and went through the admission process in the normal way.' This confirmed the college's line that Prince Edward was no more privileged than many others accepted on a mixture of headmasters' reports, examinations and interviews – though on the question of privilege it was tactfully not mentioned that not all students are, as Prince Edward was, guests of honour at beginning-of-term lunches given by the Master.

Prince Edward arrived at the 500-year-old college at the beginning of October, amid tremendous excitement, a host of implied personal invitations from female students who vowed they would 'make him feel at home,' and advice from Ted Dexter, a former Jesus student and eventual England cricket captain, that 'he should keep his drinks very long, his romances very short, and his work somewhere in between.' There was plenty to speculate upon. Would the Prince join unruly university clubs? Would he be caught walking on the courtyard lawns which are reserved only for dons? If so, would they extract the customary £20 fine from him? What did the senior tutor mean when he said that Prince Edward would be 'mixed up with women' and that 'his horizons will be that bit wider' as a result? And who was the lucky lady who would make up his bed every morning?

Prince Edward was allocated a suite of balconied rooms in North Court – part of a three-storey block built in 1965 – with views across the River Cam. The contents of his apartment were fairly standard – a single divan bed, a wardrobe, a kitchen with a two-ringed stove, a green-topped desk, bookshelves and armchairs. Like all resident students his allocation was indicated by a highly-polished wooden board affixed to the outer wall of the block, announcing his name 'HRH The Prince Edward' in painted letters. But similarities with the lives of the other four hundred undergraduates at the college ended there. Concessions to security – strict if unobtrusive – were inevitable, so his windows were bullet-proofed, while a whole landing, normally shared by four students, was reserved for him and his bodyguard alone. Detective-Inspector Richard Griffin was the man detailed to trail the Prince from his rooms to classes each day, to attend lectures and tutorials with him, to accompany him on cycle rides through the town, and to and from the many social and cultural activities which the university offers.

The Prince took to his college existence like a duck to water. There was a group photograph to mark the start of university life for him and his new colleagues, and a freshers' dinner at which he tucked into prawn cocktail, lamb chops and carrots, apple pie and cream. He was frequently seen cycling along the streets of Cambridge – once illegally on the pavement – accompanied of course by his detective, and both on gleaming new machines, a Raleigh and a 5-speed tourist Falcon Londoner. He was responsible for doing a certain amount of his own laundry, in the college's private laundromat. By the middle of the first month he had become a member of the Very Nice Society, an association of indeterminate aims, but whose habit of hugging and squeezing one another every time they meet wins at least the doubtful honour of a second look. He found himself by turns the unwilling and willing butt of jokes – unwillingly when a group of revellers burst into a local pub, got themselves thrown out, then embarrassed the publican by claiming that one of them was Prince Edward; and more willingly when he was mentioned in a series of sketches in the Coarse Acting Show put on in February by GROTS – the Graduate Randomly Organised Theatrical Society.

But he took his own more serious interest in drama. In October he put himself in for an audition to join the cast of *The Crucible*, the Arthur Miller play which the college's drama company put on that autumn. The Prince was given a leading role – that of the American Judge Danforth, the sexagenarian deputy governor of a district in the throes of a 17th-century witch-hunt. The Prince's make-up did not age him terribly convincingly, but all were impressed by his acting abilities. 'The part fits him like a glove,' said the director. 'He has tremendous presence and authority on stage.' The reviewers agreed. 'He never needs to raise his voice to a shout to make his passion felt,' said one of them, adding that 'it is strangely devoid of all royal intonation.' In February and March, he helped to produce the Cambridge University Light Entertainment Society's Rag Week Revue *The Glitter Ball Prizes*, the proceeds of which were destined for children in Botswana. 'I have to make sure everyone gets their cues right, and that all the props are in the right place,' he explained in a local radio interview, 'so I'll be quite busy.' The show, which poked fun at everything from Russian spies to the Greenham Peace Women and, of course, royalty, was a sell-out and raised £600. All tickets were sold in advance, even though, as the Prince warned, 'I shall be on stage, but *not visible*, I hope.' A theatre spokesman disclaimed public interest in its royal stagehand as the reason for the show's success. 'The word has evidently got around that it is a good show,' he said. As a publicity stunt for the review, Prince Edward was out and about in Cambridge wearing a flat cap and driving a taxi, on the roof of which a couple of daring young things were performing the Charleston. The stunt was his idea; 'I wanted to promote the show and do something that would be a crowd-stopper,' he explained, clutching a glass of champagne and fixing the last of a huge bunch of balloons to the back of the taxi.

Prince Edward was visited by both the Queen and Prince Philip during his third term at Cambridge, and by Prince Charles, who probably embarrassed him by giving him a very public peck on the cheek as they met. That all took place in May, when the royal undergraduate was revising heavily for his first year examinations early in June. By the end of the month, the news was released that he had passed part one of his archaeology and anthropology tripos, with a lower second grade – 'respectable' according to his senior tutor, whose explanation that this was the most common level of pass came at about the same time as the statistics showed that lower seconds counted for only a third of the year's successes – upper seconds for a half. Nevertheless, the Prince had successfully spent a well rounded year, and the Queen threw a celebration party for him and his fellow students at Windsor Castle a few days later.

Prince Edward broke new royal ground in his choice of sport at Jesus College – rugby. Before he had been there a fortnight, he was playing his first game for the college's second team, patriotically dressed in dark blue shirt, red socks and white shorts, to face a team from Trinity College. It was a humbling experience: Jesus lost 26-3. 'There's a lot of room for improvement,' said his skipper of Prince Edward's début performance. 'He must improve his technique in the attack, and particularly his binding in the scrum. But he's very fit.' The following week he took a slightly more active part against Girton College, though making only a small contribution to his team's 18-4 victory. But he distinguished himself by losing his temper after receiving a below-the-belt blow during a scrummage, lashing out with a flailing punch on his assailant's back. 'He was quite right to punch me,' said the wrongdoer, medical student Hugh Bethell. 'I was fouling him. I got what I deserved.' Subsequent games were not without incident. At the end of October, Prince Edward was involved in a collision when he and a player from the opposing St John's College team simultaneously dived for the ball. The Prince came off worse – he lay still on the ground for a minute, evidently concussed, then had to be carried off. His team, already losing 15-6, went on to a 27-point defeat, while Prince Edward was seen by the doctor. 'He was lucky not to have been knocked out,' said his senior tutor. Three weeks later he was back on the winning side, when Jesus won 10-0 against Selwyn College – though not before he had suffered an enormous rip in the side of his shirt.

His middling success on the rugby field mirrored his fortunes as a yachtsman. The previous August he had joined his father Prince Philip off the Isle of Wight for Cowes Week, receiving instruction on a New Zealand team boat, *Lady Be,* skippered by the round-the-world yachtsman Peter Blake, in one of the principal races, the New York Yacht Club Challenge. Blake, who had met Prince Edward during the latter's nine months as a house-master at Wanganui

Collegiate in 1982-3, and had offered to take him sailing at Cowes, acclaimed his protégé's achievements. 'The Prince has had a very good day's racing,' he said. Prince Edward had already come with reasonable credit through a couple of races in smaller craft: partnered by John Terry, he came ninth out of thirteen in *Spanish Lady*, borrowed for the Flying Fifteens race at the beginning of the week, and he followed this with third place in a three-man Aquavit the next day.

Prince Philip, a seasoned yachtsman and devotee of Cowes Week for some thirty years, enjoyed mixed fortunes at the 1983 meeting. He finished fourth in the Glazebrook Challenge Cup, the major race of the second day, sailing *Yeoman XXI*, which he had chartered from his friend Sir Owen Aisher, then came 12th in the Sir Walter Preston Cup the following day. Better luck awaited him later in the week when he competed in the Royal Southampton Yacht Club's Queen's Cup, but even then he could only manage third place, despite having his cousin King Constantine of Greece – a gold medallist in the Dragon Class in the Rome Olympics of 1960 – as part of *Yeoman XXI's* crew. It was probably doubly galling for the Duke that the winner of the first leg of the competition – nine minutes ahead of him – was another cousin, Prince Michael of Kent, sailing Mr Ernest Juer's yacht *Intuition*. In this, Prince Michael was watched by two more Cowes Week royal regulars, his sister Princess Alexandra, wearing a sporty matelot top and jaunty yachting cap, and her husband Angus Ogilvy. Prince Michael's connection with yachting has increased in recent years, a connection well illustrated by his keen interest in Peter de Savary's challenger for the America's Cup, *Victory 83*. Having supported her launch and trials in 1983, he was disappointed to learn of her defeat by an Australian rival, but both he and Princess Michael travelled to Newport, Rhode Island as guests of de Savary in September, to watch the Australians take the Cup away from the Americans for the first time ever.

Though he was elected Commodore of the Royal Thames Yacht Club at its 1983 annual general meeting in October, Prince Charles' presence at Cowes Week is these days something of a rarity. With his additional family responsibilities, he prefers to devote his sporting energies to polo, an activity at which he continues to excel. He finished the 1983 season in resounding form, playing three times for his team Maple Leaf (who themselves enjoyed a brilliantly successful season), helping them to win at Cowdray Park, Smiths Lawn, Windsor, and at the finals at Cirencester of the National 17-goal championships, the County Cup. He also played in the first polo international between England and Scotland at Scone Palace, the Perth seat of the Earl of Mansfield, early in September. Surprisingly, he was picked to play for Scotland: 'We were the first to ask him,' said the Perth and Dundee Polo Club manager, proudly adding that he knew the Royal Family would be at Balmoral at the time. Conditions were less than ideal – 'It's extremely slippery,' the Prince told journalists. 'I'll probably fall off, much to your pleasure' – but he still managed to score twice in a 6-6 draw. Each player received a horse blanket for participating, and Prince Charles sportingly put his over himself!

Despite the close season misfortune of losing one of his ponies – a four-year-old filly called Concorde which broke a leg after bolting into the path of a car near Windsor and had to be shot – Prince Charles began the 1984 season with a stable of thirteen horses, all but two of which were home-bred. He played for a variety of teams, and with inconsistent success. In May he helped Ingwenya win the Rodney Moore Cup, but was on a losing Windsor side in another match the same day. A week later he played for the visiting Rajasthan Polo Club against Laurent Perrier at Windsor, and lost 7-3 in front of the Queen. Victory came more easily when he played for his old team Les Diables Bleus at the end of the month. They won the Aramis Trophy, then the Abela Cup – in which he put them ahead for the first time at 8-7 – at Windsor, but after a promising start in the Queen's Cup at Windsor in June – they won 10-7 in the quarter-finals – Les Diables Bleus lost 7-4 in the semi-finals to the eventual Cup winners Foxcote. By this time, Prince Charles' individual performance was improving noticeably: he had developed some confident and accurate long passes and turned in a strong performance when captaining a losing Old Cambridge side against Old Oxford at Kirtlington in mid-June. Although on the following day he injured his right leg when his horse collided with another during an abortive attempt at the Summer Cup at Cowdray Park, he was back in action a week later to score three goals for Windsor Park in the Horse and Hound Cup, helping them to win 7½-5. Later that month, they won the Royal Windsor Cup after a 5-4 victory in the final over The BB's, and Prince Charles received his winner's medal from the Queen. The same day, Windsor Park were thrown out of the Archie David Cup when Dauntsey Squirrels beat them 5-2. Notwithstanding a defeat in mid-week at Cirencester, Prince Charles played for Les Diables Bleus in the Charles Heidsieck Cup and won 7-6. The Princess of Wales was present on both occasions.

By now, Prince Charles was playing more regularly and frequently than in any previous year. By the end of July he had appeared for one or other team on some two dozen days – mostly weekends – which included the birthdays of his wife and son and his own third wedding anniversary. On that last occasion, he played for an England second team against Spain for the Silver Jubilee Cup, part of a grand ceremonial event, rich in colour and brass band music, and dignified by the presence of the Queen. Unfortunately, she did not see her son's team win, though the match went into extra time before they succumbed to a 5-4 defeat. That result mirrored Prince Charles' luck the previous week when Les Diables Bleus lost the Texaco Trophy at Cowdray Park after a thrilling and open match ran into extra time to give their opponents an 11-10 victory. Fortunately, Prince Charles had already been on the winning side in three previous matches that month, by the end of which his tally of team victories during the season had gone up to thirteen, as against ten defeats. It remains to be seen whether his handicap will go up from four to five, as predicted by manager, Major Ferguson, in March in consequence of the Prince's greater participation in the game.

Since what has become popularly known as 'the advent of Lady Diana,' Prince Charles' polo matches have taken on a whole new public significance. At first, this was due to the mistaken impression that the Princess was by no means as keen on the sport as her husband – a rumour which she scotched long ago: now people flock to Smiths Lawn or Cowdray Park in the hope of seeing both her and her chic, sporty line in casual clothes. Slacks of various colours and patterns were a great favourite in 1983, some of the pedal-pusher variety showing rather more than royalty is accustomed to display in the way of calf, while in August she wore a heavy knitted cardigan – another area in which she has reintroduced a threatened species – illuminated with colourful weather scenes including rain, sunshine, clouds, lightning and a rainbow. 'She has summed up the day perfectly,' commented the Meteorological Office, observing wryly that on that very day the summer heat-wave broke up in a series of storms. More popular still was the bright red jumper, closely patterned with white sheep motifs, which she had worn over two years earlier for a photocall at Balmoral. This time, one – but only one – of the white sheep had been replaced by a black one. Whether she was trying to identify herself as the black sheep of the Royal Family proved an unanswerable question, but the design itself caught on. Two and a half thousand of them were sold by their designer Sally Muir from her shop *Warm and Wonderful*, at £60 each, and the idea was so popular that by September one of the shop's former staff was sued for selling jumpers featuring sheep on them at her own newly-established premises.

The Princess' fashions quickly became a subject in their own right during the year, her liking for bold, even vivid colours for day clothes matched by a striking line in evening gowns, from the traditional crinoline to modern, slinky, figure-hugging numbers which signalled a distinct transition from the youthful and girlish approach into a more mature and feminine phase. More than half of a sample of British women voted her Woman of the Year in a poll in October, while the *Sunday Times* revealed in the results of its second annual international fashion survey – 'money, taste, self-awareness and being seen are the important factors' – that no fewer than seven countries, from Mexico to India, had voted her among their top ten, Eire and El Salvador putting her at the very top of their lists. (Princess Michael of Kent came a strong royal second, favoured by five countries and achieving first place in Saudi Arabia.) In February, Princess Diana was voted International Best Dressed Woman by twenty New York fashion editors on an interpretation of the votes of American fashion magazine readers. They called her 'the world's most influential woman of fashion today – in spite of those hats and impending motherhood – a symbol of the young conservative swing.' She was also described as 'not only the year's overwhelming favourite for her personal elegance, but the inspiration for a sweeping trend away from eccentricity and towards dressing up.' This was well-timed praise indeed. At the end of that very month, the Princess actually drew wolf-whistles when she arrived at a pop concert in a cream and black tuxedo, complete with black bow tie. 'Diana has set the fashion world reeling – again,' said one expert. 'Just when we'd got used to her feminine frills, she surprised us all by wearing a man's dinner suit to an official engagement. She's proved she's still full of fun.' A few men disagreed. 'Outrageous,' blasted one, while another accused her of 'knocking our sartorial self-esteem.' Others, who classed the exercise as 'unfeminine' drew the wrath of two ladies from Newport, Isle of Wight, who said that it was not after all considered 'unmasculine' for Prince Charles to wear a kilt.

Meanwhile, magazines and newspapers were quick to pick up the theme, rushing to offer the cheapest copies of the outfit to their readers, as indeed they did three weeks later, after Diana had worn an Edwardian-style drape coat with velvet collar and bootlace tie to a health centre in West London. Truly, the whole world seemed at her feet. An American buyer at London's Fashion Week in October seemed to speak for everyone when he said, 'Until the Princess of Wales, British fashion was not our main concern. Now we cannot afford to ignore the London scene.' Everything from the highlights in her hair – someone christened them 'Di-lights' – to her simple yet novel use of jewellery; from her generously-plumed hats to those famous butterfly-bow tights she wore in March – everything served to make Diana an international fashion criterion. Even the Prime Minister, speaking at a reception for British designers at 10 Downing Street in March, spoke of her as 'a marvellous fashion-seller with a great sense of adventure.' In May, the Princess blushed when told by a Glasgow professor that 'for five centuries the perceptive heads of the Spencer clan have married women of surpassing beauty, and the daughters they begat have relegated Cleopatra to eclipse.' The French magazine *Marie-Claire*, generous only in its damning criticism of her 'terrible hats, outdated hairstyle, the lovely face hidden too often by veils, unsuitable feathers, fringes and collars, and badly matching accessories' was dismissed in Britain as suffering from republican jealousy, as Diana's praises were sung time and again in numerous articles and books devoted to her striking taste in clothes.

This phenomenon had a rather unfortunate flip side. 'If only Di would take the Queen shopping,' sighed fashion editor Eve Pollard in September. 'The Queen needs less pomp, more style. She has a slim, trim figure but she is apparently bored by fashion, and shows a distinct lack of interest in modern trends.' 'I suggest that Diana persuades the Queen to chuck out all those frumpish stoles that she is partial to,' advised another critic, while a visitor to the Burrell Collection which the Queen opened in Glasgow in October reported, tongue in cheek, 'After months of nothing but shots of the sylph-like, forever elegant Diana, there was something reassuring about the sight of Her Majesty's dreadfully dull matching hat and coat with a hemline too short to be chic and in a colour too dowdy to dazzle.' Anthony Holden pointed out in April that 'recent pictures suggest that the Queen now opts for clothes that reflect her true age. No longer does she have that aura of perpetual middle-agelessness.' The view was shared by those who had been dismayed almost to the point of rudeness with the Queen's choice of day-wear for her State Visit to Jordan the previous month.

It was clearly not a year for the Queen to relish in terms of popular affection for her choice of fashions, and probably one she will be quite happy to forget. It all seemed to begin with the selection of clothes she wore during her North American tour of February and March 1983, and in particular a spectacularly-ornamental evening dress designed by Hardy Amies for a State dinner on the West Coast. Amies was rankled by the continuing criticism which seemed to centre on this garment, and in August blasted opinions based, in his view, entirely on photographs rather than on 'the reality of an outfit in flesh and movement.' He did, however, suggest that the Palace might pay more attention to the demands of television – a word, he said, which is never mentioned within its four walls. In March, his autobiographical book was published, and he took the opportunity to think again. 'It was a mistake,' he admitted. 'We should not have offered the Queen a neckline which from the photographic point of view interfered with the magnificent jewellery she chose to wear.' But he nevertheless maintained that 'the Queen chooses, with impeccable taste and a wonderful sense of appropriateness, outfits which are always totally suitable for the occasion. It is as if the Queen knows her audience.' Her clothes, he added, were those 'of a well-bred lady who would hate to flout convention.' Lo and behold, and as if to illustrate the point, the tide of opinion immediately turned in the Queen's favour. She was congratulated on the choice of hats she wore on a four-day visit to Germany in May – though none of them was by any means new; she was described as always looking 'nice and stately', and complimented on having energy which exceeded that of many young people, and on her 'peaches and cream complexion' which made her 'the envy of countless women of the same age.'

Certain it was that the spotlight for royal fashions turned towards the Royal Family's junior members during the year. The Princess of Wales apart, two of the most carefully watched royal fashion exponents were Lady Helen Windsor – 'a great beauty', in the eye of Court photographer Norman Parkinson – and Lady Sarah Armstrong-Jones, the twenty-year-old daughter of Princess Margaret and Lord Snowdon. Though Lady Helen was formally photographed two years ago wearing grand, traditional gowns, both she and her cousin have achieved rather readier publicity by their devil-may-care use of rather unprepossessing, very practical and decidedly un-royal clothes as they go about their equally un-royal everyday business. Essentially, they wear what they like when they like, and if this means washed-out jeans, wrinkled tights and bomber jackets that have clearly seen better days, then they seem content to let the world criticise if it must. Lord Snowdon, who buys his daughter a copy of *Vogue* each month, has more than a sneaking admiration for her choice of clothes, explaining that in his view she wears the sort of clothes that blend with her surroundings, 'like we all do. That's what dress sense is all about – being able to know what is right for each occasion.'

Even some of the male members of the Royal Family became candidates for the fashion buffs' attentions. Viscount Linley caused quite a stir when he arrived for the wedding of one of Lord Mountbatten's grandchildren in March, wearing his hair blonde-rinsed. The reaction he provoked was a tolerant one – more so certainly than that drawn by Prince Charles, who seemed to have disappointed early hopes of a sartorial renaissance by a return to oversized, rather crumpled suits, and baggy trousers. These induced an imaginative response from a couple of Savile Row tailors. 'Just a fancy waistcoat would begin to put him on a par with Princess Diana as a leader of fashion,' pleaded one, while the other envisaged him looking good in a wide-shouldered leather jacket, peg-top cords and a designer-knit sweater. But novelty belonged to Prince Andrew, who had arrived back from a Canadian holiday in August with a beard, and his hair parted so centrally that for a time he looked like a serious challenger to Prince Michael in the King George V lookalike stakes. The beard came off again after five weeks – the result, it appears, of considerable ribbing from the rest of the Windsor clan at Balmoral – while his hair was subjected to a vigorous cropping shortly before his summer leave from the Royal Navy ended in mid-September.

Meanwhile, his nephew Prince William was making his own early impact on fashions for a younger age group. The blue-smocked rompers he had worn for a set of official photographs early in 1983 became a best seller by the end of that year. The sales of embroidered romper suits, once considered terribly old-fashioned, soared and one Derbyshire factory specialising in baby clothes reopened after a seventeen-month recession, with double the work force to cope with the new demand. 'Prince William,' said its managing director gratefully, 'has changed babies' fashions overnight.' And the navy blue snow suit emblazoned with the letters ABC, which Prince William wore for a press photocall in the garden of Kensington Palace just before Christmas, sent the fashion writers searching urgently for details. It was evidently a French import, obtained through a Marble Arch children's wear shop called *Bimbo*, which had also provided Princess Anne with the christening gown worn by her son Peter in 1977. Prince William's suit had a predictably excitable impact on the American fashion world, so much so that one transatlantic telephone call was made to Buckingham Palace, asking the significance of the letters ABC. 'They are' replied the Queen's press secretary with patience and a notable lack of passion, 'the first three letters of the alphabet.'

In the continuing saga of a future King, this ten-minute photo-session was significant, showing the world that Prince William could now literally stand on his own two feet – even if it was only to stare rather uncomprehendingly at the barrage of press-men before him. It provided a visual complement to the many reports of his progress and behaviour which reached the public during the previous autumn. In October, for instance, the Princess of Wales told children who contributed to a book of bedtime stories for Prince William, 'He is likely to chew the book up: I shall have to keep it out of his hands,' and three weeks later she was telling housewives at St Austell that whenever she put her finger in his mouth, he was inclined to give it a pretty severe bite. Highgrove staff quickly learned that all movable objects had to be put well out of reach – a message received too late at Balmoral where, while his nanny's back was turned, Prince William pressed a button to set off the alarms, thus activating a well-rehearsed security drill and putting the Aberdeen police on red alert. 'We all got quite a fright,' said one of the security officers, 'but everyone saw the funny side of it after the panic had died down.' Whether Prince Charles was amused when, one morning, he came down to put on his gumboots and found that his son had filled them with golf balls, is another question, but William continued being William. 'A mini-tornado,' was how his mother described him in March. 'Full of mischief,' added Prince Charles, talking to children in Botswana the same month. 'He tends to break everything in the house.' In April, Princess Diana eyed a glass bowl on show at a Glastonbury training centre and mused, 'It would be fatal to have a glass bowl like that around with William about.' Stories of the young Prince's mischief began to horrify some people, including one lady from Axbridge who sternly advised that 'parents and nannies should take swift disciplinary action, or we could have a teenage vandal as heir to the Throne.' Chocolate, the Princess admitted, didn't work – 'he doesn't like it,' she said in March. But one way of keeping Prince William quiet, according to his mother, was to let him watch the children's television programme *Blue Peter*; another was to hand him the feeding bottle; yet another, as the Royal Society for the Prevention of Accidents discovered to their concern, was to let him take the wheel of the Queen's Land Rover. Although Prince Charles allowed this to happen on a private road on the Balmoral estate, the Society was not placated. 'Usually the Royal Family is very safety conscious. But putting a child in the driving seat of a car is very dangerous.' Perhaps Prince William's future lies in the traditional family world of horses. In October, the Shetland Pony Stud Book Society, of which the Queen Mother is President, offered the Prince and Princess of Wales a two-year-old gelding called Lion – 'chosen specially for his temperament to be the child's perfect pony' – for their son. Lion will stay with his breeders until he is fully broken in at the beginning of 1985, then spend time in Leicestershire being schooled before Prince William is allowed to ride him.

Another, more controversial gift to Prince William was the toy version of a Jaguar car which workers at BL in Coventry were busy preparing for his second birthday. Two-fifths life-size, the vehicle was built by apprentices, while sub-contractors from other companies provided some of the fittings and parts. Real leather seats, a walnut fascia and thick-pile carpets, in the best royal style, were the aristocratic features of this product, the cost of which was estimated at anything up to £60,000 – three times the price of a full-sized model. A spokesman at Jaguar dismissed that estimate as 'preposterous' and said it could be done for a few hundred pounds, but all those responsible seemed so coy about divulging the actual cost, that belief in the maximum figure inevitably stuck. A Labour MP said that the money involved would have been better employed generating jobs, while a union convenor at the plant complained on behalf of a 'resentful' workforce, and suggested that the finished product should be auctioned off for the benefit of charity.

The controversy did not, however, spoil the run-up to Prince William's second birthday in June, for which Mrs Nancy Reagan, a coffee-morning guest at Kensington Palace early that month, had bought him a rocking-horse made in South Carolina, and pronounced the little lad to be 'just darling.' Because Prince Charles would be otherwise engaged on the birthday itself, and because Prince William was due to appear on the balcony of Buckingham Palace a few days before, the expected photocall to celebrate the occasion was brought forward to 12th June. The Wales' garden at Kensington Palace was again the venue for a much-reduced posse of photographers, reporters and cameramen, who busily recorded every movement of the royal toddler and his parents. Prince William joined in a brief game of football, initiated by his father, and dribbled the ball around the heavily-daisied lawn before kicking it, with more vigour than accuracy, into a flower-bed. He could actually say 'ball' as part of a vocabulary which also included 'ant' and 'tractor', and he showed great interest in a television camera, as well as a microphone which Prince Charles described to his son as 'a big sausage.' The Prince was then slotted into the safety seat of a yellow garden swing for a pose reminiscent of that in the greetings card his parents had used the previous Christmas, showing the royal trio on a swing at Balmoral, and he enjoyed a few pushes before his father enquired whether he was feeling sick yet. All in all, the quarter-hour session delighted everyone and disappointed no-one. It fascinated the child psychologists, who found Prince William's tendency to explore promising, and his signs of incipient left-handedness an interesting hereditary throwback – George VI had also been left-handed. It also beguiled the fashion experts who soon discovered that his light blue outfit had been bought from Marks and Spencer.

A few days later, Prince William made his first balcony appearance, following the Trooping the Colour ceremony, and chatted non-stop to his distant cousins Lord Fredrick and Lady Gabriella Windsor, and closer cousins Peter and Zara Phillips – who in fact got even closer as they both gave him a simultaneous kiss on each cheek. That appeared a delightfully spontaneous gesture, but it seemed to have been prompted by a suggestion from the Princess of Wales, herself no stranger to kissing on Palace balconies, and who eventually picked her son up and pointed out the sights below. Prince Charles also carried him for a few minutes, and William had great fun toying with the medals and lanyards on his father's scarlet uniform. Prince William's birthday itself was inevitably something of an anti-climax, though Prince Charles was given a miniature Welsh harp for his son when he visited St David's University College at Lampeter that day, and a couple of newspaper magazines ran articles in celebration. One reminded its readers that Prince William was already an eligible bachelor, and scanned the courts of Europe for possible brides. The best qualified year-old royal babies were Princess Madeleine of Sweden, Princess Theodora of Greece, and Princess Marie-Christine of Austria – the daughter of a Princess once much favoured as a wife for Prince Charles. Among the purely British contenders for future Queen were Lady Gabriella Windsor and Lady Edwina Grosvenor, the daughter of Prince William's godmother the Duchess of Westminster. The other birthday tribute came in the form of an imaginary open letter from Prince Philip to his grandson, in which the patriarch bemoaned the behaviour of his two younger sons, regretted his own deprived childhood, deplored some of Prince William's early habits, suggested that he develop an equally early interest in horses to please his grandmother, and warned him of future pressure to marry. The spectre of history repeating itself had already appeared!

Despite this wealth of detail about the Prince, sightings of him during the year were fairly rare, though the comings and goings to and from Balmoral gave those in the know the chance to see him being carried on and off royal aircraft at London and Aberdeen. He gave his first, rather uncertain royal wave on one such occasion at the end of October, prompted by a proud Princess Diana. That apart, only the occasional eagle-eyed passer-by or patient paparazzi photographer would spot him being wheeled through Kensington Gardens or at Highgrove or Gatcombe from time to time, or even, as once happened, round London Zoo. For most people, it was nowhere near enough. A survey conducted in August showed that local councillors all over the country were anxious to host him in their respective municipalities. 'The public are dying to see more of him,' affirmed the Mayor of Scarborough, and his counterparts in Bournemouth, Newcastle, Northampton, Bristol and Glasgow all agreed. A Buckingham Palace spokesman promised that 'now he is bigger and more active, I am sure more will be seen of him,' but in events it proved a forlorn hope. Early in December Prince William's great grandmother, Barbara Cartland, talked at length about him, evidencing a bright responsiveness by the fact that 'you tell him something only once, and he remembers,' and then delivering something of a backhander to Earl Spencer with the revelation that 'the boy's looks are improving. When he was born, he was exactly like my son-in-law.' Lord Spencer himself was clearly amused by his grandson. 'He started to recognise me from my enormous feet. He stops at my shoes, then looks slowly up,' he said. Added to all this, there was promise from a Surrey palmist that William's habit of sticking out his little finger indicated a future mastery of words. Then there were precise details of his height – 2ft 10", his weight – 34lb, and a tooth count – 11, all of which raised public hopes that he might feature in the Queen's Christmas broadcast. For the second year running, those were hopes disappointed.

Indeed, and for the first time in thirty years, the monarch's Christmas message seemed to disappoint a lot of people. Available to a world-wide audience of 150 million including, through the medium of sign language and subtitles, the deaf, the royal message was one of the longest of its kind, lasting fifteen minutes. The Queen began by comparing travel and communications between 1911, when her grandfather had visited India, and 1983 when she had done the same, a theme illustrated by film of Her Majesty operating a mock space-shuttle landing while in the United States that March. The message then diverged into something of a preoccupation with India, with lengthy footage of a conversation between the Queen and Mrs Gandhi about Commonwealth affairs, and a word of praise for India's self-sufficiency in food despite a 60% population increase in 22 years. The Queen then went on, 'But in spite of all the progress the greatest problem in the world today remains the gap between rich and poor countries, and we shall not begin to close this gap until we hear less of nationalism and more of interdependence.' She declared this a prime aim of the Commonwealth, illustrated by current technical cooperation and exchange schemes. There were a few rare sparks of royal humour, offering support for the Queen's final assurance that 'I always look forward to being able to talk to everyone at Christmas.'

At first there was nothing but praise, not so much for the content of the message as for its technique. Professor John Honey, a linguistic expert, applauded the Queen's delivery and described her as 'a superb exponent of spoken English. It should be taken as a model by anyone who sets out to be successful in public life.' Her accent compared well, he said, with the 'upper-crust, cut-glass pronunciation' of earlier years – a trait which Prince Charles had inherited but 'can get away with,' and of which both the Princess of Wales and Prince Andrew – 'he would make a top newsreader' – were happily free. Former royal news reporter Godfrey Talbot joined in the plaudits, describing the Queen's diction as 'purged of upper-crust accent, deeper in tone, admirably classless, classic and clear.'

Within days, however, criticisms began to be heard. 'More of a travelogue,' ventured one dissident, supporting the view of many people that it was a bitty, boring message, fragmented by so many film clips. Others found that far too much time was devoted to Mrs Gandhi; yet others that the balance in favour of Commonwealth issues left the Queen with nothing to say by way of encouragement to her British subjects at a difficult time. Exception was taken to her assertion that the world's greatest problem was the gap between rich and poor, and cited everything from East-West tension to the burning of fossil fuels as alternative candidates for that doubtful superlative. Yet greater and more vociferous objection was made to her statement, referring to Britain's membership of the Commonwealth, 'We are fortunate to belong to a world-wide comradeship.' Why should we be proud, ran the argument, of an association with tyranny and terror in Africa? A flurry of these sharply-voiced reservations soured the New Year, though by no means as effectively as a speech delivered at Leicester in mid-January by the Ulster Unionist MP, Enoch Powell. In it, he emphasised his well-known distaste for the consequences of coloured immigration by accusing the Queen of 'speaking recently as if she has other countries' interests more at heart than those of the United Kingdom, and that she is more concerned with a minority of newcomers than with the greater mass of native Britons.' This, he declared, was dangerous and it led him, as a Privy Counsellor loyal to the Crown, to question not so much the attitude of the Queen, but the wisdom of those ministers who, in advising the Queen of the content of her speeches, 'give the Crown a voice outside the United Kingdom which threatens its place within.'

The offending theme in the royal message appeared to involve the Queen's encouragement to think 'less about nationalism and more about interdependence' in an effort to defeat poverty. For some, her words betrayed a mollycoddling policy towards developing countries who might well be better encouraged to stand on their own two feet. For others, including her own Press Office at Buckingham Palace – 'the Queen has all her peoples at heart,' said Michael Shea – it did no more than confirm that the Queen was non-racial, third-world minded, and a woman who not only put Christian teaching into practice, but cared about all the citizens of the Commonwealth of which she was personally chosen as Head in 1952. Furthermore, it was confirmed both from Buckingham Palace and from 10 Downing Street that, although the Queen accepts ministerial advice – as constitutionally she must – for almost every speech she makes, the Christmas broadcast is an exception. She personally chooses its theme each year, writes at least three quarters of it and personally approves the rest, and only submits it to the Government as a courtesy and to prevent any chance of embarrassing anyone. In fact, it was later claimed that the draft of the offending speech had been sent to Mrs Thatcher, who felt no need to comment adversely upon it.

Positions were immediately struck. Mr Powell was criticised for not having had the courage to attack the Queen directly, and for comparing badly with his sovereign in terms of breadth of vision. The Queen was also criticised, this time for having been 'sadly misled by her advisors,' talking too simplistically about a 'gap' between the rich and poor nations when in fact there is no specific dividing line, and for failing to address herself to the appallingly difficult question of how the poor could actually be helped. Predictably, the Crown's arch-critic, Willie Hamilton MP, took both sides to task, condemning Mr Powell for 'using the Queen to peddle racism,' and branding the Queen as 'a clockwork doll.' Former Prime Minister Harold Wilson sympathised with the Queen in a neat turn of phrase which described her as 'a victim who can hardly stoop to answer,' while the author and Parliamentarian Robert Rhodes James defended her even more positively. 'Many people were grateful for what she said,' he confirmed. 'She is in the business of unity.'

Right-of-centre newspapers attempted to bridge an embarrassing conflict of interests in their own policies. The *Sunday Telegraph* led with a statement that 'the Queen's commitment to the Commonwealth is personal' though 'not all her subjects will share her commitment or her admiration for Mrs Gandhi. The Queen is therefore bound to displease some of her British subjects.' The *News of the World* echoed the sentiment and suggested the Queen should have delivered two broadcasts, one for the Commonwealth and one for her United Kingdom subjects. The *Daily Star* thought that Mr Powell was 'simply voicing the resentment and disquiet' which parts of the Queen's speech evoked, while the *Daily Telegraph*, finally convinced that the Queen was in fact speaking for herself, regretted that Mr Powell had not used his position as Privy Counsellor to advise the Queen in private of his anxieties, and had thus taken his grudge against the monarch's sentiments maladroitly to the public.

By this time, a flood of readers' letters inundated Fleet Street editors, expounding theories and opinions on all aspects of the issue, with a few more thrown in for good measure. One correspondent deplored that the speech wasn't broadcast live: 'If the Queen can't face the cameras on Christmas Day, then scrap the broadcast,' he added. Another held out at length on the reasons why the Commonwealth was 'in a mess.' Yet another seized on the opportunity to place the very existence of the Crown in the crossfire, claiming gleefully that 'republicanism is simmering just below the surface.' There seemed no agreed answer to the original point, though Mr Powell tried again to clarify the question of ministerial advice. Lord Blake, a veteran historian and political biographer who was to repeat his arguments in a lecture on the theme of monarchy at the Guildhall the following July, took issue with him, averring that the Queen's Christmas Day and Commonwealth Day messages were the only ones not requiring ministerial advice. Mr Powell responded by asking when this convention was first declared, arguing that if it was declared by ministers of the Crown, then 'ministerial advice that ministerial advice is not needed is still ministerial advice.' Lord Blake riposted that the convention, like most conventions, just grew and that in any event 'if ministerial advice is not needed, then ministerial advice that it is not needed is also not needed.' And with that donnish and somewhat abstruse banter, the argument, now well over a month old, was by tacit agreement at last put on ice.

Time was when Christmas was the only season of the year to see or hear royalty speaking to the masses, and the extent to which times have changed was no better illustrated than during 1983-4. Christmas television programmes themselves seemed peppered with royal themes: the BBC repeated its summer showing of a Coronation anniversary tribute called *Nobody Minded the Rain*, which documented the preparations for and proceedings of the Queen's crowning in 1953; and screened a 50-minute presentation called *The Princess and the People*, a report devoted to Princess Diana's year and which, according to its producer, 'clearly shows her progress from diffidence to complete confidence as the year wore on.' ITV responded with a recording of the charity Christmas carol concert attended by the Princess at Free Trade Hall, Manchester a few days earlier, and its own documentary called *The Royal Year*, which primarily featured the major royal tours, and ended with a snappy and entertaining two-minute sequence showing all fifty of the outfits which the Princess of Wales took with her on her journeys abroad.

ITV chose Boxing Day to show something of a scoop acquisition – a recording of the interview which Princess Anne had given to Michael Parkinson for Australian television during her short holiday there the previous October. The hour-long interview, conducted before an audience of 350, was informative, good-humoured and surprisingly entertaining. Ten years before, Michael Parkinson had scorned the sort of intense media interest in Princess Anne's engagement to the then Lt Mark Phillips that had prompted an army of journalists to flock to King's Cross Station to see the betrothed couple return to London after a weekend break at Balmoral. 'The only justification for this,' he said then, 'would be if *he* had come off the train wearing her frock and *she* had sprouted two heads.' But time had mellowed him into a geniality which proved the perfect foil for Princess Anne's witty and swift answers. She related a superb joke which gently mocked the Australian accent, was unconcerned that people criticised her for wearing outfits several times over, denied that she was too serious – 'It's difficult to take an intelligent interest in everything *and* wear a grin,' she explained – and didn't regret her sometimes harsh remarks to or about the press: 'They asked for it,' she insisted. She was even persuaded to describe the attempt back in March 1974 to kidnap her, and told how she had been 'scrupulously polite because I thought it would be too silly at that stage to be rude.' And she confirmed what many people would probably suspect if they ever had occasion to think about it – that, but for being royal, she would like to be a truck driver. Her reason? 'It would have kept me safely out of the public gaze.' The remark inspired the managing director of British Road Services to invite her to drive a 38-ton juggernaut during her visit to its training school in Birmingham the following April, and to suggest to her, after she had done so, 'If you get fed up with your present role, you are welcome to a job.'

Parkinson was little short of overjoyed with the interview, which also included Captain Phillips. 'I thought they were both tremendous subjects,' he said. 'I finished up a dedicated fan.' The Save the Children Fund, of which Princess Anne is President, was also happy, having benefited to the tune of £6,000 from Princess Anne's otherwise unrewarded appearance, as well as netting a further £5,000 as she had featured in a commercial television phone-in programme the previous day. Revelations on this occasion included the Princess' belief that women 'are more likely to improve things by quiet endeavour than by stridency,' and that the strangest gift she ever received was a set of surgical instruments, now kept in a display cabinet in a downstairs lavatory at Gatcombe – no doubt to the surprise of unsuspecting visitors! Further and much needed publicity for the Save the Children Fund came with an interview Princess Anne gave to Leonard Parkin for ITN's *News at One* programme in December, while the following April a lengthy film report, with the Princess giving a talk-over commentary, was devoted to her two-week trip to Africa to visit the Fund's many projects in some of the most deprived areas of the world.

In the meantime, Prince Andrew had tried his hand at media performance for the first time. In October, he spent a day with a film crew at Avonmouth, making a television appeal to raise funds to restore the famous Brunel ship, *SS Great*

Britain. He had become Patron of the appeal three months earlier, and when the filmed presentation was shown in November, it projected Prince Andrew as an articulate, clear and confident public speaker. The same month brought the fruits of his interview with David Frost, ostensibly on the subject of the *SS Great Britain*, to British television screens. The 25-minute discussion – 'not at all personal,' Buckingham Palace warned those who might be inclined to view for the wrong reasons – devoted much time to Prince Andrew's experiences in the Falklands, and revealed that he had actually seen the *Atlantic Conveyor* destroyed by an Exocet missile. 'It is an experience I shall never forget,' the Prince stated; 'seeing it hit, and the bits and pieces that rained down. It is still a vivid memory, and I think it will be there for a long time – horrific.' Of the wartime experience generally, he said, 'I think being shot at is one of the most character-forming experiences of one's life,' but added, 'You tend to become a sort of zombie. All you do is eat, sleep and fly.' David Frost, an old hand at interviewing everyone from presidents to pop stars, was duly impressed by his royal subject. 'He's a natural,' Frost said, 'and so relaxed, you'd have never have guessed he hadn't been on television like that before. Our chat was very relaxed, and he was tremendous fun to be with.' That was hardly news, for in the same month, Prince Andrew appeared unexpectedly in the television show *This Is Your Life*, and in the equally unexpected role of lure. The subject of the programme was to be the well-known Court photographer Norman Parkinson, a close friend and photographic adviser to Prince Andrew. The producers of the programme persuaded the Prince to make a date to meet Parkinson at the Hamilton Galleries in London to view an exhibition of photographs together. Parkinson agreed, and the trap was easily sprung – though it brought vociferous condemnation from its victim as 'the lousiest, cheatingest thing I've ever had done to me.' After the programme, he cooled off and admitted, 'I'd always resolved not to go through with it. It's too private, like opening your fly buttons. But Prince Andrew is such a great decoy; he has great charm.'

But Prince Andrew's trial by television was not yet finished. In July, he consented to be interviewed by Selina Scott for TV's breakfast television show. The interview took place on board *HMS Brazen* – which, as we shall see, he had recently joined, and which proved an appropriate location for him to confirm that he had joined the Navy 'to get away from it all.' He explained that he had always been an individual who found it difficult to make friends, and that his appreciation of his own photography had made him realise he was something of a recluse. As if to disprove the point immediately, he asked Miss Scott for her telephone number after the interview, but she refused to give it: 'I think he asked me as a bit of a joke,' she said. But she did admit to signing her name, at his request, on the nose of his helicopter, and she added seven kisses underneath. That too, presumably, was a bit of a joke. During the same month, Prince Andrew's Falklands experiences led him to feature in a recorded commentary for the 104th Royal Tournament, whose theme was 'The life of a young naval officer in peace and war.' He described his own reactions to the minute-by-minute existence on board ship in the thick of battle. 'The sound of Action Stations always sends a shiver down my spine,' he explained. 'That's when your training takes over – or so you hope. You might think that that's the time to be afraid. But it's total concentration.'

Prince Charles, one of the more seasoned royal broadcasters, seemed less in evidence, perhaps because of the rather overwhelming effect of his sister's and brother's appearances on television and radio during the year. He featured briefly in a documentary called *Secrets of the Coast*, screened in September by Television South West, and gave a long interview for the BBC radio programme *Soundings*, broadcast on Easter Day. This proved probably one of Prince Charles' most delicate media assignments, for it brought into sharp contrast the world of privilege in which he lives, and the social deprivation of inner cities which, through organisations like the Prince's Trust, he is attempting to alleviate. He condemned inner cities – a modern euphemism for slums – as 'one of the most appalling legacies of the Industrial Revolution,' for which repair and renovation would involve 'mind-boggling' investment. But, he insisted, 'if we are going to arrive at a reasonable situation, more must be done.' He was well aware of the apparent irony of himself, a wealthy person, appearing to be concerned at mass unemployment and its social consequences. 'I keep thinking,' he said 'How on earth can you motivate people who live in an environment where boredom and despair are endemic? It's difficult for me to say: "Why don't you do this or that", because people can turn round and say: "Well, it's all right for you."' But he pointed out that, whereas his privileged position might allow him to 'just sit back and do little except enjoy the benefits,' the accident of birth or wealth was to his way of thinking justified only by the return of obligations. If he sold up everything in order to distribute his liquidated wealth to others, he explained, 'it would be a four-day wonder. There would be headlines about it for a bit, and a lot of people would think I was quite dotty. I am not sure how much I could achieve after that. This business about wealth is a great problem, but if you have it, as I am lucky enough to, then I believe there is a great deal you can do to try to improve circumstances for as many people as possible.' One of the young unemployed people who also featured in the programme spoke in dismayed, desperate tones about life on the dole in inner London. 'It stinks,' she said. Prince Charles confessed in reply that 'at 35 – probably the half-way point of my life – I am thinking, and worrying about life. The reason I am involved with trusts is because I hope in some way I can make life a little less "stinking" for some people.'

Like Prince Andrew, his cousin Princess Michael of Kent endured her baptism of fire before television camera and radio microphone during the year. In January, at about the time of her thirty-ninth birthday, she followed the example of her close neighbour, Princess Margaret, and was featured on *Desert Island Discs*, the BBC radio programme which presupposes that its guest celebrity of the week has been cast away on a desert island and has the choice of eight records to enjoy during an unspecified time of isolation. Princess Michael's choice, which reflected the mid-European influences of her upbringing, included an excerpt from Strauss' *Die Fledermaus*, Mozart's third violin concerto, the fifth symphonies of Beethoven and Mahler, and a passage from Dylan Thomas' *Under Milk Wood* which, she said, had helped her when she began to perfect her English. In a fragmented conversation with her host, Roy Plomley, she gave the lie to a widespread belief that members of the Royal Family suffer from delicate constitutions which make them, and them alone, prey to any kind of strain. Speaking of the Princess' official duties, Mr Plomley sounded almost horrified when he recalled that, 'there was one occasion, I believe, when you were on your feet for 1½ hours.' Princess Michael seemed almost lost for words that such an experience should merit even a conversational mention. 'Well,' she replied, not without a tone of contempt, 'there are worse things.' She revealed that she was very superstitious, like most Aries subjects, and that she had been 'told I am going to have trouble with my Taurus daughter, but she's such a good little girl at this stage that I think not.' Indeed, there seemed to be very little friction in the household. Though Prince Michael does not like hunting any more than his wife enjoys bob-sleighing, he accompanies her to local hunts 'out of love for me.' That does not, however, prevent her from 'terrorising' him when he comes home from the shoot and leaves 'an awful lot of dead birds all over the hall.' But she did not succeed in terrorising Mr Plomley, who refused to allow her to take one of her cats to the island as a luxury. 'Luxuries have to be inanimate,' he explained. 'I want my cat with me,' demanded the Princess. 'It's the cat or nothing.' 'Sorry,' said Mr Plomley. 'No cats allowed.' 'You don't understand,' came the reply. 'There's method in my madness. It's got to be Oriental and preferably pregnant. An Oriental cat is one hell of a hunter.' Eventually, the protagonists agreed to continue the argument after the programme was off the air.

Within a month it was announced that Princess Michael was to be a guest of Maria Aitken's rather more sophisticated television chat-show, *Private Lives*, recorded in February for transmission in April. She proved to be, as Miss Aitken put it 'a wonderful raconteuse,' telling of close encounters with lionesses in the South African bush, and a hurried departure from Prague when the Soviet tanks rolled in in 1968. She opened up a shopping bag full of her favourite oddments, including a pair of dark glasses 'in case I get bothered when out shopping,' and revealed that she had been so entranced by seeing her first English-language film, *Breakfast at Tiffany's*, that she had always harboured an ambition to sing *Moon River* publicly. Unfortunately for her host and the viewers, she didn't do so on this occasion, but it was some kind of consolation to see her featured that same month in a *Sunday Times* interview, in which she mapped out a typical day in her busy and varied life. She told how she had invented Griselda – a wicked witch with a motor-powered broomstick – as the star of the bedtime stories she told her children, and how she always has a cold because Prince Michael insists she goes out riding early in all weathers. Her only newspaper is *The Times*, while her preferred lunchtime meal is a non-fattening salad. She gets most of her children's clothes from Marks and Spencer, and she and Prince Michael work at their files last thing at night – no matter how late that may be – because they are always collected up first thing next morning. She is still at work on two royal books, including the much-researched biography of Elizabeth of Bohemia, since to write 'a good book' is one of her many aspirations. Another, she confessed, was to get onto the front cover of *Horse and Hound* on merit. It did not take long for that illustrious journal – now celebrating its centenary – to respond. It announced that it would 'be honoured when Princess Michael of Kent's ambitions are fulfilled – it will certainly be one of our most attractive front pages.' Two days later, the Princess' clear round at Amberley Horse Trials was considered reason enough for *Horse and Hound* to oblige with amazing speed, by printing front and centre page pictures depicting the Princess on her hunter Sprite II within three weeks.

One of several interviews given by Prince Philip during the year was to the weekly magazine *Woman*. It centred, unsurprisingly, on possibly the Duke's most urgent and continual theme, the protection of wildlife, and it was published to coincide with yet another of his foreign tours as President of the World Wildlife Fund. He particularly deplored the destruction of tropical rain forests, an example he cited in support of his main argument, namely that 'by the middle of the next century we will have destroyed ourselves far more certainly than we will ever do by nuclear war. There could arise a situation where there is not enough green stuff on the globe to absorb the amount of carbon dioxide we are producing each year.' He was not opposed to the concept of human beings exploiting natural resources, provided that exploitation did not outrun the regeneration process – a point he made during his subsequent twelve-day trip to Hong Kong, Thailand, Malaysia and Jordan. In December he was infuriated by the scandalous affair of 24 golden-headed lion tamarins, an extremely rare species of monkey, which had been smuggled illegally from their natural habitat in Brazil, and sold to a trader in Belgium.

He was equally dismayed when, two months earlier, a greater sulphur-crested cockatoo belonging to the Queen was stolen from Whipsnade Zoo, and when, later, he heard that the Explorers' Club, of which he was a member, had staged a dinner in New York consisting of hippopotamus and lion meat, he was so 'appalled by the exhibition of bad taste' that, along with the Aga Khan, he resigned immediately. He was not appeased by the Club secretary's protestations that none of the food available represented endangered species, nor amused by the menu at a subsequent dinner which included pheasant described, in a tit-for-tat move against the Duke, as 'the bird Prince Philip enjoys shooting.'

Despite a somewhat less-travelled year on behalf of the World Wildlife Fund, the Duke continued his efforts which have already spanned two decades on its behalf. At home, he took a gloomy view of the year 2100, when the world's population would be doubled, and warned that the increase in human population was the biggest threat to wildlife – 'probably the most significant cause of the degradation of the environment generally, and the gradual extermination of the species.' Two months later, in March, he launched a £3,000,000 appeal for plant conservation at Kew Gardens, again with the warning that 40,000 of the world's flowering plants – some 15% of all known species – could be extinct in seventy years time. In May, he was in Washington to launch a campaign against the multi-million pound trade in animal skin imports, and took the opportunity to describe people who bought or kept tropical fish as sufferers 'from some psychiatric problem.' Fish breeders were instantly offended. 'He should try looking in the mirror,' said one.

Earlier the same month, the Duke had visited Austria, where a problem typical of his fears was under discussion. Europe's last virgin-forested estuary nature reserve, near Hainburg, was under threat from a project to build a hydro-electric complex and power station on the River Danube. For the government of Austria, which supported the project despite having ratified a conservation convention back in 1975, the Duke had harsh, uncompromising words, deploring its failure to stick to international agreements and to address itself to the potential loss of rare plants and animals. He was rewarded, immediately, with a rebuke from the Austrian Chancellor, who termed his remarks 'inappropriate and superfluous foreign demands', and with an equally harsh message from pro-project demonstrators in Vienna, who described the Fund as 'irrelevant.' Prince Philip denied that the Fund was 'trying to interfere in any way with the process of government in Austria. But if countries do not abide by conventions, it completely pulls the rug out from under the conservation movement.' He won his case. At the end of June, the power station scheme was rejected – though the matter remains under appeal.

The Queen was one of several other members of the Royal Family involved to one extent or another in the growing international preoccupation for wildlife. The plight of Britain's swans was brought to public and royal notice in September, with a Save Our Swans campaign designed to protect them against human neglect and wilful cruelty. As the Queen owns all unmarked swans in Britain, the campaign's organisers appealed to her for a contribution to its expenses. This was refused: the Queen may donate funds only to recognised charities, and the campaign could expect nothing till it registered. But in March the Queen, clearly concerned at the problem, commissioned a survey by the Edward Grey Institute at Oxford University, to investigate the dangers to swans and their causes. Preliminary findings that the number of swans on the Thames had dwindled from over a thousand in 1954 to less than two hundred today, and that over the whole country numbers are being reduced by up to three thousand a year, put the Save Our Swans campaign into overdrive, and they immediately announced an appeal for £100,000 to build a bird sanctuary. And, as if to illustrate how a little can go a long way, a pair of swans donated by the Queen to the Borough of Maidstone became the first to swim on the Medway for fourteen years – and in June they produced three cygnets. In October, Prince Charles announced that he had earmarked five acres of his Highgrove estate to be converted into meadow-land for the cultivation of wild flowers. He also began negotiations to set up a national nature reserve and a marine reserve on Duchy of Cornwall land in the Scillies. That autumn, the Queen Mother had become gravely concerned about the fate of a 1½-mile avenue of 240 ilex trees which had for 150 years graced the approach to the Sussex estate of Goring Hall, a former home of the Bowes-Lyon family. Almost half of the trees had contracted an incurable and terminal disease called ganoderna, and in August the Worthing Council condemned 77 of them to be felled. The Queen Mother heard of the proposal and her request for a report on the necessity of such drastic action prompted the Council to have second thoughts. On the advice of tree surgeons, only 43 of the ilex were brought down, and the remaining seventy were saved after being administered extensive surgery.

The Queen Mother had somewhat less success at the one activity with which she never fails to be immediately identified – horseracing. In the National Hunt season which ended in June 1984, she had nine horses in training, but only three of them earned their keep by winning races for her. Of these, by far the most impressive was her 11-year-old gelding Special Cargo, back in excellent form after he broke down in 1982 and had to have two carbon fibre implants in his legs. He rewarded the skill and patience of those who spent eighteen months nursing him back to fitness by a superb win in the Grand Military Cup at Sandown in March – a 12-length victory which made a nonsense of his disappointing February form, and which prompted his trainer, Fulke Walwyn, to consider him a potential Grand National winner 'if his legs stand up to racing.' It also made him a respected favourite for the rest of the season. He won two more races that month – at Lingfield and again at Sandown – and was reckoned to be firmly on course for the Whitbread Gold Cup at Sandown at the end of April. Despite a less than comforting fifth place at

Cheltenham in the meantime, he did indeed carry off the Gold Cup, finishing his season by bringing home over £25,000 prize money for his royal owner, and proving that his stamina over a 3½- mile course was a promising pointer to an Aintree appearance before long.

Two of the Queen Mother's six-year-olds, Sun Rising and Sunyone, also produced victories for her. Sun Rising, who showed great ability over hurdles in 1982-3, made a dreadful mistake at Warwick in December when he hit a fence on his very first steeplechase, and had to be content with third place. Eleven weeks later, however, he justified the bookmakers' confidence in him by winning a novice handicap at Windsor over 2½ miles. Meanwhile, the mare Sunyone won a novice hurdle at Huntingdon – an impressive début which also gave the Queen Mother her first ever win on that course – though in two subsequent races she failed to reach the frame. Dismal luck accompanied the Queen Mother's other horses. The nine-year-old Master Andrew, one of her more celebrated eightieth birthday presents, failed to match his previous season's form and, despite high expectations, brought home only one prize – for third place at Ascot in January – out of three races. A five-year-old newcomer, the New Zealand-bred gelding Harbour Master, was raced during only two months of the eight-month season, and failed to equal or better the third place he achieved in his third outing at Sandown in December. There were no wins or places from either Barrogil Castle, Highland Piper or Highland Line, in spite of promising form in 1982-3, and notwithstanding general expectations that Barrogil Castle – so called after the former name of the Queen Mother's Scottish residence, the Castle of Mey – would 'be at concert pitch' for his February début. So, thanks mainly to her useful servant Special Cargo, the Queen Mother had to be content with comparatively modest total winnings for the season amounting to a little short of £40,000.

One of the Queen Mother's string of horses which stood out for other reasons was a son of the illustrious Brigadier Gerard, the five-year-old Army Council. Formally trained as a flat-racer by William Hastings-Bass, he was sent late in summer to be trained by Bob Champion, the man who defied the onslaught of cancer to win the Grand National in 1981. *The Times* hailed this departure from the Queen Mother's usual practice of keeping all her horses in training at Fulke Walwyn's stable, and said that her decision 'will go down well with those who have grown to appreciate the contribution that each have made to the sport.' Champion gave Army Council a thorough grounding for his first race at Newbury in November, and was rewarded with fourth place in the Queen Mother's presence. After another confident race at Cheltenham, Champion had high hopes: 'I must admit I fancy the horse a lot,' he said. 'It would be marvellous to give the Queen Mother a victory.' Disappointingly, that never occurred. Army Council repeated a fourth place performance at Folkestone in February, but otherwise brought nothing back from his six outings, and this in spite of carrying three different riders. But, as the Queen Mother once said, 'that's racing.' And as one of her jockeys, Jonjo O'Neill said when he was chosen to ride Army Council in December – his first outing in the Queen Mother's colours – 'the Queen Mother must be more effective than anyone else when it comes to spreading the gospel of jumping. Pardon me, Ma'am, for saying so, but you obviously get one hell of a kick out of going racing, and your enthusiasm rubs off on the rest of us.'

The sentiment is not without evidence. In December, the Queen Mother went along to Warwick racecourse – her first ever visit there – to attend a special lunch in honour of 73-year-old trainer Walwyn, and to watch the afternoon's races which had all been specially named after him. It was in one of these – the Fulke Walwyn Novice Chase – that Sun Rising came in third, but unfortunately she had left the meeting before Walwyn's own horse, one of four he had taken with him to the course, won a race.

It is well known that, for a time at least, the Queen Mother's enthusiasm for racing infected Prince Charles, and it was probably in tribute to his somewhat brief participation over the sticks in 1980 and 1981 that the officials at Chepstow named a race – the two-mile Prince of Wales Chase – after him in November. He consented to this on the condition that the race should be open to mares only, a decision which, according to the Clerk of the Course, 'shows how keen he is on the perpetuation of the steeplechase breed.' The Prince's continued interest in horseracing was illustrated the same week, when he opened the new British Racing School, launched at Newmarket by the Apprentice Schools Charitable Trust. The school deals with all aspects of stable life, and boasts a seven-furlong all-weather gallop, and an indoor riding school. 'If there is a ratio between enthusiasm and success, this place is going to provide the biggest success story ever,' said the Trust's chairman, Lord McAlpine, rejoicing in the prospect that the school will provide a more solid foundation than at present exists for would-be jockeys, trainers and stable managers to base their future careers.

The idea of members of the Royal Family taking up their own careers, once something of an unusual notion, is one to which we are gradually becoming more accustomed. Once upon a time the trend was reversed: those royals who had taken up careers, like Prince Michael, the Duke of Kent and the Duke of Gloucester, eventually gave them up in order to satisfy public demand for their services on the royal round – though the Duke of Gloucester in particular has succeeded in continuing some aspects of his chosen career of architect with his official duties: in September he was appointed vice-chairman of the Government's new heritage body, while in January he opened a major exhibition of Arab architecture at the Royal Institute of British Architects, at which he was accompanied by the Crown Prince of Jordan. Some of his cousins, particularly those with no prospective obligations to carry out royal engagements, are now managing to shake off the restrictions of their birth, and follow a line of their own.

Most conspicuously successful among them is Viscount Linley, the 23-year-old son of Princess Margaret, whose wood-working career is now entering its third year. By September he was preparing for a ten-day exhibition of his latest furniture for the benefit of wholesalers at Palm Beach, Florida. One of his new pieces was a leather inlaid wooden chest, another a screen which operates by the use of novel magnetic hinges. While in Miami to promote his stock in November, he revealed that among his customers were the Prince and Princess of Wales, who bought a glass inlaid wooden table for their dining room at Highgrove. In October he and his three colleagues at their Dorking workshop held a private showing which included some of his tall, multi-coloured wood screens, now finding a market at several hundreds of pounds each. He also designed a nifty and brightly-coloured table and chair set – marketed the following year for just over £100 – whose main selling feature is its ability to fold up into a portable package only inches thick. Viscount Linley revisited Florida in January to represent over a hundred British craftsmen at the new Charles Nesbitt Fine Arts Showroom. He was thrilled to be the spearhead for what was in effect a promotional campaign, primarily because, as he has several times before said, 'they are very receptive to new designs and there seems a lot more opportunity to sell in America.' By March, however, the Dorking workshop team began to split up. One of them, Peter St Pier, whose father owns the converted bakery they all rented, gave notice that all was not well. 'With any creative characters, you are for a while inspired by each other,' he said. 'Then that tends to get stale. We all want to expand and I am not keen to expand under the same roof.' Viscount Linley confirmed that 'the business has been going well, but some of us feel it is time for a change.' Negotiations to take over other premises nearby began with the hope of a move by the early summer. Sure enough, at the end of July, a new workshop was ready at Betchworth, just a few miles away, and Princess Margaret came to perform a less than serious opening ceremony, cutting a wooden ribbon with a tree-saw. Lady Sarah Armstrong-Jones, and Lord and Lady Snowdon were among the fifty or so guests who attended the champagne celebration, with music provided by a five-man steel band.

Viscount Linley's sister, Lady Sarah Armstrong-Jones, completed her first year foundation course at Camberwell School of Art in December and began a year's sabbatical with a term's study of stained glass techniques in Cambridge. When that came to an end, she began to look around in other directions, trying, as her father Lord Snowdon said, 'a month here and a month there to see which way she may go. She will be doing various things to widen her outlook.' She spent some time learning to gild wood, with her father's cousin Thomas Messel, and was showing an interest in fabric design when, in mid-March, she accompanied Lord Snowdon on a three-week working holiday to India, to help him on a commission to take still photographs of the filming of *A Passage to India*, which Lord Brabourne, husband of Countess Mountbatten, was producing. She finished up being a wardrobe-mistress, and when she returned to Britain at the end of April, she continued her association with the film by working as an assistant to one of its production staff, Richard Goodwin, at his studio in Rotherhithe. Lady Sarah's second cousin and close friend, Lady Helen Windsor, having passed one 'A' level in Practical Art in 1982, passed one of her two retakes – the History of Art – this year, though by September a career had not been settled upon. 'Nothing has been decided yet,' said a spokesman, 'but this latest result means that she can pursue a career in the art world.' Eventually, she took up a job as a receptionist at the Mayor Gallery in Mayfair, travelling by underground to and from the Knightsbridge flat which she leased with two other girls at the beginning of 1983. In January 1984, it was announced that she would be going to Paris for six months to polish up her French and widen her horizons. She admitted that her ideas were as yet vague, though she was convinced that her future lay in art. 'I am not quitting the art world whatever happens,' she said.

Meanwhile, her brother George, Earl of St Andrews, was continuing his studies at Downing College Cambridge, just a year ahead of Prince Edward, while his first cousin, James Ogilvy, the twenty-year-old son of Princess Alexandra, began his at St Andrew's University in Scotland, after spending a short-term commission with the Scots Guards (of which his uncle the Duke of Kent is Colonel) in Singapore during August and September. Conditions, he said, weren't bad, but he seemed less than enthusiastic with the idea of 'living off bananas and coconuts.' In July 1984, James' younger sister Marina completed her school career at St Mary's, Wantage – the school which Lady Helen Windsor attended before going to Gordonstoun – and has emerged as a keen swimmer and horsewoman, as well as a gifted actress who has starred in many school plays. She was selected that month as one of the venturers for Operation Raleigh, the scheme sponsored by the Prince of Wales and designed to expand powers of leadership in young people. The scheme has proved exceptionally popular, and Marina was lucky enough to find herself one of only 14% of the 8,500 applicants to secure a place.

Preparations for Prince Edward's projected career at present alternate with his further education. A month before he went up to Cambridge, he began a probationary commission as a second lieutenant with the Royal Marines at Lympstone, having already qualified on merit ('because of *what* he is, not *who* he is,' as the Marine's Commandant-General emphasised) in a three-day assault course described by his recruiting officer as 'the start of the road to Hell and back.' 'We like to get our pound of flesh,' he added, 'so he'll have to be kept up to date.' Accordingly, the Prince attended a two-week course of training in September, which provided some idea of what he could expect when eventually he embarks on his full year commando course, while at the same time his training officer could not emphasise too strongly the importance of maintaining a rigorous programme of physical exercise while studying at Cambridge. Prince Edward's interviewing officer, Lt Canning, spoke in blunt, forceful manner about his recruitment. 'We give special treatment to none but the enemy,' he warned. 'I didn't pull any punches about what he was letting himself in for.' Even the elements of the course had brutalising titles, like the 'beasting' promised for the first day. 'It happens to nearly all the new entries,' said the recruiting officer. 'I doubt whether they would make the Prince an exception.'

They didn't. Delights of the first day included being woken at 2 am, ordered onto the assault course, and eventually immersed in a tank of water. The following day the Prince was sent on a two-circuit run around the camp, wilting with exhaustion, and heard talk of death slides and back-pack-carrying cross-country runs to follow. He was back in training almost immediately after finishing his first year at Cambridge, spending a week on Woodbury Common in Dorset 'yomping', Falklands-style, through six miles of rivers, mud and gorse-covered moorland, with an 85lb pack on his back, and showing that he had lost none of his old fitness. He rarely lagged behind during the entire route-march, and turned in what his superiors described as a creditable performance. And all for the £12.50 a day, including a £4.50 education allowance, which he will receive as a full-time commando trainee late in 1986. Nor was this all. During the Easter vacation he spent three weeks at RAF Abingdon in Oxfordshire, with a special unit attached to the Queen's Flight. Here he learned to fly Bulldog aircraft, the piston-engined two-seaters belonging to the University of London's Air Squadron. The course was designed to up-date his rather sporadic flying experience – he had completed a three-week basic training course at RAF Cranwell in 1982, and flew from time to time at Wanganui the following year. While at Abingdon, he flew his Bulldog to RAF Benson, ten miles away, on an unscheduled mission to meet the Queen who was visiting the headquarters of the Queen's Flight. 'What a nice surprise,' she beamed.

His elder brother, Prince Andrew, had already borne the heat and burden of the day, and his service career is now well established. He began a six-month advanced training course, learning to fly Lynx helicopters, after having successfully mastered the Sea Kings from RNAS Culdrose. For this purpose he transferred to 702 Naval Air Squadron at Portland in mid-September, living in the officers' mess on *HMS Osprey* (which Prince Charles had visited at the end of 1981), in standard accommodation comprising a cabin with a living area and a desk for study. He was one of eight officers – four observers and four pilots – to join the course, and as a pilot he was allocated a permanent observer colleague, 32-year-old Lt Robin Wain, who completed his Lynx training in 1978, and the two of them operated as a team for the duration of the course. 'He will find it difficult,' said his commanding officer Tom Bradley. 'We do not spoon-feed these boys. We require them to take a responsible attitude to their training.' That seemed to pose no problem for Prince Andrew. 'I live to fly,' he had said during his interview with David Frost, 'and to fly from the sea.' By December he was on a man management course, which included being trained for pastoral care of his subordinates. 'He has been taught how to deal with personal problems,' said one of his superiors, Lt-Commander Colin Cook. 'Anything from conditions on board ship to girlfriend problems.' In February, Prince Andrew was promoted from Sub-Lieutenant to Lieutenant, which took his salary from £7,800 to £10,900. By May he had completed 100 hours of flying, passed the entire training course, complete with examinations and flying assessments, and was posted to *HMS Brazen* as the only Lynx pilot aboard the 4,000-ton frigate, and with the prospect of staying there for up to two or even three years.

The inevitable glamour of his naval career tended to obscure Prince Andrew's claim to become a serious photographer – a profession for which in March many acquaintances were predicting that he would soon be resigning his commission. Those rumours, which proved, like most, to be over-enthusiastic, followed the news that the Prince had just signed a contract for the production in November 1985 of a book of two hundred of his photographs – which the publishers, Hamish Hamilton, promised would 'show he has become a very competent photographer.' The pictures would range from architectural studies to incidents during his service career, and photographs of members of his family, including 'some nice pictures of the Queen and Queen Mother off duty.' This latter category would presumably remind his readership that his family 'do get slightly annoyed and complain bitterly that I am getting more and more like a Press-man.' Prince Andrew would also write a text, dealing with his techniques and choice of subject matter, as well as with his experiences as an up-and-coming photographer: 'the Prince is very aware of his duties and realises why people are so interested in his pictures,' explained his agents. 'But he is desperately serious about his photography and totally committed to being a good photographer.'

Prince Andrew's life on both *Osprey* and *Brazen* was designed to be as normal as that of any other officer, though monthly social functions were off limits. 'He will not be joining them,' said Commander Derek Scott from *Osprey*. 'That would mean bringing someone along, and the press might get interested. It ruins the event for everyone else.' It was a wise precaution in a year when press interest in Prince Andrew's girlfriends had been little short of hyperactive. Speculation about Koo Stark, a recurrent theme in 1982-3, continued into the following year with renewed vigour when the lady was rumoured to have been personally invited by the Queen to spend part of August at Balmoral. The implication of a serious romance recognised and approved of by the monarch was intensified by the claim by the senior editor of Burke's *Peerage* that, 'I have now learned that the Queen likes Koo,' and by the appearance of Miss Stark's portrait photograph, taken by Norman Parkinson, on the front cover of a German weekly. The reality proved otherwise, hope of respectability foundering on an ill-starred and rather embarrassing television interview – 'a contender for the prize of worst made and most irritating television show of the decade,' commented one reviewer – in which she talked of affairs of the heart, claiming, with an earnestness which belied the events of the previous ten months, 'You have to be subtle because men's egos are fragile.' In the aftermath, she sought refuge abroad, a planned holiday in France proving abortive when the French press tumbled its proposed location. Eventually, she flew to Bali, Thailand, Nepal and Australia, where she succumbed to the lure of another television interview – this time with Michael Parkinson. Her condition that her personal life, especially as far as it concerned Prince Andrew, should not be broached doomed it to failure, and the Melbourne *Age* damned it as 'the non-interview of the decade.'

Reports at the end of August that Prince Andrew had ended the relationship were resisted. The editor of *Majesty* magazine declared that the romance was far from over, and guessed that Miss Stark had herself abandoned the idea of going to Balmoral for fear of press intrusion. The belief was fuelled by reported telephone conversations between the couple, in which reunions on her return to Britain were arranged, and by Prince Andrew's sudden and unexplained absence in the first week of September from three events at which he might reasonably have been expected to join his holidaying relatives. Miss Stark added to the speculation in December by insisting that the possibility of marriage remained 'if people weren't so keen to spoil it.' But then the rumours became more desultory; understandably so, as by then she had appeared again in the nude – this time in a book of photographs taken four years before, called *Private Viewing, Contemporary Erotic Photography* – and had in November been involved in a doubtful scandal over her missing handbag – or was it merely a camera case? – in which a tape recording – or was it a letter, or both? – said to have contained some fairly steamy messages to or about Prince Andrew, were reported stolen. Police questioned her no fewer than three times, and the apparent seriousness with which the loss was taken – the Queen was said to have been sent daily details of police progress on the case – sent the continental press crawling on all fours for the mystery material. A West German periodical *Bild der Frau*, unable to come up with the real thing, published what it thought was a plausible invention which was immediately slapped down by all concerned. 'Rubbish!' snapped Buckingham Palace. 'You've heard of the Hitler diaries, haven't you,' said Miss Stark, proving that not all her subtlety had abandoned her.

By July, she was engaged to a 22-year-old bachelor, Timothy Jefferies, the grandson of the man who had made his fortune marketing trading stamps. It came as little surprise that the prospective bridegroom's mother was 'horrified', and reduced to commenting that her son had done the Queen a favour by taking Miss Stark out of royal reach. 'If she wasn't acceptable for Prince Andrew, I don't see why she should be good enough for my boy. Would anyone like their son to marry a girl of her notoriety?' No doubt the Royal Family was relieved, if not positively delighted that this particular chapter, with its long-drawn-out ramifications, seemed at last to be closed. Certainly the feeling was shared by much of the country at large, who showed little interest in the lengthy post-mortems which appeared in the press at the demise of this controversial affair.

No sooner had Koo Stark been written off as a candidate for the position of future Duchess of York than journalistic eyes began to cast around for new possibilities. In August, Fleet Street zeal exposed its own shortcomings on accuracy, when a young lady called Sophie Birdwood was reported to have spent the weekend with Prince Andrew at Balmoral. The first she personally knew of it was when, coincidentally, she arrived back from the Bahamas around the same time, 'horrified and not very amused' at being confronted by no fewer than six newspaper teams who thought she had just flown back from Scotland. It transpired that the lady in question was the Hon Carolyn Herbert, daughter of the Queen's racing manager Lord Porchester, whose weekend at Balmoral – by no means an unusual occurrence – was spent at the Queen's personal invitation. The mistaken newspapers retreated with egg well and truly on their faces, while one of those who had abstained from running the story mischievously suggested that the time had come for an illustrated edition of *Who's Who*. The lesson was well and truly learned. When, on the eve of his 24th birthday in February, Prince Andrew took Carolyn to the Royal Opera House and to supper afterwards with a group of friends, there was no talk of romance.

Other prospective candidates were not so lucky. In November, Prince Andrew was spotted escorting an unidentified brunette to Joe Allen's restaurant in Exeter Street, but a brief speculation came to nothing. Then he was seen accompanying Susannah Constantine to the photography exhibition at Hamilton Galleries – but she turned out to be a frequent companion of several of his relations, including Viscount Linley with whom she had been seen twice in the same month at restaurants in Fulham and Knightsbridge, and with whom she had travelled to Belgium the previous June. In December, the dangers of provoking publicity impressed themselves on a former girlfriend of Prince Andrew, Carolyn Seaward. She had intended to go to the London première of *Never Say Never Again*, at which the Prince was to be guest of honour, but she decided against after being warned that 'the press would get very excited and it would get out of hand.' By January there were two more possibilities. Bridget Mathey, the 24-year-old daughter of a wealthy London businessman, was said to have been Prince Andrew's evening guest at Buckingham Palace after nights out on the town – including two visits to the Royal Ballet before Christmas. When her brother informed the press, 'It's a cold trail now,' they turned to 27-year-old Clare Park, a ballet dancer turned model – she became *Vogue's* Face of Britain in 1977 – and known to the public generally for her claims on behalf of the advertisers of crispbread and moisturising cream. But all palled in the fierce, ephemeral light of February's celebrity, Kate Rabett.

Miss Rabett, a former dancer with Second Generation, made the mistake of inviting Prince Andrew to her West Ealing home for a party to celebrate his 24th birthday – not long after the couple had allegedly bumped into each other at a photographic exhibition and exchanged telephone numbers. It was in truth a very ordinary party, insofar as any party attended by royalty can be, but its telling combined surprise and homeliness in such a way that there was immediately talk of Prince Andrew settling down at last. A few doubts were raised when she was discovered to have been in several rather down-market television shows and comic strips, but her father's respectable profession of gynaecologist, and the revelation that she herself was in the process of overcoming a recently terminated love affair with a male model (who said he still hoped to win her back) lent credence to hope and expectations of another royal wedding before long. Besides, said Harold Brookes-Baker of Burke's *Peerage*, 'her pedigree is much more impressive than many members of the Royal Family.' That rather odd remark turned out to be derived from the unprepossessing fact that she was descended from the Earls Winterton, who, like most of our ancestors, it seems, came over with William the Conqueror.

Then inevitability took a hand. With the speed of light, almost a hundred transparencies showing a topless Miss Rabett did the rounds of Fleet Street in search of a buyer, found one in the shape of the *News of the World* for £15,000, and were selectively published. Her father, who knew of the pictures and their sale, despised those involved and said that the £15,000 could have been better spent 'to support a geriatric ward or feed a family for a year.' Her mother vehemently denied that her daughter had ever posed topless 'in order for someone to publish, or to make a profit,' while Kate herself denied the pictures were even of her. The photographer, Chelsea-based Philip Lindsay, insisted they were, and took this heaven-sent opportunity to provide fairly frank details – 'She had no inhibitions about undressing' – about how he got them. When a clutch of nude photographs appeared, Miss Rabett became more emphatic still. 'I can categorically state that they are fakes,' she maintained, adding – in a timely way because Prince Andrew's connection with all this had all but faded – 'I am a friend of Prince Andrew, but nothing more. We are not having a special relationship.' To prove her point about the photographs, she took out writs of libel and for the protection of copyright. They were only partially successful, and after a week of denials, she finally admitted 'a lapse of memory' about those nude pictures. There seemed to be débris all around her, and, of course, Prince Andrew had disappeared from the scene. Nevertheless, in the twelve fleeting days during which her story was current, she was said to have clinched contracts worth £15,000 and to have doubled her modelling rates to around £70 an hour.

Meanwhile, Viscount Linley's association with Susannah Constantine was certainly one of the most enduring of the year. In January, he took her to a fancy dress ball at Christie's; the same month she took leave from her job as a publicist for a disco company to join him on his trip to Florida, and then to Mustique where they stayed with Princess Margaret for a fortnight; and she was with him again in March to see an exhibition of Lord Snowdon's photographic portraits at the Olympus Gallery. But Viscount Linley persisted in denying thoughts of marriage 'at my age,' and pointed out that the friendship had after all lasted perfectly well without talk of romance for almost four years.

Journalists in Cambridge, keeping a weather eye open for Prince Edward's attentions towards the opposite sex, were rewarded with an unconfirmed report in November that Katie Furshpan, a fellow member of the cast of *The Crucible*, had succeeded in hooking him. Like many of his brother Prince Andrew's companions, she failed to attract lasting press attention, but by the end of February, the young Miss Romy Adlington proved a more worthwhile prospect. The initial information that she was a model, coinciding as it did with the height of the Kate Rabett story, proved almost too much for some. 'I never thought the time would come,' said one high-born cartoon character, 'when I longed for just one Royal to be homosexual.' And it was perhaps because everyone was rather over full of royal love stories that this one achieved a pleasant, rather cosy seriousness. Stories – almost *de rigueur* in this connection – that the young lady had been Prince Edward's guest at Windsor, Balmoral and Sandringham, were readily confirmed by her mother from the family home in Micheldever, Hampshire, and she also added that the couple had met the previous August during Cowes Week, which is always attended by the family. Like Prince Edward, Miss Adlington enjoys sailing and skiing, and there are frequent telephone calls between them. Even so, her mother was quick to point out, 'it's just a normal young relationship. I am sure it's not a long-term romance.' The sentiment was confirmed by the daughter. 'He is gorgeous and very good-looking,' she said while on a modelling trip to Madrid, adding that while they write regularly to each other, she did not want the relationship to interfere with her career. She was in no hurry to return to Britain, and was enjoying her stay in Spain. This sensible and quite straight-forward approach seemed to bring out the best in all parties, and as far as the press was concerned, the relationship was left to take its now tranquil course.

Back in London, a small-hours observer spotted Lady Sarah Armstrong-Jones driving away from the Soho restaurant L'Escargot shortly before Christmas in male company, but the gentleman's identity escaped those normally reckoned to be in the know. Lady Helen Windsor's escorts were less fortunate – indeed her liaisons, both fleeting and enduring, were followed and reported on avidly by the gossip columnists. There was general agreement by November that wedding bells would soon be ringing for her, and that her bridegroom would be 22-year-old John Benson, then in his final year studying Art at Edinburgh University. The rumours derived their strength not only from the fact that Benson had been an Eton contemporary of Lady Helen's brother, but from the stories that she had often helped him run his mobile disco at Raffles nightclub during his weekends and vacations in London, as well as from the frequent sightings of both of them travelling around London in his hand-built, cream-coloured Morgan car. In September, the association seemed to have become more formalised when they went on holiday together with the Duke and Duchess of Kent to Corfu, in place of a vacation the young couple had planned in the Greek islands but which had to be cancelled because of a typhoid scare. They were back in London again a week later, in time to attend the All-Stars rock concert at the Albert Hall, at which the Prince and Princess of Wales were also present.

At the end of October, one lone voice predicted that 'inevitably Lady Helen will do the right thing and dump him. It's bred into them.' With an immediacy for which until then only the effect of Government leaks were famed, Helen was reported to be wining and dining with Gerard Faggionato, a 23-year-old assistant at the Fraser Art Gallery, only a stone's throw from her own place of work in Cork Street, forsaking Benson's sporty Morgan for the new boy's Monaco-registered Volkswagen. Faggionato, thought to be a former escort of Lady Sarah Armstrong-Jones, protested that he and Lady Helen were 'just friends', while she merely laughed off the multiplicity of stories. 'John and I are still very happy,' she was reported to have said, 'and all this about Gerard is nonsense. I see him for lunch as much as I see anyone working in Cork Street, but he's just a friend. John is doing his degree now, so he can't come down.' And as if to confirm it, there was talk that Lady Helen was to accompany Mr Benson on a skiing holiday in January. This did not stop her being seen with a succession of other escorts, including David Flintwood, another West End Art Gallery employee; a 23-year-old Ghanaian businessman, ex-public schoolboy Isaac Ayer-Kumi; and Old Etonian Nigel Oakes. Both Ayer-Kumi and Oakes escorted Lady Helen to see the film *The Betrayal* in London in March, and it was Oakes who was in the party of four which left for a skiing holiday in the French Alps in the middle of that month, only to return to find his company OGP Limited in financial difficulties.

The prolonged and persistent talk over Lady Helen's supposed romances was heard with some concern by her parents, and one could not help feeling that the Duchess of Kent in particular could well have done without the prospect of reading speculative reports in each day's newspapers. There had already been considerable anxiety about the Duchess' health, following an unexpectedly long period of convalescence after the previous April's operation to remove an ovarian cyst had caused her to cancel all further engagements until after the summer. Her staff denied that she had fallen foul of the depressive condition that had spasmodically dogged her during the past five or six years, and by early August were able to report that she was pretty well back to full health. That month, she left with her younger son, the 13-year-old Lord Nicholas Windsor, for a two-week holiday in Canada, assuring well-wishers as she left London Airport: 'I'm feeling fine. We're going on holiday, just the two of us, to get away from it all.' The break had been planned for some time, though no indication was given as to whether it was designed to be part of the Duchess' recuperation. Her subsequent two-week family package holiday in a six-bedroomed villa near the fishing village of Kassiopi on the north-east coast of Corfu, kept her out of the country until the end of September. By that time, her spokesman from York House, the Kents' London residence, had confirmed that 'the Duchess continues to make good progress. She is starting with a very light programme of engagements.' They began on 20th October, with the première of the film version of *La Traviata* in London, and reached a tally of 22 in the two-month period to Christmas.

The Royal Family generally had a hale and hearty kind of year, free from all but a few irritant health disorders and temporary disruptions of programmes which were otherwise diligently fulfilled. Of the Duchess of Kent's two royal sisters-in-law, one, Princess Michael, suffered nothing worse during the year than the humiliating experience of a bee-sting, when she sat down without looking during a picnic in August, while the other, Princess Alexandra, caught a cold virus at Christmas which threatened her January schedule. Happily, she recovered from it in time and as usual was one of the first royals off the mark in the New Year, beaten only by Princess Anne and Princess Margaret. In November her daughter Marina, following what has almost become a royal tradition, was suddenly whisked from her school in Wantage to the John Radcliffe Hospital in Oxford for a five-day stay to have her appendix removed. She was visited, and eventually accompanied back to school by her father, Angus Ogilvy, who himself had recently undergone surgery to arrest a deterioration in his eyesight. Princess Anne caught a cold in October, but it didn't stop her paying a nostalgic visit to Harrods at 8.30 one morning, to open the new Food Hall; nor was her sense of smell so affected that she couldn't recognise the very distinctive savoury smell which lingers in the memory of all Harrods visitors long after they have left. 'As a small girl,' she said, 'I was often brought to Harrods, and one of the big features was to go through the Food Hall. The sights and smells were always very special.' It probably did her no end of good to be treated to a 'breakfast of British exports' – sausages, mushrooms, tomatoes, prime bacon, scrambled egg and fried potatoes, toast and marmalade, strawberry preserve and honey.

In December, Prince Charles also caught a cold – by way of a germ which, rejoicing in the name of respiratory syncitial virus, sounded worse than it probably was. He had, much to his disgust, caught it from Prince William. 'I have discovered during the course of parenthood,' he announced to an audience in Newcastle-upon-Tyne, 'that children give you worse diseases than anyone else.' Lord Frederick Windsor, the five-year-old son of Prince Michael, kept his one indisposition very much to himself: in October, he broke his left arm in a playground accident at the Bayswater Prep School, Wetherby's, which he had joined the previous month.

Prince Edward probably suffered the worst royal bout of ill health when, shortly after the New Year, he went down with what the medicos term infectious mononucleosis, and what the rest of us call the kissing disease. This glandular infection, common to people in their late teens and early twenties, involves a loss of appetite and energy. Prince Edward's illness was no better and no worse than most of its kind: he was laid up at Sandringham for the best part of a fortnight but was 'well on the way to recovery' by the middle of January. His return to Jesus College for the Lent term – scheduled for the 19th of that month – was delayed by four days, and he was obliged to give up rugby for the duration. He could often be seen enviously watching his College's games from the sidelines, and must have felt quite deprived at having to cancel his proposed visit with his team to the United States in March to play a series of matches in North Carolina.

That apart, the only anxieties were for the Queen Mother, whose meeting with Lady Diana Cooper at a reception at St James's Palace in March was instantly regretted when Lady Diana contracted chickenpox a day or two later, and for Captain Mark Phillips who turned up at the Cheltenham Festival that month with a black eye – apparently the result of an accidental butt by one of his horses at Gatcombe Park. There were certainly no problems for the Queen and the Princess of Wales, who were the subject of predictions at about the same time that they would live to 85 and 81 years of age respectively. These days the computer can, it seems, predict the length of each reign, based on evidence about the subject's lifestyle, pressures and worries, the taking of exercise and the pattern of eating and smoking habits. Meanwhile, the Duke of Gloucester, as Patron of Action on Smoking and Health, made an assault on the national health hazard of smoking. In an open message of support for a new plan of action following a Royal College of Physicians' claim that 100,000 people die each year through smoking, the Duke hailed the 'fight against Britain's smoking epidemic.' He must be well aware that both his father, grandfather, great-grandfather, and two royal uncles died from smoking-related diseases, and reveals that he has tried, regrettably unsuccessfully, to persuade Princess Margaret to give up what their common ancestor James I called 'the poisonous and vile weed.'

The public sympathy for the Duke's attitude to smoking was probably greater than for another cause which he had championed – the rehabilitation of that much-maligned monarch Richard III. As co-sponsor of the Richard III Society, he had attended several events in 1983 in celebration of the 500th anniversary of the beginning of the king's controversial two-year reign. One of the last of these was staged by the Oxford Union in the form of a debate – 'not terribly serious,' said its President – on the motion that 'Richard III was more sinned against than sinning.' The level of earnestness was perhaps indicated by the fact that all officers of the Union wore fancy dress, though the Duke, attending in a private capacity as a former Oxford student, stayed loyal to the black tie. He also stayed loyal to Richard III and, predictably, supported the motion.

As his mother, Princess Alice, continues her gradual run-down of public duties, the Duke of Gloucester and his wife are increasing theirs. They repeated one particular feature of their 1982-3 programme the following year by making several visits abroad in what for the Duke at least seems to have been one of his busiest years. In October, his presidency of the British Consultants Bureau took him on a six-day round trip to Jordan, Dubai and Abu Dhabi. The following March he was accompanied by the Duchess on a two-day cultural trip to Luxembourg as guests of the Grand Duke Jean, which also included a tour of the European Community institutions based there. And a journey to New York at the end of April on behalf of the Victorian Society, the English Speaking Union, and the Order of St John, with which his family have been connected for many decades, allowed him and the Duchess to stay on privately in Washington, extending their absence from Britain on that occasion to nine days.

Somehow you couldn't help feeling that this was the year of the United States so far as royal visits abroad were concerned. The Duke and Duchess of Gloucester were only two out of ten members of the Royal Family who crossed the Atlantic to spend anything from a few days to a fortnight in the republic – some, like Princess Alexandra, relatively quietly and on behalf of comparatively obscure organisations; others on missions of almost international importance. One of these involved a relative novice to the business of official foreign visits – Prince Andrew. In mid-April he flew to Los Angeles to promote British trade in the *Britain comes to Beverly Hills* sales drive. His contribution was to correct any quaint impressions of the British still lingering with the Americans. 'The British people are not just cute-accented traditionalists,' he assured his audience. 'There are producers of consumer goods over there who have not let their responsiveness to the demands of modern taste spoil their long-established standards of workmanship. We are proud of people who can produce clothes, china, silver and a whole range of beautiful things at reasonable prices.' Prince Andrew was also in Los Angeles as a focal point for Americans who were former pupils of his old school Gordonstoun, celebrating its fiftieth anniversary in 1984, as well as to attend functions in connection with the British Olympics Association, a cause well supported by many members of the Royal Family – especially Princess Anne – throughout the year. Prince Andrew had a whale of a time: he attracted a huge female following, which probably accounted for the policewoman detailed to guard him from over-enthusiasm; he enjoyed a spectacular reception and dinner with tax-exiled British celebrities, had a surprise meeting with Nancy Reagan who happened to be staying briefly in the same hotel, and was seen sporting a whole assortment of hats, including a red, white and blue Olympics cap, a sombrero, and a baker-style cap for a visit to a NASA laboratory – all to the delight of his respective hosts.

At first it proved a popular and successful trip, despite a few rumbles of disapproval from one quarter or another. A row broke out when guests at a Gordonstoun former pupils' dance, suspecting that one of their number, Wendy Allen, had been set up by the organiser and sponsor, millionaire Armand Hammer, as the Prince's partner for the evening. Press interest in her almost dominated the entire occasion, though she wisely refused to say more than that she found Prince Andrew 'charming and delightful. We had a lovely evening and he is a super dancer.' Other incidents involved a disparaging remark that the Prince was said to have made to a vendor of T-shirts at the British sales exhibition, the disappointment of crowds as he overshot time on some duties and had to rush through others, and what the picture-hungry American press saw as his distinct lack of cooperation. 'Touring this city with Prince Andrew,' said one photographer, 'is as much fun as a visit to the dentist' – and his colleagues reduced the significance of the visit to a rating of 3 or 4 out of ten.

But these were pinpricks by comparison with the incident in which Prince Andrew, visiting a construction site, took up a paint-sprayer, directed it at journalists and switched it on. It took less than ten seconds, not only for several of the victims and their photographic equipment to be covered with paint, but also for the incident to become the most analysed, most heavily criticised and certainly the most notorious royal act of the year. The press on the spot were naturally the first, loudest and longest protesters – understandably so as they took the full force on clothes, cameras and faces. 'He tested the gun, then took two steps forward and sprayed us,' said a *Time-Life* photographer, with due deliberation. 'I would expect that sort of behaviour from my eight-year-old grandson, but not from a 24-year-old royal visitor.' A reporter corroborated the second-by-second story: 'He held it up for a moment, with this most devilish grin – my nine-year-old son has a grin just like that when he is about to put a frog down your back – and just pulled the trigger.' A BBC sub-contractor condemned Prince Andrew's action as 'stupid and deliberate,' while another journalist commented wryly, 'I'll just claim from my paper on the ground that covering Prince Andrew is a hazardous assignment.' The press in London was quick to take up the theme: the *Daily Star* and *Daily Express* called him 'a hooligan' while a Sunday paper, regretting that the incident in all probability spoiled the Queen's birthday, complained, 'Some Mothers Do Have 'Em.' A tongue-in-cheek *Daily Mirror* sympathised with Prince Andrew's predicament: 'He couldn't help it,' stated its leader writer, remembering that the Duke of Edinburgh sprayed photographers with a hose at the Chelsea Flower Show in 1959. 'His oafish sense of humour is hereditary.' *The Observer* remarked that the incident nailed the myth that royalty could not answer back, while the *Sunday Express* compared the Prince's behaviour with that of the Queen Mother, who during a recent visit to the Medway towns had spent time to direct a lost child towards her parents. The *Daily Mail's* thought that the Prince was 'loosing his charm' was echoed both by Jean Rook in the *Express* – 'God Save The Queen From The Heirs Without Graces' – and by Auberon Waugh in the *Sunday Telegraph*. 'I could live a happy and fulfilled existence without seeing another photograph of this young man in any newspaper for the rest of my life,' he declaimed, adding that the press should nevertheless always persevere with their job of photographing the Princess of Wales 'even if she showed a tendency to release Cruise missiles in every direction.'

From the outset, Buckingham Palace denied that the episode was anything other than accidental, a view shared by the American officials in Prince Andrew's entourage, and by the British vice-consul who quickly expressed his regret to the journalists. From Prince Andrew personally and from his immediate staff there was a long, embarrassed silence, which prompted questions as to whether he should not in future be accompanied by a press officer in addition to his private secretary – a matter reflected in one commentator's suggestion that 'he should take on no more unaccompanied tours until he has learned more about them.' Eventually, the Prince was said to have been 'mortified' by the incident, and in a hastily-arranged television interview three days later he made a simple, unaffected apology and explanation: 'I am not used to spray guns. I was going to spray the wall. I'm sorry you got painted. There was nothing I could do about it.' It did little to placate those who knew that the Prince had been specifically advised by the work-force on the construction site not to squeeze the trigger of the device, nor others who were convinced they saw a smirk on his face as the paint was released, and heard him say afterwards, 'I enjoyed that.' There were others, however, who thought the whole matter had been over-dramatised. 'So a few photographers got sprayed,' sneered a New Yorker. 'They're big boys. They can take it.' Michael Caine, one of the British actors who had attended a dinner-dance with the Prince, almost protested too much in Prince Andrew's defence. 'Andrew did millions of positive things,' he said in a spate of hyperbole, 'and I can't understand why everyone has latched onto one silly incident. He gave the trip 101% of his efforts.' Certainly the heat of the furore far exceeded the level of actual damage. When the British consulate announced that claims for compensation would be considered, there was no shortage of speculative estimates – the highest reaching $50,000. In the event, only three claims were made: they totalled less than £2,000 and were settled quickly and without fuss. It rather put into perspective the assessment of the visit by one jaundiced commentator as 'the most unpleasant British visit since they burned the White House in the war of 1812', as well as the rumour that the Queen had banished her son from Windsor Castle for the duration of the Easter holidays – a story that lost little of its gossip value even when it was pointed out that Prince Andrew had in fact gone to Scotland as godfather at the christening of the son of the Duke and Duchess of Roxburgh.

It was in many ways a pity that Prince Andrew's first official visit to the States was so easily and conclusively soured, not least because only a fortnight earlier his visits on behalf of the Queen to the mid-Atlantic islands of St Helena and Ascension had proved dazzlingly successful and full of nothing but goodwill. These got off to a roaring start, both island communities hailing them with special issues of stamps and coins – the first on which the Prince has ever appeared in his own right – and with a blend of sentiment and jubilation which seems to flourish readily in areas so sheltered from Western culture. For the St Helenans, now celebrating their 150th anniversary as a Crown colony, it was their first royal visit since Prince Philip called in briefly in 1957, following King George VI's stop-over on his way home from South Africa ten years before, and the future Edward VIII's three-day stay in 1925. A carnival atmosphere pervaded Prince Andrew's own two-day visit, despite the unfortunate incident when the plumed and pith-helmeted Governor-General missed his footing on Jamestown's quayside during the welcoming ceremonies, and fell flat on his face! 'Feel free, have fun, join in with everyone,' the Prince was urged in the never-ending chorus of song which greeted his arrival, while his progress, white-uniformed, through the dusty streets hit exactly the right note in return – lots of informality, banter exchanged with an excited crowd, and shouted conversations with onlookers from upstairs windows beyond. At a dance that night, he picked 21-year-old waitress Deborah Yon from the milling crowd of six hundred young guests. 'She was the first face I recognised from an earlier walkabout,' he explained. 'The others were a bit young: I would have been accused of cradle-snatching.' 'I couldn't believe it,' said Deborah. 'I never really believed he was going to dance with me. I felt so embarrassed, but my friends congratulated me. He really is very cute.' Conversation between the Prince and his partner seemed to revolve around, of all things, the size of the island's Coca-Cola cans – a topic made much of, if only because it illustrated how unstuffy the visit was. 'For two days, our physical isolation has vanished and we may feel that St Helena is at the centre of the universe,' said the island's sheriff, after the population of 5,000 had sung a sentimental farewell to accompany Prince Andrew's embarkation for Ascension. The Prince confessed himself at a loss for words at this 'moving experience' and said that St Helena would always be a special place for him. Ascension Island must also have been special, for it became the strategically important mid-way point for British ships and aircraft travelling to and from the Falklands in 1982. Now this royal Falklands hero was back in much less tense circumstances, and again he reflected the prevailing mood in a way which found a ready response among Ascension's community as they took him on a tour round the island. The Prince was, however, reluctant to stereotype his style at such an early stage in his official career. 'It really is new for me,' he explained after the visit was complete. 'You play it as best you can. It was obvious that informality and relaxed attitudes were probably the best way of getting something out of the visit. They are not used to the pomp and circumstance of London.' And, as if to illustrate his point, he very unceremoniously opened a photographic exhibition featuring the island life of St Helena, back in London in May.

Prince Charles' growing tally of foreign visits was increased yet further during the year, with journeys in February and March to Brunei and Southern Africa respectively. Few people seemed to know where Brunei was, including Princess Diana: 'So that's where it is,' she exclaimed when she opened an atlas during a conversation with children at a Red Cross centre, and found it hiding in South East Asia. 'I didn't realise he was so far away.' But her husband's visit had all the trappings of a State occasion, undertaken as it was on the Queen's behalf, and in celebration of the tiny state's nationhood after 96 years of British rule. Prince Charles was guest of the Sultan, Sir Muda Hassanal Bolkiah, the 37-year-old, Sandhurst-educated, 29th ruler of Brunei, which his ancestors have governed for over four hundred years, and whose governmental departments are even now suffused with his myriad relatives. Popular and polo-mad – a factor which surely made Prince Charles an eminently suitable representative of the Queen on this occasion – the Sultan's vast wealth from his £2,500 million annual income was stamped on everything the Prince saw. Foremost among such evidence was the two thousand-roomed palace, newly constructed at a cost of £500 million: topped with two enormous solid gold domes, it covers fifty acres of ground, contains marbled halls with 20-foot-long crystal chandeliers weighing two tons each, and four thrones carved from solid English beech and hung with canopies gilded with £25,000 worth of gold leaf. Each of the senior guests from seventy countries was ferried around in one of the Sultan's hundred or so Rolls Royces, the latest of which was a six-door, long-wheel-based version in which he personally travelled. Even the comparatively modest-sounding residence for the Prince of Wales – the bungalow club-house in the grounds of Jerudong Park Polo Club, was surrounded by opulence. The club is one of the world's most exclusive, and all its 230 ponies are owned and maintained in almost imperial fashion by the Sultan. In between the official ceremonial of the six-day visit, the Prince managed (despite the early threat of monsoon flooding) to practise his game – on ponies prepared by Argentinian grooms – with his personal polo manager, Major Ronald Ferguson looking on. Just before the visit came to an end, Prince Charles played in the Sultan's team against some local opposition. Whether by courtesy, the tact of opponents, or sheer skill, the royal team won 7-2.

The brilliance and glitter of Prince Charles' Brunei visit were in marked contrast to his eighteen-day visit to Africa – a much more business-like trip made on behalf of the Commonwealth Development Corporation. The only Government quango to boast a royal director, the Corporation promotes industrial and economic progress in some forty countries, most of them the less developed nations of the Commonwealth. Not surprisingly, a few eyebrows were raised when details of the Prince's trip were published: Lesotho, deprived of a visit by Princess Anne during her African tour of 1983, was omitted from her brother's itinerary and thus remained the only Commonwealth country not to have been accorded a royal visit since independence almost eighteen years before. Zimbabwe, on the other hand, *was* included, much to the consternation of those whose anxieties still lay with the unfortunate people of Matabeleland, whose ordeal by drought was inflamed by a relentless government and army purge for dissidents. Though Prince Charles was to avoid the stricken area, his inevitable social contact with Zimbabwe's Prime Minister Mugabe heightened fears, especially among those who had not forgiven Prince Charles for conferring independence on the country in 1980, for the respectability thus bestowed on a man bent on creating yet another one party state in Africa, and nourished anxieties lest, as one opponent of the visit put it, 'the only beneficiaries will be Robert Mugabe and his military thugs who can carry on their work of reducing Zimbabwe to savagery with the appearance at least of a royal seal of approval.'

As with the earlier visits of Prince Philip and Princess Anne, the voices of protest were more strident in the anticipation than in the event. Prince Charles arrived in the country unheralded and pretty well unsung, and the greatest publicity, both within Zimbabwe and without, seemed to be connected with his trip to see the ruins of the city from which it has taken its name. The emphasis on the Prince's enthusiasm for archaeology, evidenced by the way he clambered up seven hundred feet of steepish hillside, braving a sharp downpour of rain on the way, gave a pleasant and neutral tone to a potentially controversial couple of days. In fact the entire tour was undertaken pragmatically and without undue fuss. Prince Charles piloted his Queen's Flight Andover from country to country, to be greeted almost everywhere by the dazzling smiles of school children, the shrieks of tribal dancers, the songs of women in dress of vibrant primary colours and the constant thunder of drums. In Dar-es-Salaam he amused and delighted his welcomers by trying out a few words of Swahili: in Zambia he in turn was amused by a male dance troupe in suspiciously feminine clothing. As the highlight of the Zambian leg of the tour, he piloted himself across the Victoria Falls – Dr Livingstone's so-called 'flight of angels' – before putting on a raincoat to make the pilgrimage on foot to the celebrated Knife-Edge, one of the narrowest ledges accessible to visitors to this magnificent scene. 'I hope you don't get too many suicides here,' he told his hosts. He was less keen to investigate the grizzlier wonders of a Botswana slaughter-house, and looking rather put off by the sight of so much running blood, made do with only a token inspection. For everyone, however, Prince Charles' visits were memorable for the fact that rain seemed to precede, accompany, or closely follow every one of his arrivals, bringing much needed relief to areas vulnerable to a capricious climate. In Tanzania they even dubbed him Pula – the bringer of rain. In view of such magical gifts, it was perhaps ironic that a tree he planted at an airport in Tanzania – using his umbrella as a substitute spade – was immediately flattened to extinction by the draught from his aircraft as he left. His comment was one of characteristic resignation: 'My trees never seem to last long.'

Perhaps Princess Diana's tree-planting success rate is higher than her husband's, but even her luck had already run out during her two-day visit to Oslo in mid-February. Just before she left Norway, the British ambassador asked her to plant a tree in the embassy garden – nicknamed the Royal Forest because so many members of the Royal Family have done similarly in the past. Despite an enormous amount of preparation, including some laborious digging and the use of boiling water to soften the ice-hard soil, and in marked contrast to the cheerful planting ceremony itself, the tree died within a couple of days – the conditions of a Norwegian February, as every British gardener might reasonably suspect, was just too unfavourable for saplings. It was an isolated misfortune, for this, the Princess' only official visit abroad during the year, was as successful as it was brief. It began in predictable style, with a welcome at Oslo's airport by Crown Prince Harald – like our own Queen, he is a great-grandchild of King Edward VII – and his wife Princess Sonja. Princess Diana was to stay overnight at the royal couple's farmhouse at Skaugum, some fifteen miles away. There too were the children of King Olav's daughter Princess Astrid, to present Diana with a bouquet of blue carnations in front of thousands of people who waited hours in sub-zero temperatures for this rare and prestigious occasion. Even a hard-bitten Norwegian press was astounded by the Princess' reception, and the reason for it. 'We have come to expect such a high standard of beauty,' one photographer explained, 'but she has left us goggle-eyed.' Indeed, throughout the twenty-hour visit she was a triumph of charm and patience. There primarily to see the City of London Ballet in a performance of *Carmen*, she made a special point of asking to be introduced to Karen Smith, a ballerina who was paralysed after a car crash two years before, and who was not expected to dance again. Now back on the road to a dancing career, she was overwhelmed by Diana's consideration. 'Shaking hands with the Princess was a moment I will treasure forever,' she said.

One wonders whether this much-acclaimed visit will be remembered by the Princess herself as very special, undertaken as it was in the knowledge – then unshared by the world at large – that she was pregnant for the second time. It was a secret which she could not afford to keep for long, as experience had taught her that to celebrities like herself, such confidences are privileges of only brief duration. She would not have forgotten the pressures of the previous autumn, after her September visit from Balmoral to London had coincided with the return of her gynaecologist from holiday and caused immediate and convinced talk that she was expecting again. Buckingham Palace's denial was stated in such carefully chosen words – 'If she is having a baby, it will be announced at the proper time' – that if anything, the speculation increased. She was inwardly staggered when, visiting a sweet-factory in Dundee shortly afterwards, she was actually asked whether she was pregnant. 'That's a very personal question,' the Princess chided, cleverly answering neither yes nor no, while other workers swore they detected all the signs of prospective motherhood. One said that she looked too well not to be pregnant; another that she had a 'special glow'; a third that she was 'definitely blooming'; yet another that she seemed to be acting similarly to a couple of local girls who were themselves expecting. It was enough to give the whole world and his wife justification for weighing in to dispense prediction and advice – from the astrologer Russell Grant, who foresaw that she would have five more children, to the former editor of *Debrett's*, who tackled the heady question of possible names for the new infant. The royalty correspondents of the tabloid press tapped their Palace contacts for confirmation. Almost all were agreed by the middle of September that Prince William would have a nursery companion by the early summer, and on evidence no more convincing than the usual alleged statement, like the one from an anonymous Balmoral employee, that 'we don't need an official announcement to tell us what is going on.' In the face of categoric denials from Press Officer Victor Chapman, coupled with denunciations of the rumours as 'rubbish', only the *Daily Star* trod a wary and considerate path. 'It is not something to make statements about – like a government announcing periodically that we are not at war,' it stated, remaining aloof from a hubbub of clamour which agitated the foreign press as much as the British. The French led by combining rumours old and new in a claim that the Princess, though pregnant, was able to conceal the fact because of her anorexia; while an American magazine thought it not beyond a peradventure that Diana was now carrying triplets – two girls, and a boy who would eventually force the Queen to abdicate, usurp the Throne from Prince William, and restore the British Empire. After that, almost everything seemed an anticlimax. The absence of hard news staled the story beyond recall by the end of October, with a handful of those who had confidently predicted a pregnancy the previous month explaining all away by the revelation that Diana was after all having difficulty in conceiving and was consequently, according to the faceless legion of unnamed 'close friends', tense and tearful.

When the Palace announced, at about the same time, that the Prince and Princess of Wales would be paying a two-week visit to Italy the following October, any remaining hopes of Diana producing in 1984 seemed effectively squashed. This prompted one medical journalist to suggest, early in February, that the Princess' dramatic weight loss and the influence of stress were contributory factors which had prevented conception but, that apart, talk of babies was out of fashion while the guesswork was transferred to whether the Princess would meet the Pope or visit Pompeii. So Diana must have felt triumphant when she was able, on 13th February, to announce her pregnancy after all, and to take everybody by surprise at the same time. The news was received with almost universal delight, nowhere better illustrated than in Coventry where a somewhat shy Princess was to carry out her first engagement since the announcement – a visit with Prince Charles to the Jaguar car plant at Allesley. There was much talk about losing shape as the pregnancy progressed, many questions about whether the Princess would not like a girl this time, countless enquiries about her health, and some mischievous *double entendres* from the male work-force when Prince Charles complimented them on their production record! The first baby gifts were received on that day when a pair of woolly mittens and a toy monkey were tossed through the open window of the royal limousine. The medical profession seemed equally happy with the news, congratulating the Princess on perfect timing which would give Prince William a companion at the very juncture when he could enjoy much needed company without the risk of sibling rivalry. The maternity wear business was all smiles again, in the expectation of a boom in the wake of some new Diana fashions. The Scots began to get excited when it was realised that as the baby was expected in September, the Princess would probably be at Balmoral, thus offering the prospect of a royal birth in Scotland for the first time since Princess Margaret in 1930. And the Royal Family itself was, to quote Princess Michael of Kent, 'ecstatic'. Of the prospective grandmothers, the Queen was said to be delighted, and to have been in sparkling form at the following day's Investiture at Buckingham Palace, while Mrs Shand Kydd declared, 'I am very excited. They're really happy days when they are safely in the world.' Even Prince Philip, rarely one to be bowled over by news of this nature, admitted to guests at a Windsor Rugby Club dinner, 'We are all very pleased.' As was Diana's sister, Lady Jane Fellowes, at this 'lovely news. It's smashing.'

The announcement of the Princess' pregnancy came on the eve of St Valentine's Day and gave the press an unexpected bonus to this annual theme which never fails to sell papers. Only the *Morning Star* kept the news aloof from any Valentine connection, offering it a mere factual, five lines on the penultimate page of its six-page addition. The *Socialist Worker* pulled out all its anti-monarchist stops with the headline 'Another Royal Brat' which advertised a discontented, insulting and distasteful article containing the promise that 'this little kid will grow up to be just as big a bastard as all its relatives.' Meanwhile a Liverpool gynaecologist, Professor Harold Francis anticipated that, if the royal couple should go on to have a third child, an unwelcome baby boom would follow. He cited the example of the 1960s when a 50% increase in the birth rate was 'partly due to the Queen and Princess Margaret having babies. When you consider the popularity of Diana, the situation is quite alarming.' He repeated those opinions in the March edition of *World Medicine*, regretting what he saw as the inevitable result of people 'trying to keep up with the Windsors.' Eventually, in the face of some stiffish opposition – Buckingham Palace described his suggestions as 'presumptuous', while Liberal MP Cyril Smith said that 'it's up to us how many children we want. If Charles and Diana want fifteen, then good luck to them' – Professor Francis backed down. He accepted that 'in Princess Diana's case a slightly larger family is acceptable in order to ensure the succession to the Throne. But,' he warned, 'the optimum number she should have is three.' He was joined by a representative of a group of West German women who considered that the Prince of Wales should now be sterilised, in order 'to take a great physical and mental burden' from his wife. But they at least did not have the Princess' support. 'Men don't understand women's determination to have babies,' she said during a visit to Hammersmith Hospital in mid-March, and a week later she was saying that although she didn't think she was 'made for the production line, it's all worth it in the end.' That comment followed an admission that morning sickness had begun to take its toll on her. 'I haven't felt very well since Day One,' she complained as she began to lack some of her usual public sparkle, and throughout those early months it became clear that she was worse affected even than in 1981 by the constant indispositions which took her so much by surprise.

But she still continued to think positively, hoping, she said about then, 'for a girl this time.' Prince Charles had already expressed the same wish, though his reason – 'so that she can look after me in my old age' – sent the feminists rushing around with protests urgent upon their tongues. It also sent the punters off to the bookmakers who had opened their ledgers on the choice of names and were then offering shortest odds for Elizabeth, Victoria and Alexandra, longest for Tracey. For boys, George and Richard were favourites, while Wayne and Spike extended to a 1,000-1 at the other end of the scale. In the battle of the sexes, it was odds-on for a girl, evens for a boy, 25-1 against twins, 200-1 against triplets. Until early April that is, when a bevy of well-presented gentlemen – 'they weren't exactly wearing coronets or ermine robes, but they seemed to be people who could have a little knowledge from inside,' said a counter clerk – tried to place £700 worth of bets at four different branches of the same bookmakers on the prospect of twins. Wisely, since this occurred at just about the same time as the Princess might reasonably have expected to see the results of a scan, and had been reported to have purchased two identical shawls from Harrods – the bookies closed their ledgers on multiple births. The speculation over, the sex and names of the baby introduced a rather more esoteric protest from an Exeter man who claimed that the baby's eventual baptism should be a public, rather than a traditionally private one. His argument was that baptism involved Christian witness of the most public kind, besides which there was benefit to be had from the hearing of 'baptismal promises on behalf of a royal child as the Church of England directs.' The Rev Raymond Maynard supported him – as indeed he had supported Professor Francis' population explosion fears.

Few people, however, had time for what many viewed as kill-joy attitudes, particularly as the Princess was clearly enjoying her second pregnancy – in marked contrast, it was pointed out, to Princess Caroline of Monaco, whose rather more furtive approach was eventually explained by the birth of her son Prince Andrea only six months after her marriage in December to Stefan Casaghiri. It wasn't until mid-July that Prince Charles put down all those rumours about twins: during a visit to East London he admitted having wondered whether his wife might produce them, 'but I think not.' So anybody who saw Harrods delivering two cots to Kensington Palace, or Diana buying two sets of baby towels in London, had jumped to the wrong conclusions. Meanwhile, the Princess herself was busy comparing notes with housewives and expectant mothers all over the country, counting her blessings during a June visit to Chester when opening a hospital wing at which infertile women could be treated, telling well-wishers at Salisbury that she was doing plenty of swimming and exercises, and confiding to workers at a sweet factory in Bridgend that she would eat more of their products if she didn't have to watch her weight. These casual comments became excuses for more journalistic inventions, and within the short space of two months Diana was reckoned to be on a diet of almost anything from royal jelly, honey and wheatgerm oil to keep her nervous system in order, to fried breakfasts to satisfy overnight cravings. There seemed even less authority in the stories that she had booked a room for £140 a night at St Mary's Hospital, Paddington, where Prince William had been born two years earlier, or that she had already been told that her baby would be born 'in the early hours of 27th September'. For the price of a newspaper you could also discover that Prince Charles had arranged for a 'home movie' film to be made of successive X-rays which his wife had undergone, and that, although he knew the sex of his second child as a result, the Princess preferred not to know in advance. Looking further ahead, there was mounting speculation on the identity of the lucky man chosen to take the official photographs of the new baby, and a unique revelation that the Princess would be taking it on a 1985 tour of America, which nobody else knew anything about!

The news that the Princess would soon be providing the Royal Family with an addition followed closely on the death of a man who perhaps ranked second only to Earl Mountbatten in terms of his close relationship with the Queen and her family. On 5th February, 31 years almost to the day since the death of King George VI, the 10th Duke of Beaufort died of a heart attack that he suffered the previous day. He was 83, and had enjoyed a lifetime of activity in the hunting field, an enthusiastic and genial man unspoiled by his prestigious royal connections. His marriage to Lady Mary Cambridge, a niece of Queen Mary, probably began those connections – the old Queen took up residence in his Gloucestershire mansion Badminton House for the duration of World War II – but his influence on equestrian sports brought royalty, consistently and in great number, literally to his doorstep. He inaugurated the Badminton Horse Trials in 1949, and hosted the Queen and, at one time or another, every member of her growing family at this annual classic four-day event. The Queen Mother was his regular guest each March for her annual decampment from London to the Cheltenham National Hunt Festival. As Master of the Beaufort Hunt, he began his sixtieth season in November 1983, the last in a career which had seen the patronage of major royal figures right down to the present Prince of Wales. Prince Charles will be gratified that only shortly before the old Duke's death he gave the Beaufort permission to hunt through part of the Highgrove estate. The Duke was a byword for fitness; his last summer holiday was spent salmon-fishing in Wales; his last cub-hunting season began in August and saw him up and about regularly at 6.30 each morning. He was a stickler for etiquette in all equestrian pursuits, insisting on everything from full mane-plaits to maintaining reins in the uncrossed position. Boasting 2,000 members, his Hunt supporters' club was one of the largest in the country, while his car registration plate MFH1 symbolised his devotion to a family pack of hounds – unique in its antique pedigree – dating back to the days of the 5th Duke in 1728. By October 1983 he had calculated that he had led his Hunt on almost 3,900 single days.

In life, his closeness to the Royal Family brought him a stack of ceremonial honours which included the Garter, the Royal Victorian Chain, and the office of Master of the Queen's Horse, which he relinquished to the Earl of Westmoreland in 1978. In death he was honoured by the presence of the Queen and ten other members of her family at his simple half-hour funeral service, conducted by his personal chaplain at the Badminton church of St Michael and All Saints. Its congregation of 250 comprised mostly tenants and estate workers, while a further three hundred village mourners heard the service relayed in a marquee outside. His three favourite hymns were sung, Psalm 121 intoned, but there was no address. His coffin, ready-built on his own instructions from wood felled on the estate, was draped in his personal standard. Six weeks later came the national tributes, expressed at no fewer than three memorial services held, almost simultaneously, at Gloucester, Bristol and the Guards' Chapel in London. Five members of the Royal Family and a host of the famous, from aristocrats to charity workers, marked the day. Among them were his 86-year-old widow and his successor as 11th Duke – the 56-year-old David Somerset, a second cousin and heir to the bulk of the 52,000-acre estate under a trust set up by his predecessor to avoid death duties. He runs the Mayfair art gallery, Marlborough Fine Arts, and having been joint master of the Beaufort Hunt since 1974, led the pack on the Saturday following his cousin's death. Married in 1950 to Lady Caroline Thynne, daughter of the 6th Marquis of Bath, the 11th Duke has four children, of which the eldest son, 31-year-old Henry Somerset, took the courtesy title of Marquis of Worcester. The late Duke's will was published in June, and showed a disposable fortune worth £3½ million. That did not include much of the land and family heirlooms, of which widely reported estimates of value amounting to £125 million were dismissed by their new owner as 'ridiculous exaggeration.'

The Duke of Beaufort's death cast a shadow over the following April's Badminton Horse Trials. Flags were flown at half mast over the estate during the whole event, and although the Queen attended, as she nearly always does, the Royal Family was not out in its usual force, neither did any of them stay with the Beaufort family at Badminton House. For the first time ever, the Dowager Duchess was in the Royal Box alone, and it was here that she saw the Queen presented with a memento of her late husband, in the shape of a plate bearing a picture of him out hunting. The Queen herself kept a relatively low profile, forsaking the usual haycart for a tent close to Badminton House in which she watched parts of the trials on closed-circuit television. The site of her Crown Equerry, Sir John Miller, commuting between the royal tent and the Badminton tote office clutching a copy of the *Sporting Life*, led to suggestions that the Queen was using him to place bets on runners in the week's National Hunt racing! As usual, Captain Mark Phillips competed at Badminton, which meant that Princess Anne was there to see him, which in turn meant that any of the two hundred thousand spectators who cared to watch could see her two children indulging in their usual mischievous frolics. Six-year-old Peter spent his time climbing scaffolding, larking around with his friend Harry Wallace, and getting into a few scrapes with sister Zara, who at almost 3 years old proved herself no soft touch for anyone. She was seen giving as good as she got during a rough and tumble with Peter, but when her brother delivered a sharp cuff to her ear, Princess Anne decided to arbitrate. She did so in compelling fashion – a length of her tongue and an impatient smack on the bottom for both of them. Nor was it much of a time for their father, since he was obliged to retire his horse, Classic Lines, after two refusals at the difficult Vicarage Vee fence in the cross-country. Thus, not only did Classic Lines pass up the chance of fulfilling his promise as a 7-year-old some three years before, but his rider's withdrawal from the event effectively deprived him of the opportunity to represent Great Britain in the July Olympics: Captain Phillips had the previous December been left off the short-list for Los Angeles, but with the proviso that a good showing at Badminton could lead to a reconsideration of his prospects. The Badminton winner was Lucinda Green whose horse, Beagle Bay gave her an early and successively convincing lead which ensured that, for the sixth time, she received the Whitbread Trophy from the Queen. Two other horses were not so lucky; one broke a leg during the competition and had to be put down; another – a bay gelding which Prince Edward had been called upon to name Jubilee during the 1977 horse trials, collapsed and died of a heart attack.

Classic Lines' performance at Badminton was unfortunately not untypical. He had refused at a fence at the Burghley Horse Trials at Stamford early the previous September, forcing Captain Phillips, watched by his wife and children, to retire; he fell, on a rain-soaked course, at Wylye at the end of that month; and he was withdrawn from the Brigstock three day event early in April, when a cut to the side of the mouth, sustained a fortnight or so before, failed to heal in time. Captain Phillips' luck was much more conspicuous with Fieldsman and Blizzard II, two 10-year-old horses he rides under his contract with Range Rover. Blizzard II missed much of the 1983 season after straining a tendon, but came back in August to a promising 3rd place in a three day event in Sweden, in which British riders took four of the first five places. The following month, Captain Phillips rode him to fourth place in the dressage at Wylye, though he was overtaken in subsequent stages of the competition. Despite being unplaced at the Rushall Horse Trials in March, Captain Phillips took Blizzard to Switzerland for an international event in which he came a respectable thirteenth and contributed to the overall victory of the British team. It was on Fieldsman, however, that he notched up his greatest home success of the season – first place in the TI Glow Worm section at the Windsor Horse Trials at the end of May. Perhaps the family connections encouraged him. The Queen and Prince Philip were there; the event was held, for the first time, on the Prince of Wales Field, and Princess Anne helped to design the course!

The absence of the pressure which participation in the Olympics would otherwise entail enabled Captain Phillips to bring on a modest string of novice horses, which in due course will replace his present stable. The most exciting prospect was the six-year-old gelding Distinctive, a well-built animal which he bought as a yearling, and which repaid Range Rover's sponsorship handsomely this year with a consistent tally of second-place ribbons at Crookham in March, at Brigstock in April, and at Stowe in July. At each of the last two events, Captain Phillips also rode another novice horse, Four Sure, into second place, and these two now seem certain successors to the likes of Classic Lines, Blizzard and Fieldsman in two or three years' time. Meanwhile, Captain Phillips was busy extending his international contacts. In October, he went to Australia – for the second year in succession – to take part in several cross-country events, finishing fourth in the most important of them all, the Melbourne Cup competition. November saw him in New Zealand, heavily involved in instruction courses, show-jumping competitions and, of all things, refereeing a superstars event. Late in February he travelled to Japan, where he won the Tokyo Grand Prix on a borrowed horse, then followed up with first place in a speed class event, and secured second place – losing by only two seconds – in the Hermes Cup. The following May took him to the U.S.A. where he was invited to compete in the Lexington three day event, on a course very similar to that arranged for the World Championship there in 1978. He led after the cross-country, but lost four points in the show-jumping arena, and finished a commendable third.

Though Princess Anne has been conspicuous by her absence from equestrian competition in recent years, she is making progress, albeit slowly, in bringing on her own younger horses. The most promising prospect appeared to be Mission Lake, a competitor twice in the autumn of 1983, and an eventual winner in a dressage event at Congresbury, Cheshire at the beginning of March. In addition, Princess Anne's support for the sport generally continued in the course of her public engagements. Speaking at a British Equine Veterinary Association meeting at York back in September, she had defended equestrianism against those who criticised it on the grounds of a tendency to cruelty, and had at the same time questioned whether certain veterinary aspects might not be investigated. In November she agreed to open a Northampton factory which produces machines for horse therapy. She visited two main agricultural shows during the year, one of them in weather so foul that she became a walking advertisement for Barbour rainwear. But perhaps her and Captain Phillips' most outstanding contribution to their favourite sport was the inauguration in August of the Gatcombe Park Horse Trials. Princess Anne staunchly defended her husband's right to take full credit for this event: 'Nothing to do with me,' she insisted during a radio interview the following March, 'short of the fact that I hammered in a lot of stakes and pulled up a lot of thistles.' Perhaps it had more to do with the producers of Croft Original sherry, whose £10,000 worth of sponsorship enabled the idea to get off the ground. A further £10,000 came from the BBC who secured sole television rights and a commentary from Princess Anne herself. But the spark came from Captain Phillips, who maintained the initiative throughout a long preparatory period, despite some fairly strong criticism from various quarters. Some of it was directed at the severity of the 2¼-mile course which he had designed. He agreed that, while it was 'a true advanced course – quite big,' it was perfectly straightforward and contained no traps. As proof to the unconverted, he took Classic Lines round the course in a television preview, performed a clear round – even over the two back-to-back Range Rovers – and immediately silenced his critics, the RSPCA among them. Lucinda Green called the course 'formidable in parts but brilliantly built,' and her husband David showed that it could be done by winning the entire two day event. More criticism came from the people of Gatcombe, who on the day suddenly found the village almost completely cut off by road blocks designed to facilitate the flow of traffic into the Park. Captain Phillips' organising agents, International Management Group were duly apologetic and promised better planning for the second meeting in September 1984. But despite his best efforts, Captain Phillips could not shake off the constant doubts about the event's financial success. Estimates, some patently uninformed, that up to 40,000 spectators would be needed to break even, put undue pressure on him to justify the venture when only half that number turned up – at £7 a car-load – to watch a field of 160 competitors, or simply to enjoy the sensation of picnicking on royal soil. But he professed himself pleased with the attendance. 'We've got a nice crowd here,' he said. 'Everybody seems to be enjoying it and that's the main point of it. I don't mind the picnickers. That's what we expected. The more the merrier.' And with 80 acres of parkland packed with stalls, displays of almost anything from the Duke of Beaufort's pack of hounds to the Scorpion tanks demonstrated by Captain Phillip's old regiment, the Queen's Dragoon Guards, and a host of celebrities led by Prince and Princess Michael of Kent and including Anthony Andrews, Angela Rippon and Jackie Stewart, it certainly seemed an enjoyable occasion. At the end of the day, it was considered sufficiently successful to induce Croft Original to undertake sponsorship for the following year's event.

Princess Michael's attendance at the Gatcombe Horse Trials was the prelude to another year in the saddle, as she joined her royal neighbours in their passion for horsemanship. Shortly after those trials, she visited another equestrian event at Mayfield in Sussex, riding round the course before the competitions began, though not taking part in them herself. In April, she *did* compete, making her eventing début at the Tidworth Army Trials by riding two horses, Benny's Gold and Sprite II, in the novice section. The Princess was quick to point out beforehand that she too was only a novice, yet she cleared all forty obstacles faultlessly on Benny's Gold. That gave her the confidence to try for the Amberley Show event in Gloucestershire a month later, when again she performed a clear round over 23 cross-country obstacles, finishing halfway down the field of 38 on time points. A hunting enthusiast as well, Princess Michael is a regular rider to hounds with the Cotswold Hunt and the Beaufort, whose opening meet she attended in November. Having now completed her third hunting season, she is joined by Viscount Linley, whose first hunting appointment was with the Belvoir in Leicestershire shortly after Christmas. 'Lord Linley coped very well and said he enjoyed himself,' said the Hunt's secretary. Prince Charles, meanwhile, saw much less hunting this year than previously. With four horses stabled near Melton Mowbray, he was well placed for hunting with the Quorn, Cottesmore and Belvoir Hunts, and by November had gone so far as to equip himself with one of Scotland Yard's £12,000 mobile tracking devices, to enable his bodyguards to know exactly where he was even though the chase took him out of their sight. But by the turn of the year, the Prince was much less in evidence. Possibly this was due to a nasty fall which he suffered at a high fence while out with the Cottesmore in January – 'One of those days,' said the joint master. 'There were a lot of empty saddles.' Then again, it might have followed another in a long line of annual national scoldings which the Royal Family received at about that time on the issue of bloodsports.

Two of the late Duke of Beaufort's most oft-quoted maxims in his implacable defence of hunting was that it comes second only to war in drawing the nation together, and that the fox would rather die at the hands of the huntsman than by any other method. He would certainly have spent the last month of his life in almost apoplectic dismay as the Royal Family's traditional pursuit – not of foxes, but of game – came under fire over Christmas and the New Year. It all began with the publication of news pictures showing a Sandringham pheasant shoot in which Captain Phillips, accompanied by his brothers-in-law Prince Andrew and Prince Edward, was nothing if not quick and enthusiastic with the gun. Beside him was son Peter, gleefully imitating his father with a toy pistol. In one succession of photographs, the boy was seen watching the Queen's black Labrador retrievers as they brought back the kill in their mouths, then actually receiving one of the dead birds from his father. The League Against Cruel Sports rounded on the holidaying royals as never before. 'It is an absolute tragedy,' said one of its officers, Mr Richard Course. 'It makes me extremely angry as I imagine it would most people. The majority of parents in this country spend their time teaching their children not to pull the legs off flies. Now Mark Phillips gives his young son a dead bird he has just shot.' A child psychologist, Dr James Hemming, thought that particular incident 'distasteful,' and said it was 'crucial that children should develop sensitivity and respect for living things.'

As it happened, Prince Philip had already recorded an interview, transmitted in a New Year's Eve television programme, in which he defended bloodsports – a category, he said, into which fox-hunting had been inappropriately slotted. He saw no contradiction between his presidency of the World Wildlife Fund and his participation in the shoot. He criticised hunt saboteurs whose efforts, he said, were misdirected, though 'they are perfectly entitled to their animal welfare point of view.' He defended game-keepers as essential to the good and efficient organisation of hunting, citing as an example of bad organisation the situation in Kenya, where hunting has been so improperly run that there is now a free-for-all in which the animal population levels have plummeted. 'The result is that it has now become a poachers' paradise, because no-one is interested in conserving the animals. If you are involved in any kind of hunting operation on a sensible scale,' he continued, 'the hunter is the only person who wants that species to survive.' The RSPCA gently begged to differ, one of its spokesmen stating that 'I do not think his argument holds water.' Richard Course was characteristically more forthright; he called Prince Philip's arguments 'rubbish' and said he should be sacked as president of the World Wildlife Fund. 'So far as I am concerned,' he said, 'he has never done anything useful in his life for conservation – though it is not too late for him to start.' One of Mr Course's colleagues accused the Prince of 'talking about keeping vast areas of land for a privileged few to enjoy their killing. It stinks of arrogance and hypocrisy to say that only those people know how to conserve animals.' Another colleague, Chris Williamson, took issue with Prince Philip on the question of game-keepers – they were, in his opinion, 'responsible for slaughtering many thousands of other creatures who prey on those they are rearing.' From the country at large the Duke came in for some virulent attacks for his 'hideous rites' and 'real 1984 double-speak' before the matter descended into pure abuse. 'Nauseating,' wrote one enraged listener. 'Like the braid and medals on the numerous uniforms he wears, his right to hold the office of president of the World Wildlife Fund is as unreal as Alice's Wonderland.' Even the Queen Mother became trapped in the cross-fire when the treasurer of the Hunt Saboteurs' Association deplored her practice of salmon-fishing, and said that, given the opportunity, he would push her into the River Dee. 'An unfortunate joke,' he admitted later, 'but even so we intend to harass anglers all over Britain until they stop that barbaric sport.'

Not to be put down, even by the strength and spontaneity of these attacks, Prince Philip took a tilt at the saboteurs in May, in a letter he wrote in support of the Campaign for Country Sports, an association recently established to counter the growing trend towards bringing the issue of bloodsports into the political arena. 'It is extremely important,' wrote the Duke, 'that all country sports organisations, including the anglers, should stand firmly together and present a united front. I hope the campaign will attract more attention to the important part played by country sports in rural and wildlife conservation.' Not surprisingly, the Duke found himself criticised by the Hunt Saboteurs' Association for dipping into politics himself: its secretary even challenged him to a meeting so that he could ask the Duke exactly what he had meant. Richard Course had no doubts at all, however, that the Duke had made 'an amazing and ill-considered statement. It is the first time,' he continued, 'that a member of the Royal Family has defended cruel sports such as hare-coursing and stag-hunting by urging organisations to stand together.' Prince Charles on the other hand attracted positive praise in March, in the wake of a report that his hunting activities had been drastically reduced, and that he had neither shot pheasant nor stalked deer during the previous eight months. 'We are very pleased when anyone gives up shooting,' beamed the RSPCA, 'and all the more so when it is someone of Prince Charles' stature. He has set a shining example.' The Prince's old, eccentric friend and critic, Spike Milligan, added his congratulations: 'I give Prince Charles eight out of ten. If he gives up hunting as well, it will go up to ten out of ten.'

Certainly the Princess of Wales had no difficulty achieving ten out of ten, if the year's popularity polls were anything to go by. She came top in a Christmas poll, commissioned by the *Sunday People* to find the most popular woman of 1983, while she and Prince Charles were voted Outstanding Couple of the Year – eight points ahead of that other successful partnership, Torvill and Dean. A personality poll in the *Sunday Mirror* placed the Princess first not only as top personality, but also as men's idea of the ideal woman, the woman other women would most like to be, the most charming personality, and a contender for men's vision of the ideal mother. She came second to Olivia Newton-John for beauty, and seventh for attraction to men. *The Times* assumed a more objective stance, but still considered that she had 'enhanced and more importantly survived her unchallenged position as the media market leader of the planet.' There was certainly no shortage of genuine personal tributes from people with no axe to grind. Photographer Norman Parkinson popped up again in December to state that he would give 'almost an arm to photograph Princess Diana, but the opportunity hasn't come my way. You can't make the approach,' he explained. 'You have to wait for the magic call.' To her step-grandmother Barbara Cartland, the Princess 'embodies the romantic heroine. She reads my books and is a very good example of what my heroines are like – sweet, understanding and compassionate, as she likes children.' But of all the eulogies she received during the year, perhaps she will most value that of a regimental sergeant-major at the Royal Hospital at Chelsea. 'Forget Vera Lynn, forget Lilian Gish,' he said. 'The Princess of Wales has well and truly taken over. She is now our pin-up girl. We have a picture of her in every room.'

Prince Andrew, recently suggested as the next James Bond – 'that devastating smile, those broad shoulders, and all that combat training,' sighed one admirer – was about the only male member of the Royal Family to achieve the sometimes doubtful credit of a mention in the national popularity ratings, and in any event was eclipsed by the storming progress back to the nation's bosom of his sister Princess Anne. Buckingham Palace were much gratified in October at her increased popularity, which it ascribed to the greater publicity she was receiving. That was certainly true, but publicity, though a fickle asset, has almost always a reason behind it. It was rather simplistic to put it down merely to the rapidly increasing number of engagements Princess Anne is undertaking these days – though that, at a time when the mathematics of public appearances seems to count for everything, is at least one good reason. Without doubt, the Princess' public character – or its reporting – has improved: the straight-talking, unsuffering, caustic woman of two or three years ago is now projected as caring, brave and warm and witty. She was described in January as having taken a leaf out of the Princess of Wales' book, but that explanation, too, is facile. Having shaken off successive rumours and doubts about the state of her marriage, and shown that despite her admission of being unmaternal, she is as capable as anyone of bringing up two delightfully-playful children, she has gone about her royal business in a way quite dissimilar from her sister-in-law, and has won applause for the traditional royal qualitites of hard work and concern rather than simply for glamour. The process of transformation began undoubtedly with her lengthy African and Middle East tour on behalf of the Save the Children Fund in Autumn 1982, and it was strengthened by another tour – this time confined to the North and West of Africa – in February 1984. Undertaken on the ground that, as Princess Anne had said the previous December, 'there is no better way of knowing how the money raised is spent than by going to see for yourself,' the tour was one of familiar dangers and discomforts. The risks of disease were counteracted by a succession of expensive and sometimes highly painful inoculations: in all, Princess Anne had no fewer than nine, including those for meningitis, hepatitis and rabies. The discomfort – dust, humidity, swamps, sleeping conditions which Buckingham Palace said would be 'basic', and mosquitoes – to say nothing of the heart-rending encounters with advanced and widespread killer diseases – made the trip one of the most challenging of her life.

Her visit to Morocco was comparatively brief and certainly only a shadowy prelude to what was to come. It was at the next stop, the Gambia, that she began to witness what she had come for – 'to see for herself how appalling conditions really are.' At a leper colony she saw unfortunates who could only crawl around on all fours, and one man who not only lacked hands and feet but was also blind. At a hospital, she learned how the staff were running out of vital penicillin supplies, having only sufficient for emergencies over the next fortnight. She visited several water wells, where the precarious battle to keep a parched land irrigated is frequently lost, and a mother-and-baby care centre which promotes human survival against all the odds. And she was touched by the pitiful but sincere personal tributes they paid to her. 'Glory to God you have come here,' persisted one elderly leper, while a newly-confined mother named her baby Princess Anne in honour of the royal visitor. In some ways, the more festive side of her visit – involving her attendance at the celebrations of the 19th anniversary of the Gambia's independence – made the pastoral aspect even more tragic. But there was more real tragedy to come when she moved on to Upper Volta, where the Fund had worked for ten years to save its population from the creeping economic paralysis that comes with the expanding Sahara Desert as it sweeps down from the North. Here, where rain is the make or break factor of all forms of life, the drought had reached truly dreadful proportions. At one village, Princess Anne was told that three children had recently died of starvation, and that others would certainly follow. Some yet surviving were too weak to stand on their beds; those who could were pot-bellied and spindle-limbed from inadequate nutrition. Cattle and other livestock stood emaciated after continual monsoon failures. The Princess did visit one oasis created and nurtured by the Fund, where coconuts and fruit trees flourished. Yet these were hopelessly inadequate at present to provide the quantity of food necessary to stave off disaster – thirty thousand tons of millet was needed as a matter of urgency. Eventually, even the Princess was constrained to accept how hopeless the situation was. In these appalling conditions, surely prayer was the only answer, she suggested, convinced that no practical alternative to faith existed. When she returned home, she admitted how difficult it had been to keep her head in the face of such incessant horrors. 'You have to stay remote,' she explained, 'or you'd just crack up.'

The experience failed to discourage her – indeed quite the contrary. By June she had arranged to pay similar visits to Fund projects in India and Bangladesh, and throughout the year seemed to be concentrating all her efforts towards rounding up more and more support for its work. Apart from the £11,000 she raised from her two interviews in Australia the previous October, she had received a Land Rover from the Carmen's Company, and a Ford Sierra from the Dagenham plant in celebration of the production of its half-millionth model. On various public engagements she picked up cheques for a few hundred pounds here, a few thousand there, which her hosts had collected or donated as their contributions to the Fund's unceasing efforts, and she attended function after function – gala evenings, balls, film and theatrical shows – put on specifically to raise money for what is clearly to be the Princess' favourite charity. The combination of her interest and the Queen's visit to the Fund's project in Dhaka in November led Princess Anne to launch an appeal at the end of February, run by the Townswomen's Guilds, to raise £¾ million for a second Bangladesh centre, and she was duly grateful to her mother – if a touch modest on her own behalf – for the Queen's 'timely visit to Dhaka and the inspiration it has given.'

So there could be little wonder at Princess Anne's increasing popularity in 1984. The African tour was almost completely devoid of the brilliance usually associated with royal visits, and what little there was became overwhelmed by the surrounding desperation. Almost immediately after her return, forty MP's tabled a Commons motion paying tribute to her courage and determination, while the director of the Save the Children Fund affirmed the simple truth that her obvious concern for people really endears her to our doctors, nurses and local staff: 'She is magnificent at it.' Her own insistence on complete informality was reflected by her indifference to the traditional images projected by royalty's choice of clothes, and in those two weeks she proved that crowned heads could be as popular in sombre green shirtwaisters, tough khaki skirts, culottes, headscarves and sturdy desert boots as in the most dazzling evening dress and most glittering tiara. She was described as 'a latter-day Florence Nightingale, Queen Victoria or member of the SAS' and it was once suggested that the Queen should create her Princess Royal in recognition of her achievements. Others were content to exorcise perhaps the most vivid memories of the Princess' blunt-spoken past, by referring to the effects of the past couple of years on the Princess' reputation as her 'de-naffing.'

It may have seemed as if her activities on behalf of the Save the Children Fund could not possibly have left her with sufficient time to devote to other organisations, but the British Olympic team needed some £2 million from public subscriptions to enable it to go to Los Angeles in July 1984, and Princess Anne, as President of the British Olympic Association, became the leading light of the nine-month drive to achieve that goal. By November 1983, with a quarter of the target figure already collected, she launched an appeal for the remainder, with simple, hard hitting, home-truthfulness. 'If we want our sportsmen and women to compete next year – never mind win,' she said, 'then we must have the money. If you're not interested in seeing the Union Jack run up some American flagpole...' and she went on to lay it on the line to the doubters. And for those who doubt the ability of Britain's first family to give a lead where it is most needed – especially where the cause affects people's pockets – the royal push to send the British Olympic teams on their way provided the classic example. Prince Philip became patron of a ball at Grosvenor House which raised £30,000, and launched the Round England Run in which 300,000 children from five hundred schools joined in a sponsored race from Land's End to John O'Groats. The Queen sent a cash donation to the British International Equestrian Fund Olympic Appeal, Prince Michael of Kent attended a Peugeot car launch in Surrey to help raise funds for the bobsleigh team, Princess Anne and Captain Phillips were at a ball at the Savoy in London to raise £25,000 for the yachtsmen, and the magnificent, if controversial dinner Prince Andrew attended in Los Angeles in April raised no less than £200,000. Both Prince Michael and Princess Anne travelled to Sarajevo in February to watch various events in the Winter Olympics: Prince Michael to support the bobsleighers; Princess Anne primarily to witness the monumental ice-dancing victory achieved by Torvill and Dean. That earned them not only a gold medal and a place in the history books, but also a rare and appreciative telegram from the Queen: 'Many congratulations on a superb performance which we watched with great pleasure, and which brought a well deserved gold medal.' Two months later the champions were presented to the Queen at a lunch in Nottingham, after Her Majesty had visited nearby Southwell Minster to make her annual distribution of Maundy money.

April's Maundy Service somehow seemed to be one of comparatively few familiar royal landmarks in a year which witnessed the unavoidable or deliberate breaking of traditional royal routine. We have already seen that the Queen was, for the first time in fifteen years, absent from the Remembrance ceremonies in London, but this departure from past form seemed more understandable than the Queen's decision not to hold any formal ceremony in connection with the Order of the Garter, an event customarily held on the Monday following her official birthday in June. The explanation for the decision – that the Queen did not wish it to be thought that the Garter service was a necessarily annual event – baffled many if for no other reason than that, since the end of the war at least, it **has** been an annual event; the highlight of the great ceremonial mid-June season. Pragmatically, there was an argument for discontinuing the practice on an annual basis: it was that the costly and time-consuming functions of Garter Day might well be played out every three or four years, in much the same way as the service of the Order of the Bath, or of the Royal Victorian Order, for the purpose of installing new knights who are from time to time appointed to fill vacancies. But, whatever the reason, the Queen has clearly changed a tradition in deciding that even ceremonial considerations are not sufficient to justify an annual celebration of the Order's six hundred-year-old history.

In place of this year's Garter ceremony, the Queen travelled to Scotland to attend the Royal Highland Society's Show at Ingliston, then celebrating its two hundredth anniversary. It was one of two major agricultural events graced by the Queen within six days – the other being the South of England Show at Ardingly in Sussex. As Patron of this event, the Queen had arranged to visit the previous year's show, but the general election intervened. When, in January, she promised to make good the enforced postponement, the organisers were thrilled: 'The news that our royal Patron has accepted an invitation to be with us has delighted us all.' But perhaps it is inevitable that part of the Queen's official programme should be set aside for such visits, for she has more than a passing interest in agriculture. Her farms at Windsor, Balmoral and Sandringham continue to flourish; one of her Jersey cows won the Dairy Cow of the Year award, as well as the Jersey breed championship, at the Newbury Agricultural Show in September; and in January she inaugurated her own award for home-bred cattle, the Queen Elizabeth II Cup, to be presented at the King's Lynn Christmas Stock Show.

Another missing link in the annual royal round was the customary – though by no means irrevocably fixed – State Visit paid to the Queen each autumn by a foreign head of State. In October 1983, President Jayewardene of Sri Lanka was due to carry out a four-day visit to London as guest of the sovereign, a fixture rearranged from the previous June after it to had become a casualty to the British general election. But by August, Sri Lanka had problems of its own, with an uprising by the Tamil minority, which threatened the country's stability to such an extent that a state of emergency was declared, keeping the President at home and unable to receive the Queen's hospitality in return for his own for her back in October 1981. He did pay an official visit to Britain the following June, and called in on the Queen at Buckingham Palace, as indeed did several national leaders during the year. Among them was President Mitterand of France, a brief visitor to Buckingham Palace one afternoon in October to accept the Queen's invitation to pay a State Visit to Britain a year later, and who was in England again in April to open a new nuclear fission plant near Oxford in a joint ceremony with the Queen. (Coincidentally it was eighty years to the month since the conclusion of the *Entente Cordiale* which followed King Edward VII's celebrated visit to Paris in 1903.) Other official guests of the Queen included President Reagan, who lunched with her after both had attended the D-Day celebrations in Normandy in June, and President Pertini of Italy, who accompanied her to the *Genius of Venice* exhibition in London in February, and who said glowingly of his host, 'I am very fond of the Queen. We talk together like friends of long standing. She is open-minded, straightforward and speaks her mind.' The previous December, President Gemayel of the Lebanon, who at the height of his country's civil chaos toured the West to sound out prospects for solutions, also found time to call upon the Queen, and two months earlier President Machel of Mozambique, who arrived at Buckingham Palace to be invested by the Queen with the Order of St Michael and St George. The bestowal of this, one of Britain's foremost personal honours, to a Marxist ex-guerrilla was seen by many as odd, if not positively untoward: 'Where is the British bulldog now?' questioned one critic. 'Not only toothless, but seemingly blind as well.' But the President's mellowing attitude towards the West, indicated primarily by his conciliatory gestures towards neighbouring South Africa, gave hope that the Queen's award might serve to assist the process of persuading him away from his Communist mentors. Meanwhile, other guests of the Queen included foreign royalty, like the King and Queen of Tonga who in October made their first visit to Britain since the Prince and Princess of Wales' wedding, and the Crown-Prince and Princess of Japan, paying a three-day unofficial visit in March, which included a trip to Oxford where their son Prince Hiro is a student.

Britain did, however, witness one State Visit during the year – undertaken in merry style by the Amir of Bahrain. One would perhaps not expect this diminutive, middle-aged potentate, whose nickname of Jolly Jack respectably conceals his reputation for having a ready fund of risqué jokes, to be accorded more than the standard royal treatment, but the Amir is a good friend of Britain and, like many middle-Eastern dynasts, makes no secret of his admiration for the British Royal Family personally. So, in place of the predictable, sometimes rather uninspiring ceremonies of welcome in London, the Amir was brought from Heathrow Airport, where Princess Alexandra and her husband had gone to greet him onto British soil, to Windsor Home Park, where the Queen and her family – Prince Philip resplendently swathed in the Order of Ahmed the Conqueror, which the Amir had given him during the Queen's visit to Bahrain in 1979 – welcomed him at the Royal Pavilion. From there, he was accompanied by Her Majesty in the 1902 State Landau towards Windsor Castle, in a visual delight of colour and pageantry not seen there since the visits of Queen Juliana of the Netherlands in 1972 and Queen Margrethe of Denmark in 1974. The Amir's stay was punctuated by several engagements common to such visits, like talks with the Prime Minister and a luncheon at the Guildhall, but the choice of Windsor as a home base meant that tea with the Queen Mother was taken at Royal Lodge, Windsor rather than at Clarence House; that the splendours of Windsor Castle took over from those of Buckingham Palace as the setting for the Queen's welcoming banquet; and that sight-seeing visits gravitated around Berkshire and not around the capital. The Amir was, for instance, taken to see the Royal Mews at Windsor, the Queen's training stables at Highclere and West Ilsley, and to Madame Tussaud's royal exhibition at Windsor station – an item which was retained on His Highness' itinerary despite the restriction which his Muslim faith places on him against clapping eyes of images of the human form. The Amir's reciprocal banquet was, however, given in London. It took place at the Dorchester Hotel and was one of the most informal of its kind. No speeches, no royal toast – in fact no alcohol at all!

The Queen was not yet finished with the business of breaching long-standing royal practices. Her presence at the Derby each June has become almost an inviolable tradition, but even Epsom was forsaken this year. Queen Elizabeth the Queen Mother, the Duke and Duchess of Gloucester, Princess Alexandra and Mr Angus Ogilvy, and Prince and Princess Michael were there as usual, but the Queen had more important official work to perform across the Channel. For Derby Day was also the fortieth anniversary of D-Day, and the Queen led Britain's commemoration of the beginning of Europe's liberation by travelling to France in *Britannia* for a day of international ceremonies on those historic Normandy beaches. At dawn that morning, *Britannia* sailed under Pegasus Bridge near Caen, the first target for the Allied invasion in 1944, and the Queen and Prince Philip made their first stop in the town for a visit which was meant to be strictly private. The townspeople decided otherwise, however: they had the dockside cleared of lumber for the day and decorated with bright flowers; the belfry of St Etienne's Cathedral – built by William the Conqueror – was repaired as a concession to the legend that its fall would signify the end of the British monarchy; and there were huge numbers of people in the streets shouting 'Vive la Reine' as the Queen came to pay her respects both to the mayor of Caen and to William the Conqueror himself, who is buried in the Cathedral. The royal couple were then taken by helicopter to attend the public D-Day ceremonies. The choice of helicopter as a means of transport was not thought to be the Queen's favouite decision of the day, but security made enormous demands upon the French organisers – 'We are taking no chances, even though we appreciate it is not an occasion for disruption,' said a French security organiser – and the timing of a packed programme of engagements made it imperative that, for the first time since her visit to Northern Ireland in 1977, the Queen should travel in this way. Her agreement was all the more thankfully received in view of her known aversion to helicopters, and a French official gratefully said that it made all the difference to their timings.

So the Queen and Prince Philip flew to Bayeux to visit a military cemetery. They did not see the few graves of German soldiers which had been daubed with black paint and slogans by French patriots, but there were 3,900 British buried here, and the Queen was able to speak to some of the 53 widows who, after a long and somewhat acrimonious struggle with the Government, had been brought over by the Ministry of Defence. One of them was quick to forget this bitter episode in the wake of her meeting with the Queen. 'She has been marvellous,' she said. 'This memory I shall keep forever.' At Arromanches the Queen took the salute of three thousand veterans whom she addressed in a speech which revealed how important this day was for her. 'There are only a few occasions in history,' she said, 'when the course of human destiny has depended upon the events of a single day. June the Sixth 1944 was one of those critical moments.' There was a thoroughly domestic air about the parade, with Household Guards and a few Chelsea Pensioners on hand to lend ceremonial colour, and a fly-past of Spitfires and Dakotas to bring those wartime memories flooding back. But the main ceremony of the day took place at Utah Beach, where the Queen joined the Kings of Belgium and Norway, the Queens of Denmark and the Netherlands, Grand-Duke Jean of Luxembourg, Presidents Reagan of the United States and Mitterand of France, and Prime Minister Trudeau of Canada in a joint commemoration consisting of speeches, a service, and aerial, naval and military displays. With *Britannia* docked nearby, the Queen hosted her royal cousins for lunch.

The Queen was not the first member of her family to reach Normandy for these celebrations. The previous day, Prince Charles had crossed the Channel to Ranville, where six thousand men of the 6th Airborne Division had parachuted in to prepare for the 1944 invasion, to commemorate which the Prince began his engagements by watching a drop by 68 present-day paratroopers. He also attended a ceremony with veterans and widows of the fallen at a cemetery in the town, where 2,500 soldiers are buried. 'For me, forty years afterwards,' he said, 'this is an occasion to pay homage to those men who died so that my generation could live freely.' The pride felt by the veterans as they marched past was reflected by the Mayor of Ranville who said that 'having the Prince with us is our second proudest day.' The proudest day, he explained, was when each citizen realised that the town had been the first to be liberated. The Queen Mother did not visit France, as her husband, King George VI had shortly after the invasion in 1944, but she did not forget D-Day either. In early June, she unveiled a plaque at the wartime headquarters of General de Gaulle in Carlton Gardens, a gesture not only of British recognition of the contribution made by the French Resistance to the Allied victory, but also of the Queen Mother's personal regard for de Gaulle and of de Gaulle's respect for George VI – two factors which survived the often difficult and suspicious relations between de Gaulle and

Churchill. The Queen Mother also visited Portsmouth during D-Day week, to open a new museum devoting its permanent exhibition to the Allied invasion, and boasting the superb Overlord Tapestry – the largest embroidery in the world. That the Royal School of Needlework had fashioned it made it especially important to the Queen Mother, who is its patron, and who was naturally proud to see her late husband depicted with General Eisenhower at Arromanches ten days after its liberation. Her visit to Portsmouth gave the Queen Mother the opportunity to 'recall the pride we felt in the courage and resilience shown by young and old alike in the face of grievous destruction' during her visit with the late King to the city in 1941.

The Queen Mother was the sole adult member of the Royal Family not to have gone abroad officially during the year. Quite apart from the more heavily publicised foreign tours undertaken by the Queen, Prince Charles, Princess Anne and Prince Andrew, the Gloucester, Kent, and Ogilvy families were out of the country on several occasions, and even Prince Edward was given his first foreign commission when he was sent out to Wellington, in view of his recent connections with New Zealand, to represent the Queen at the funeral in December of the country's former Prime Minister, Sir Keith Holyoake. As is the tendency these days, most of the minor royal foreign visits were either business trips – like the Duke of Kent's journey to Korea in October on behalf of the British Overseas Trade Board, or the Duke of Gloucester's visit to the Middle East that month for the British Consultants' Bureau – or connected with the armed services, like the successive summer visits of the Queen, Prince Charles, Princess Anne and Princess Alice to regiments in Germany, or Prince Philip's brief journey to Canada in July. There was one, more ceremonial occasion the previous September as yet another outpost of Empire achieved its independence. This was the two-island territory of St Kitts and Nevis, whose West Indies location made it a prime candidate for one of Princess Margaret's now almost annual official trips to the Western Atlantic. First settled by the British in 1623, St Kitts was granted internal self-government in 1967, and was the last of five similar West Indian territories to request total independence for its 45,000 population. The Princess was received with the full ceremonial honours reminiscent of many similar occasions in the late 1950s and 1960s, when royalty was despatched throughout the Empire to dispense independence – a 21-gun salute, peals of church bells, the gleeful explosion of fireworks. And, of course, the hauling down of the Union Jack and the raising of the national flag as the Princess handed over the constitutional instruments of self-government. As always, she followed her official visit with a brief holiday in nearby Mustique – her second vacation within a month. At the end of August, she had gone to Florence with her two children, after an earlier Italian holiday as guest of Sir Harold Acton had been postponed – on the advice, her host surmised, of her doctors, who thought that the current temperature of up to 110°F would be unsuitable.

At about the same time, another part of the old Empire was preparing to receive its fourteenth visit from the Queen, with a tour in July that would encompass New Brunswick, Manitoba and Ontario. Preparations, well under way by Christmas after the Queen had said she was 'very much interested' in going to Canada and 'would do her best' to keep her engagement book open, continued apace into the New Year, when the official announcement was made. The plans suffered a setback in March, however, when Prime Minister Trudeau announced that he would be retiring in June. The implications for the new Prime Minister, Mr John Turner, were somewhat daunting. On the one hand, he was pressed by his advisors to call an election immediately, to cash in on his party's undoubted popularity in the opinion polls. Such a move would entail a statutory eight-week campaign which would engulf the dates of the Queen's proposed visit, and effectively cause her to stay away, as she always does when her host country is in the throes of an election. On the other hand, he could refuse to put the royal arrangements into disarray, and risk losing any election at a later date. His Opposition deplored the prospect of an election in the near future, though ostensibly on the grounds of inconveniencing royalty and offending royalists. 'Rudely interrupt the Queen's visit,' protested one Conservative front-bencher, 'then let's see what the people of Canada think about it.' Everything seemed to come to a standstill for several weeks until, only seven days before the royal visit was scheduled to begin, Mr Turner paid a flying visit to Windsor Castle to inform the Queen that he intended to call an election for early September, and to ask her permission to postpone her tour. The Queen agreed – she had little option to do otherwise. But the measure of her understanding – not shared by many of the tour organisers, who condemned the postponement 'just so a politician can win votes' – was indicated by her willingness to reset the tour dates for late September and early October. It would mean that she might miss the birth of her fourth grandchild, and that the Queen Mother's scheduled visit to Venice in October would have to be put back, but it fitted in nicely with the her own private visit to stud farms in Kentucky and Wyoming in mid-October, so the dates were fixed accordingly. Meanwhile the Queen, left with the second half of July free of engagements, was no doubt grateful for the unexpectedly early break in her royal duties, though she attended a Buckingham Palace garden party which the Queen Mother was to have hosted in her absence, and held a dozen or so audiences which otherwise would have had to wait until the autumn.

One royal visit which did go ahead – almost, it seemed at one time, against all the odds – was the Queen's State Visit to Jordan in March. Announced the previous Autumn, the tour's endangered prospects were exposed in December by reports of concern for security, following the most recent of nine major bomb explosions in Amman – the work, it was generally thought, of a Syrian-backed terrorist organisation opposed to King Hussein's Palestinian policy, and to his allegiance to Iraq against Syrian-supported Iran in the Gulf War. The terrorists – members of a fanatical Palestinian faction – had also vowed revenge on Britain for having gaoled three of their number after the attack in London on an Israeli diplomat, which had contributed to the renewal of the war in Lebanon in 1982. These issues made security a lasting and sometimes tortuous consideration for Buckingham Palace, though at the Press Office in January, Michael Shea, who had just been to Jordan to help prepare the arrangements, said, 'The Queen is aware of security factors wherever she goes, and the plan is that the Queen will go unless advised otherwise.' He was angry with several of the British newspapers, whom he accused of 'having an axe to grind' in their alarmist editorials: his fury was first directed at the unlikely target of *The Times*, while others were quick to follow its lead, thinly disguising their anti-Jordan stance with the issue of the Queen's safety. *The Sun* called Jordan 'a ramshackle, fly-blown kingdom' governed by a 'playboy' monarch of 'doubtful dynastic claim' to its throne, and mocked the Foreign Office, which it considered the only likely beneficiary, with its 'Arabian lobby of pinstriped sheiks who fancy they are still living in the days of Lawrence of Arabia.' *The Express* was less red-necked on the issue, pointing out that the risks did not justify the likely benefits in view of the uncertainty of King Hussein's future, and that it was the wrong time and wrong place to pitchfork the Queen into a complicated Middle East imbroglio.

The longer the discussion went on, the greater were the counter-anxieties that any postponement or cancellation of a visit designed to reciprocate one made to London by King Hussein nearly twenty years before might adversely affect Anglo-Jordanian relations, and jeopardise the King's standing in his quest for a solution to the Palestinian problem. So, with five weeks to go, the Foreign Office insisted the tour was definitely on, while elaborate security precautions were put in hand. The British Embassy in Amman was almost ringed with enormous concrete barriers disguised as flower-holders, designed to prevent bomb attacks by suicide squads driving vehicles full of explosives into the compound. The Queen's aircraft, a British Airways Tri-star, was not only refitted in the way a royal aircraft normally is, but was also supplied with an anti-missile device under each wing, to detect missiles on the ground or in the air, fire flares to deflect any weapon on course for the aircraft, and destroy it in the air subsequently if necessary. The editor of Jane's *Fighting Aircraft* confirmed that it was 'not novel for a passenger aircraft to carry an anti-missile system of this sort,' but its somewhat grotesque appearance on the Queen's plane, the training of its pilots to take sudden steep dives and climbs if necessary, and King Hussein's orders that any aircraft seen approaching the Tri-star should be shot down without question, brought home to many people how seriously every possible threat to Her Majesty's safety was being taken. In London, the Jordanian Embassy insisted that 'Amman is a much safer city than many others: the Queen will be perfectly safe,' while in the Jordanian capital a British official, with mischievous reference to Michael Fagan, said that 'there was little chance of an intruder getting as far as King Hussein's bedroom.' Many had suspected that any terrorist attack would be launched before the visit, in order to persuade a cancellation, rather than during the visit, and this seemed to be the case when, on the eve of the Queen's arrival, a bomb went off and twenty-five sticks of gelignite were defused outside the hotel in Amman where most of the foreign press were being accommodated. News, which followed directly, that the British ambassador had advised an immediate cancellation was denied by 10 Downing Street in a statement which confirmed that 'after consideration of all the information and advice available, it was considered that the visit should go ahead.' Questioned by journalists, the Jordanian Information Ministry dismissed the bombing: 'The bomb you heard was marked for your attention,' a spokesman said. 'It was a little bang for propaganda effect only.' The British ambassador's fears, if indeed he had harboured them at all, were also allayed. 'I have no qualms at all,' he said. 'They will be in good hands.' And King Hussein gave his personal guarantee to that effect.

With less than convincing smiles on their faces, the Queen and Prince Philip left London for a hesitant start to their visit. They made for Cyprus, staying overnight at Episkopi airbase, before leaving for a comparatively lengthy flight to Jordan which took them on a roundabout route over Egypt in a pointed and determined attempt to avoid overflying Syria. They arrived safely at Amman's Marka Airport to be greeted by King Hussein and his tall, elegant, American-born fourth wife, Queen Noor. Eleven of the King's children were also there, two of them – Princess Haya, his nine-year-old daughter by Queen Alia who died in a helicopter crash in 1977, and Prince Hamzeh, his three-year-old son by Queen Noor – to present bouquets to the Queen. Then, after the usual welcoming ceremonies, a huge convoy bristling with Browning machine guns, and escorted by clattering helicopters overhead, took the royal party in silver-grey cars at 50mph over roads lined with soldiers every fifty yards, and almost totally devoid of spectators, to the royal palace complex. Strategically positioned on the crest of one of the hills on which Amman is built, the complex was constructed by King Abdullah, whose assassination in 1953 brought his grandson King Hussein to the throne. There are, in fact, four palaces within its walls, including a guest palace where the Queen and Prince Philip stayed during the early part of their tour, and the Basman Palace where, on the evening of their first day, King Hussein hosted a spectacular banquet in their honour. The splendour of the occasion, with the royalties fairly studded with Orders and decorations, was matched by the politically-motivated sentiments propounded by the Queen, whose speeches rarely touch on any matter too specific to be remotely controversial. She was on this occasion almost fulsome in her praise of King Hussein's efforts to resolve 'the tragedy which has befallen the Palestinian people' and which had 'affected no country more than Jordan. The world has been deeply impressed by your efforts, in the face of so many discouragements and setbacks, to achieve a negotiated settlement of the problems of the Middle East. We have greatly admired the way in which you have guided your country through so many difficulties. In doing so, you have come to symbolise for us those qualities of courage and statesmanship which have made that achievement possible. In an area of turbulence and of almost continuous and tragic conflict, you have made Jordan a beacon of stability and orderly progress.'

The stability referred to by the Queen was nowhere more evident than in the easy-going atmosphere of the royal stables, which she visited as part of the next day's engagements in Amman. These are managed entirely by Princess Alia – at twenty eight years old, King Hussein's eldest daughter and, like Princess Anne, a former Benenden pupil – and consists of over a hundred pure-bred Arabian horses, which she hopes will soon qualify her for membership of the World Arab Horse Association. Built up in the last twenty-two years, the stud was inaugurated to prevent the disappearance of the Arab breed from Jordan, and the Queen was delighted with the latest evidence of success in the shape of a brood-mare with a strong, almost frisky two-day-old foal. She was no less delighted with a gorgeous Bedou saddle, hand-made by Arab craftsmen and fully decorated with red and black braids and tassels. In all, the visit was a pleasant contrast to the Queen's rather more solemn pilgrimage to the Martyrs' Memorial, where Jordan's war dead, from the time of the rebellions against Turkish rule seventy years ago, are commemorated, and it set the tone for the rest of the day. At the King Hussein Rehabilitation Centre, for instance, the Queen found herself chatting to a Royal Jordanian airline hostess who was recovering after a car crash five days before. 'It was a real tonic,' the patient said afterwards. 'I feel better already.' But the biggest surprise was for forty British children who had waited to see the Queen the day before, when her car journey from airport to palace proved just too fast for them to see her, or she them. The Queen heard of their disappointment, and arranged that they should be invited to a reception the following day when she explained everything to their delighted parents. 'The Queen told us that she saw us waiting yesterday, but could do nothing about it because the car was going too fast – but that she was glad that she was able to see some of us here now,' said one.

The reason for the ever-present security – four huge American tanks had guarded the Queen during her visit to the royal stud, for example – made itself felt on the third day of the tour, when the Queen and Prince Philip visited a valley farm owned by a former Jordanian ambassador to Britain, for a briefing by the the King's brother Crown-Prince Hassan on the political, military and territorial predicament in which Jordan found herself. Referring to a map on which this was illustrated, the Prince began a long lecture, filled with complaints and accusations of alleged Israeli injustices against Jordan, and her plans for expanding Jewish settlements on the West Bank, conquered by Israel in 1967. He pointed out the visible buildings of the Israeli-occupied town of Jericho, drew the Queen's attention to the grinding rumble of Israeli jets, and explained that Israel wanted to increase her West Bank population to 1.4 million within the next twenty-five years, to equal the expected Arab population there. The Queen called the map 'depressing' and the prospects 'frightening' – private courtesies which immediately caused dismay in Israel where even then invitations to the Queen to pay a State Visit there as well were being contemplated. Following the briefing, King Hussein personally drove the Queen and Prince Philip to the shores of the Dead Sea, where at Jawan, also known as Lot's Lake because of the salinity of the waters, a picnic of truly royal proportions awaited them. Enormous tents, flying national flags, had been erected, in which a major-domo, six cooks, two coffee servers and dozens of waiters stood ready to attend the royal guests as they lounged on long, silk-upholstered sofas and huge, soft cushions, with a selection of dips, mounds of rice flavoured with almonds, pine-nuts, sultanas and currants, spit-roasted lamb kebabs, sherbets and sorbets, and coffee poured from fine gold and brass pots heated over small fires. And all, of course, within the sound of helicopters combing the nearby hills for snipers and ambushers.

That afternoon, the royal party left for Aqaba, where King Hussein has a country palace on the shores of that controversial gulf town, within sight of the Israeli port of Eilat. From here, the following day, he took his guests to Petra, which the Rev. John Burgon immortalised as 'a rose red city half as old as time.' It is in fact a comparative youngster, built two thousand years ago as a trading centre for the Nabateans, but it is no less grand for all that, and the Queen took the correct tourist action by hopping out of her car just before the city was reached and walking the last hundred yards or so through the sheer cleavage in the rocks so that the full effect of the hidden city could be revealed in the most dramatic way – a sudden vista of porticos, canopies and columns all lit by the eerie shafts of angled sunlight filtering down. Unfortunately, security considerations even here meant that most of the indigenous cave-dwelling families had to be kept away from the huge tombs and monuments which the Queen was to inspect, but a few were allowed to see her. Luckiest among them was a New Zealand-born woman who had married a Jordanian souvenir-seller, and had given up her Western way of life to join him in Petra: she exchanged a few words with the Queen as her young son slept soundly on her shoulder. It was a delightful trip, relaxed and relatively low-key, the perfect note on which to end a tour which once seemed unlikely to materialise at all. After the Queen left the following day, King Hussein gave a brief interview to say how delighted he was with everything, and how grateful to the Queen for her resolve to follow her government's advice not to put the visit off. There was praise, too, back home for 'a truly magnificent sovereign' whose courage, which no-one had ever doubted, was 'as much part of her public performance as the handbag she carries.' The last word, as is often the case, came from Buckingham Palace. 'The tour,' said Mr Shea, 'has been an enormously successful and very enjoyable one.'

The potentially controversial tour of Jordan was matched, in spirit if not in scale, by a few embryo controversies at home. In January, the Prime Minister's refusal to allow the Social Democratic Party a representative at the annual Remembrance Day ceremony at the Cenotaph sparked off a row in which the Queen, as leader of the nation's homage, could have become involved. That prospect arose when Mrs Thatcher's suggestion that Parliamentary representation, the Prime Minister and Leader of the Opposition apart, should be concentrated in the person of the Speaker was denounced by the Liberal leader Mr Steel as 'impertinent.' And, he added, 'I do not suppose Mrs Thatcher has had the gall to put this preposterous proposal to the Queen.' Whether she did or not, we do not know, but in due course the SDP was given a place at the Cenotaph, which David Owen would take up in November 1984. He was less successful in securing a seat at the Queen's banquet for the Amir of Bahrain at Windsor Castle in April, though the Queen was kept out of any possible controversy here in view of existing governmental guidelines on the scope of the invitations she can make. By summer, however, there was a danger that the Queen might be involved in the bitter tangle of the miners' strike, which had begun in April. She was due to open a new power station in Yorkshire at the end of June, but the fear of violence by pickets, the sensitive nature of any official business in the heart of a coal-mining area, and anxiety lest the Queen should be directly identified with the dispute led to the visit being called off a week before it was due. The issue posed questions as to how concerned the Queen was with the worsening situation, and speculation based on a brief statement by the Lord Lieutenant of South Yorkshire began to fill the newspapers, who vied with each other to present the most grossly exaggerated tales of what the Queen had said to the Prime Minister, or to her own family, or to her staff. It took a letter from a retired miner, asking the Queen if she could please intervene to stop the dispute, to give her the opportunity of reaffirming her loyalty to her strictly constitutional duties. 'Her Majesty profoundly hopes,' came the reply from Buckingham Palace, 'that a way to settle this dispute will soon be found, and takes advantage of her weekly meeting with the Prime Minister to follow closely the development of this and other matters.'

The following month, the Queen received an invitation to take tea with the Peace Women at their makeshift camp at the Greenham Air Base. It came from a woman who had just attended one of the Queen's garden parties, but like most private invitations to tea, whether from little girls celebrating their sixth birthday or elderly couples on their diamond wedding, it was no doubt politely refused. The previous April saw the Queen brought into the issue of the Greater London Council, then as now threatened with abolition under a government bill in Parliament. Ken Livingstone, an articulate and persuasive left-winger, had just been obliged by the GLC, of which he is the leader, to reverse his earlier decision not to invite the Queen to perform the opening ceremony for the new Thames Barrier, and he was quick to make capital out of the sovereign's ready acceptance of his eventual invitation. 'The Queen is trying to tell us something,' he claimed quite seriously – 'that she does not agree with the abolition of the GLC. I have no doubt at all that, if the Queen was opposed to the GLC and supported the government's policy, it would have been difficult to persuade her to open the barrier.' It was a surprising statement for a man of his political maturity, and the fact that it was probably worth a try did not prevent it from meeting with instant assaults from two quarters at least. The Tory leader of the Westminster City Council called it 'a disgraceful attempt to drag the Queen into his political campaign against the government,' while Buckingham Palace affirmed, in its usual neutral way, that 'the Queen is doing it because the barrier is a major feature of London. It does not imply political opinion at all.' For an issue so early soured, the eventual opening in May was all sweetness and light. The Queen and Prince Philip approached the massive steel barrier in the royal barge *Nore*, accompanied by, among others, Mr Livingstone's stubbornly royalist mother, who had travelled down from her home in Lincoln, and bought a new outfit just for the day. She chatted non-stop with Prince Philip, who asked her all about Lincoln and its cathedral, and pointed out London's own landmarks to her. Her son had **not** bought a new suit, but had had his old one dry-cleaned, and when he welcomed the Queen to Woolwich Reach, with a bow almost as low as Mr Punch's to Princess Mary, every camera in the world seemed to click to record the moment. He was unabashed at the obvious irony of the rampant socialist doing homage to a monarch, and pronounced the Queen 'a very nice person.' Prince Philip was even nicer, exchanging a volley of witticisms with Mr Livingstone as the Newham Borough Band played a selection from Handel's *Water Music*, and klaxons and ships' sirens hooted their welcome. And, with the press of a button and the declaration that 'the power of this great river flowing through our capital has been tamed,' the Queen put the finishing touch to the eight-year-old project to defend a 45-mile flood-plain against a tide which on two occasions as recently as 1978 came within half a metre of breaching the existing defences.

The Princess of Wales came up against the GLC controversy when she visited the Albany Trust Centre at Deptford in

May. Some of the workers there, fearing for both the centre and their jobs, asked her to sign a petition against the GLC's prospective abolition. When she refused, on the grounds that 'I have to be very careful, you know,' they asked her to do what she could to save the centre if the abolition bill went through Parliament. She came up with a clever compromise undertaking, wisely avoiding any political opinion: she would speak to her father, Earl Spencer about it, before he voted in the House of Lords' debate due in a few day's time. We do not know what the direct effect was, but the bill was voted down and the GLC remains very much alive. The issue marked the high point of any royal involvement in political controversy, though those two incorrigible free-speakers, Prince Philip and the Prince of Wales, managed to find other hotly-disputed matters to pronounce upon. The nuclear debate was raised again when Prince Philip published a book in February entitled *Men, Machines and Sacred Cows* – which was little more than a classified selection of many of his articles and speeches on various matters in the past decade. One of them involved his support of nuclear weapons as a means of preventing global war, a conclusion based on what he saw as 'the successful deterrent effect of nuclear weapons. They have prevented escalation and certainly appear to have discouraged armed conflict between east and west in Europe.' A former Labour Minister, Mr Bob Brown, was unimpressed if not positively rattled. 'I would have thought,' he commented, 'that the Queen's husband would be well advised not to involve himself in pronouncements which are the subject of political controversy.' There was no audible disagreement, however, in March when, giving his first lecture as Chancellor of Edinburgh University, he condemned the tribal factor in society for its perpetuation of violence in Northern Ireland, war in Lebanon, and soccer hooliganism, and criticised the Church for doing too little to prevent those evils. 'Church leaders of all denominations,' he stated, 'raise their voice for peace, but that is rather like being against sin. Considering that most religions preach brotherhood and tolerance and peace, it might be thought that this was one human activity in which the tribal factor played no part. Unfortunately, the tribal factor in religion has achieved not only untold good, but has also been the cause of some of the worst violence the world has ever seen.' Nor did anyone disagree with him when, in July, he pointed out the irony of British industry's ability to 'beat the pants off the rest of the world' on the evidence of commercial initiative, designing talent, management competence, productive skills and cooperative enterprise, while at the same time, regrettably, 'our most successful export has been jobs.'

There was widespread sympathy, too, for Prince Charles' agonised puzzlement, expressed at a Jewish Welfare Board dinner in March, over social attitudes among the young. 'They seem to despise the old,' he said. 'Often they think nothing of beating them up, outside or inside their homes, just for the pension books they have picked up. We badly need to discover the meaning of this supposedly old-fashioned value which recognises old age and accords it the respect it deserves.' He also deplored the trend towards the social ostracism of the old, who 'find themselves in homes, cared for by devoted people, but cut off completely from the society of younger people,' and said that in this respect the Jewish and Asian populations in Britain had much to teach those of native stock. He expanded the argument at a Bermondsey probation centre the following day, putting the blame for these social ills on umemployment – 'a particular cause,' he said. 'A lot of young people have told me that boredom leads them into petty crime.' And he pledged funds from the Jubilee Trusts and Prince's Trust to help, on the basis that 'young people have talents which have gone the wrong way. If we could only help to develop them the right way, we might get somewhere.' His reference to unemployment caused the Prime Minister some embarrassment in the House of Commons the next day, but she said that the Prince was wrong, and that a recent study under the auspices of the Social Science Research Council had concluded that there was no significant connection between unemployment and crime. Auberon Waugh, writing that weekend with his usual nail-on-the-head cynicism in the *Sunday Telegraph*, thought that, however sincere Prince Charles had been in his pronouncements, they stood condemned for being weak. 'The young will certainly think twice before misbehaving again,' he scoffed. 'Perhaps the Prince is wasting his talent. He should have been a bishop.'

For an issue which really raised the roof, you would be hard put to find a better example than Prince Charles' now celebrated tirade against the nation's architects. He was speaking in May at a banquet given at Hampton Court Palace by the Royal Institute of British Architects, then celebrating its 150th anniversary, to honour Charles Correa, an expert in the development of low-cost housing schemes in India. Prince Charles had little time for the usual courtesies of such an occasion before he launched himself into what was obviously a carefully-planned attack on the profession of his hosts. He condemned architects for 'consistently ignoring the wishes of the mass of ordinary people in this country,' and cited several examples of what he saw as the unfortunate results of recent architectural decisions. The planned extension to the National Gallery, for instance, was likened to 'a vast municipal fire station, a monstrous carbuncle on the face of a much-loved and elegant friend,' while the proposed development at the Mansion House was labelled 'yet another glass stump, better suited to downtown Chicago than to the City of London.' 'What are we doing to our capital city?' he demanded. 'What have we done to it since the bombing during the war? It is hard to imagine that London must have had one of the most beautiful skylines of any great city. Why can't we have curves and arches that express feeling in design? Why has everything got to be vertical, straight, unbending, only at right angles – and functional?' What a contrast in attitude, he considered, to Prince Albert's individuality and fascination with architecture, and to those comparatively few architects today who are willing to restore old Victorian and Georgian buildings which the Prince Consort loved so much.

The storm of argument which followed hard on the heels of his astonishingly frank, impassioned and forthrightly-expressed speech lasted for the best part of six weeks. Initially there was tremendous praise, not just for his sentiments but for the superb choice of occasion – seen by one of his supporters as a typical RIBA self-congratulatory beano – on which it was delivered. Others sounded almost relieved that Prince Charles was sympathetic to most people's indifference and hostility to buildings which were nothing but businessmen's paradises. The chairman of Save Britain's Heritage came immediately to the Prince's side, and said that 'millions of people feel that too much of the old has been needlessly destroyed, and too much of the new is needlessly tasteless.' Lord Gowrie, the Minister for the Arts, commented somewhat cagily that the speech was of 'immense value' to architects, while a former RIBA President said it was 'dynamic, and could spark off a revolution in the profession.' *The Times* was in no doubt that Prince Charles' words had 'carried the attack into the very tent of the profession.' Others, more simply, complemented the Prince's cry from the heart with another one: 'God Bless the Prince of Wales.' Even Willie Hamilton, whose customary annual attacks on the Royal Family were conspicuous by their absence during the year, said that he thought Prince Charles 'has a valid point. I would go along with it.' A few people, while agreeing with the Prince's sentiments, tried not to put the blame solely on architects. 'His questions,' said one, for example, 'will remain rhetorical until money is available for grandiose designs.' Another thought that the Prince might have investigated the degree of blame attributable to planners, pressure groups and politicians, while another gently reminded him that he may have spoken out of place about the two London schemes while their futures were still the subject of Environment Department scrutiny. Yet another thought it curious, if not ill-mannered, that an occasion staged to honour one man was turned into something quite different, and left little or no glory reflected upon the real hero of the hour. The rest of Prince Charles' critics were firmly out of sympathy, and the longer the argument went on, the bolder they became in expressing themselves. RIBA's president wrote an early letter to say that 'society gets the architecture it deserves,' and to wonder whether it wouldn't 'be marvellous if the Duchy of Cornwall commissioned a modern building.' Later, he became more direct, counselling the Prince to 'think more about modern architecture, because it is here to stay,' and cited many examples of recent building which had resulted from public enquiries and popular polls. He also deplored, by implication at least, the distinct lack of positive royal support for architectural proposals and progress during the twentieth century. Another critic who thought the Prince had not grasped the full arguments in favour of the Mansion House project reflected another's opinion that he should have picked a wider target for his criticisms – the Tower of London, for instance, which is surrounded by 'banal office blocks and car parks,' instead of two instances 'where quality has at least been attempted.' More virulent attacks were not long in coming. One opponent thought Prince Charles' speech 'half-baked, and the familiar sound of peevish abuse.' It reflected, according to another, a 'coarseness of response' and merely repeated 'stale gossip which should not have been too difficult to pick up.' 'On with mediocrity and shabbiness,' proclaimed yet another, sarcastically 'and down with anything progressive because, don't you see, the ordinary person doesn't understand it.'

As the discussion grew more intense, it spawned all manner of side issues which received public airings in their own right – community architecture, concepts of modernism, the New Brutalism of the '50s, High Tech of the '80s, the identity of so-called 'ordinary people', Prince Albert's contributions, the character of downtown Chicago, uptown San Francisco, New York, Dallas, Baltimore....and just as the dialogue began to show signs of retreat, news came through that the Royal Opera House had named their man to design a new £55 million extension. Prince Charles had been known to favour Ted Cullinan – 'a man after my own heart' – for the job, but the Royal Opera House decided otherwise and opted for the much more modernistic Jeremy Dixon. Dixon was quick to make any necessary peace with Prince Charles, with whom he agreed 'that people should like the buildings they have around them,' and he promised that the royal patron would find his design 'very relevant' and 'not avant-garde.' And within a further week, RIBA announced that it had floated the idea to Prince Charles that he might become involved in some way or another with the direction of architectural development in the future – say on a permanent commission or advisory body. 'The Prince realises that he has stuck his neck out,' said a spokesman in July. 'If you complain that the kitchen is dirty, then you have to do something about clearing it up. What Prince Philip has done for wildlife as President of the World Wildlife Fund, Prince Charles could do for architecture.' Perhaps this will be a case where controversy is usefully converted to yet another royal involvement in national life.

There were sufficient other, more minor, controversies to irritate the Royal Family during the year, though few of them achieved greater status than that of mere talking points. In October, Stephen Knight, about to launch his book *The Brotherhood*, revealed how Prince Charles has always been adamant in his refusal to join the Freemasons, a body of some 700,000 of which the Duke of Kent was re-elected as nominal senior member in January, in which his brother Prince Michael is Grand Master of one of its Grand Lodges, and of which the Queen herself is Grand Patroness. Mr Knight revealed that Prince Charles owes his firm line to the Queen Mother, who did not relish her own husband's membership of the society, and to the Duke of Edinburgh who, though he reluctantly followed King George VI's lead, regards the whole thing as rather a silly joke. Two other books threatened royalty's private pursuits rather more directly. One was being prepared, according to its author Stephen Barry in August, to reveal more secrets of his life as valet to Prince Charles, and promised a tougher, more controversial tone than his first effort the previous year. It would tell how ordinary the Royal Family is in private life – 'wonderfully middle-class,' Mr Barry revealed, 'except they wear crowns' – and how the only thing that separates them from the rest of us is that they have four palaces or private homes, three hundred staff, a yacht, three helicopters and three aircraft at their disposal. As if convinced that few people would pay very much to read what they already knew, hot on his heels two months later came Vicki Hodge, who thought she had something worthwhile to reveal about Prince Andrew and Princess Margaret, from her few peripheral contacts with them in the past. Much later, in May, she claimed that at least one of her contacts had not been quite so casual: in a three-part preview of her well-ghosted book, she talked of an eight-day affair she had had with Prince Andrew when his ship, *HMS Invincible*, docked in Barbados early in 1983. In what was a 'totally harmless and really very lovely' relationship the Prince, she alleged, became her lover and confided in her about his family, his other girlfriends and his career. Apart from one of the other girls who was with her in Barbados at the time, no one seemed willing to come forward to support her story, which was vehemently denied by the owner of the villa in which the incidents were said to have taken place. But it did not prevent the author from scooping an estimated £40,000 for her efforts, nor deter her from assuring everybody that she had no regrets, despite a disapproving 'no comment' from Buckingham Palace, and the deprecations of one leader-writer who called her story 'a fantasy which exists in the mind of that raddled, middle aged-trollop.'

One celebrity of more dubious sexual proclivities had something of a brush with royalty when the singer Boy George met Princess Margaret at an awards ceremony in London in May. It turned into one of those bewildering episodes in which everything reported to have been said was denied but, in the absence of first-hand evidence, remained half-believed by a credulous public. Boy George had apparently wanted the Princess to pose for a group photograph after the ceremony but she, said not to have recognised him earlier, was then reported to have refused to 'be photographed with that over-made-up tart. I am too old for that kind of thing.' If those words ever did leave her lips, they had hardly done so before London almost shook with the rattle of handbags. Boy George initially reacted with, 'I don't give a damn. I didn't want to talk to her anyway. She doesn't mean a thing to me; my fans mean a lot more.' Kensington Palace, equally bristling with fury, denied that 'the Princess would ever dream of saying such a thing.' The singer remained unconvinced, and demanded an apology, saying that 'if Princess Margaret goes out to represent the Royal Family, she should behave.' Besides, he added, 'I bring more money into this country than she does.' One newspaper canvassed its readers for their reactions and found 65% of them in sympathy with Boy George. One columnist claimed to have solved the misunderstanding, with the explanation that Princess Margaret had likened Boy George's face to a mask from the *Commedia dell'Arte*, and that this very up-market comment had been misheard for the reported controversial remark. But it was Viscount Linley who apparently calmed things down between his mother and the singer. He and Boy George met in a restaurant in Soho in June, and the Viscount assured him that Princess Margaret 'knew very well who you were, and was not at all happy that her comments were misrepresented.'

Viscount Linley was himself no stranger to the passions kindled by a stray remark when, back in October, in answer to the question: 'What gift would you present to your worst enemy?' he replied, 'dinner with Princess Michael.' This casual, even chuckled answer to a hypothetical enquiry fairly exploded into public consciousness despite the Viscount's immediate protestations that it was not given or intended to be taken seriously, and Princess Michael's own good-natured disbelief that he had even said it, and the announcement by each that they both liked and got on well with each other. In private, the Princess was said to have been very hurt, though at a public function a few days later she clearly saw the funny side of things and gave as good as she got. 'If there are any men among you,' she said, 'who are responsible for the three sackloads of mail I received this morning, all assuring me that you are in fact the worst enemy of a cousin of mine, then when can you come to dinner?' In the inevitable taking of sides, there was little sympathy for Princess Margaret's normally uncontroversial son. 'What a right royal little sneak!' said one of Princess Michael's supporters. 'He has a lot to learn. Today's lesson should be to say sorry to Princess Michael.' Another imagined that Princess Michael's gift to **her** worst enemy would be a table made by Viscount Linley, with one leg propped up by a copy of Nigel Dempster's book about Princess Margaret. In one quarter, however, the issue was seen as evidence of a simmering royal animosity against Princess Michael, and a host of silly, tired, rehashed tales of past contretemps, brought forward as supposed evidence of the fact, prompted a member of the public to point out that 'there are enough people going about sniping at the Royal Family without its own members joining in as well.' In time, as one would expect, the matter was quietly shelved. Princess Michael said she had received an apology. 'We are now the greatest of friends and I shall look upon it all as a terrible misunderstanding.' It was certainly not the only misunderstanding she had to clear up. In the New Year, a long-held suspicion that the Michaels' country retreat at Nether Lyppiatt was haunted broke surface after two priests were reported to have performed ceremonies to exorcise the ghost of a blacksmith hanged there in the 17th century for sheep-stealing. The Prince and Princess were said to have stayed away from the house that night – 25th January – when, according to legend, the ghost returns on horseback to the scene of the execution. The story was strengthened by the testimony of another priest who had visited the house shortly before the royal owners bought it. 'I was not at all happy about the atmosphere,' he said. 'I sensed things in the house that I did not like.' But the priests who carried out the ceremonies insisted that they amounted to nothing more than a house-blessing, comprised of prayers and the sprinkling of holy water. And Princess Michael herself dismissed the stories a few months later as 'Silly. There aren't any ghosts. Let's be quite clear about that.'

In July, the grounds of Nether Lyppiatt were opened to the public for the second time, to raise funds for the Red Cross – despite the tragedy of Kitty, Princess Michael's five-year-old Burmese neutered tom cat, which had disappeared on a similar occasion the previous July. Kitty had been a wedding present from Prince Michael, and his wife was devastated when neither her exhaustive searches of nearby fields, nor the issue of photographs, nor the offer of a reward succeeded in recovering him. Eventually, three weeks later, Kitty was found dead in a timber-yard at nearby Brinscombe, after having evidently been struck by a car. Princess Michael came to the yard with her gardener to retrieve the body – 'She was in tears as she walked away with the bundle of fur,' said the wife of its proprietor – wrapped it in a linen cloth, and buried it under a favourite tree in the garden of the house. The following week, Prince Michael had replaced the much-lamented Kitty with a pair of twelve-week-old Burmese kittens, bought from a breeder in Monmouth. 'Of course they will never replace Kitty,' said the Princess, 'but I am absolutely delighted with them.' She thought she would wait to see what they got up to before giving them names, but within a week her son Lord Frederick had persuaded her to call them Bessie and Jessie. The happy outcome attracted a wealth of good-humoured jokes, such as whether the kittens would be housed in the Royal Mews, or would have the honour of a christening by the Pope. This latter witticism was a none-too-thinly veiled reference to another happy event for the Prince and Princess – the recognition of their five-year-old marriage by the Vatican, after a long and complicated application for Papal blessing in which the dominant issue involved the Princess' insistence that her children would be brought up as Anglicans. The Roman Catholic journal *The Universe*, unconvinced that the Princess had done enough deserve the dispensation, was told by the Archbishop of Westminster that she had conveyed and would continue to convey to her children her 'genuine love and knowledge' of the Catholic church, and that her efforts had impressed the authorities in Rome. The nub of the matter seemed to be that she had assured them that, if her children wished to convert to Catholicism of their own volition, no obstacle would be put in their way – an improvement, it was felt, on her stance five years earlier that they would be not only baptised but also raised in the Church of England. Not surprisingly, the Vatican's decision, which culminated in a service of blessing at Westminster Cathedral shortly afterwards, was seen as highly selective. One partner of a 'mixed marriage' was deeply resentful of the 'red-carpet treatment doled out' to the royal couple, and pleaded for similar consideration on behalf of 'many more of us whose souls were cast into outer darkness.' Meanwhile, Thomas Troubridge, whose marriage to the Princess had been annulled in 1978, became engaged to a daughter of Lord Penrhyn, and they were married the following June.

The rumour-mongers who thrive on predicting impending marriage for Princess Margaret, seemed to have been on holiday for several months in 1982 and 1983, and may also have been cheated by the absence in the New Year publication of Cabinet papers under the thirty-year rule, of any reference to her liaison with Peter Townsend which became public in 1953. But it took only a few well-placed whispers to link her once again with Norman Lonsdale, the businessman who has been her companion on several occasions in the past three or four years. This time, the Americans were at the root of it, using Princess Margaret's brief October stay at the Virginia home of the attorney Neil Phillips as the foundation for a story that a secret wedding was being arranged there between her and Mr Lonsdale. Mr Phillips, admitting that the Princess was staying with him, explained that her friend was at the time on a business trip to Rome, but by then the speculation had reached New York, and the Princess' staff in London and Washington had to step in to squash the 'idiotic' things that were being said. 'As far as I know,' said a Clarence House spokesman, 'she is not getting married again.' And from the British Embassy in Washington, the Princess' private secretary Lord Napier issued a statement denying 'any truth whatsoever' in the story. 'Certainly news to me,' confirmed Viscount Linley, and the rumour obligingly died down.

Not so, however, the more persistent rumours about Princess Anne and Captain Phillips, whose marriage easily survived the continual separation of partners heavily committed to their respective duties and pastimes, yet invariably seen in good company with each other on the comparatively few occasions when they were brought together in public. 'The sort of life we lead means that we are apart quite a lot,' Princess Anne had said in a magazine interview in September, 'but lots of working couples suffer the same problem.' Nevertheless, the Australian press, gleefully anticipating a visit by the Princess and Captain Phillips the following month, during which they would at times be working apart, were not to be dissuaded that their marriage was effectively in ruins. 'There are a lot of areas in which uninformed gossip has been going on for years,' retorted the Princess when she got to Australia. 'We did after all arrive in the same car tonight!' Her easy, dismissive tone was not echoed by her husband, who said that, even after ten years, 'it is difficult. We try to ignore the stories.' And he mouthed a despairing 'Oh God, not that again,' when the following July the fact that he and Princess Anne would be staying in separate hotels in Los Angeles was taken as yet another indication that the couple had broken up in all but appearances. Buckingham Palace's repeated explanations that the arrangement was purely logistical – Princess Anne was visiting the city officially while Captain Phillips, there as a contracted commentator for an Australian broadcasting company, was obliged to stay in the same company as his television crew – were to little avail, particularly when Captain Phillips failed to accompany his wife to America for a short visit earlier that month. Again, Buckingham Palace denied any significance in the arrangement. 'It is not his job to accompany the Princess,' they insisted. 'His job is as a farmer and horseman.'

Princess Anne was at least accorded the courtesy of being excluded from the sometimes savage slings and arrows propelled by the Central Television satirical show *Spitting Image*, which began a weekly series in March. A prime example of the lengths to which television comedy must needs go if it is to retain the attention of a public satiated with the blandishments of respectable sit-coms, the series was pretty well unsparing of all public figures, from politicans to pop stars, and from national do-gooders to international crooks. Though it did not feature the Establishment as its major target, its weekly helping of glove-puppet royal satire assured it of a perpetual audience – though not, if the royal spokesmen were to be believed, at Buckingham Palace. 'We never take action before programmes are shown,' said one, in reply to a question as to whether attempts had been made to keep the programme off the air, 'but we have no plans to watch it.' For a while, Central Television's plans to screen the series were in doubt when, at the end of February, the Duke of Edinburgh visited their studios in Nottingham. In a move which many saw as cynical and hypocritical, but which the producers put down to 'a matter of courtesy,' the series, due to have begun the previous weekend, was delayed until the next, when Prince Philip was at a safe distance. As far as the scriptwriters' thoughts about the Royal Family were concerned, the series left little to the imagination. Prince Philip himself was portrayed as a good-natured, indulgent father, giggling at practical jokes and protecting his errant and thoughtless son Prince Andrew from the ever-present wrath of the Queen, following successive amorous adventures which the Prince neatly encapsulated in a song entitled *I'm Just A Prince Who Can't Say No*. Prince Charles, by contrast, was seen as a bumbling, almost half-witted heir-apparent, doing his plodding, obedient best to keep mother, wife and child happy against all the odds. The Princess of Wales, though never seen, was projected as an uncommunicative spouse, full of capricious whims and Sloane Ranger-type phraseology, while Prince William bawled ceaselessly from beneath a monstrous frilled baby cap. 'To involve a baby like this is cruel and insensitive,' remonstrated Mrs Mary Whitehouse – herself a recurrent victim of the show. Tory MP Mrs Jill Knight agreed. 'People must have sick minds to produce a caricature of a baby like this,' she protested. 'I find if wholly offensive.' Central Television, falling back on the well-tried apologia that 'we believe Prince William's parents have a good sense of humour,' failed to see the inconsistency of satirising some, but not all, of the senior members of the Royal Family. Both the Princess of Wales and the Queen Mother were spared, on the grounds that they were very popular. 'If we'd gone ahead, we'd have upset an awful lot of people,' a spokesman admitted. One would have thought the Queen one of the most popular members of the Royal Family, yet she too was depicted as a grotesque parody of herself, her interviews with Mrs Thatcher alternating with her references to horses, and her joint headgear of tiara and headscarf proclaiming the well-acknowledged truth that, when she is off duty, she is most at ease when in the company of her four-legged friends.

Unfortunately for the Queen, even her horses gave her little consolation during the year. Success on the racecourse was an intermittent luxury, particularly in 1983 when, with three months to go before the end of the flat-racing season, her racing manager Lord Porchester described it as 'a bad season for us.' It was a premature comment in a year when the Queen earned some £50,000 prize money for her efforts, but it was entirely understandable in the wake of the death in early August of Special Leave, while training at Ian Balding's gallops at Kingsclere. A year before, Special Leave had been tipped as a possible Derby winner for the Queen, but his chances of breaking the royal Epsom duck were at first diminished, and at length extinguished by an abscess and a hopelessly wet Spring which left the ground too soft for his liking. His death, an inevitable consequence of having shattered a hind leg bone 'into twenty pieces', as Lord Porchester put it, was 'very upsetting' for the Queen. But, her manager continued, 'she is a racing person, and she knows that the odds are stacked against you. You have to be philosophical, but winners are important to maintain the standard of our racing operation.' So indeed is cash. The Queen's winnings in 1983 were probably little more than 50% of her outgoings, which is perhaps why she sold one of her best-bred mares, the nine-year-old Circlet, in November for £240,000. A few other horses, like the small-time winner Red Duster and the well-made but disappointing colt Sheildag (sold at Ascot in November for £6,200) changed hands, to leave the Queen with eight horses of three or four years old to represent her interests in the 1984 Flat. In the first half of the season they proved disappointing: by the end of July, the Queen could savour the joy of winning only twice – once through her middle-distance colt Musical Box, who also achieved second place twice, and once thanks to Rough Stones, who was thought to be on the upgrade after winning at Goodwood in May, but who failed the following month at Royal Ascot. After fairly commendable two-year-old performances, the colt Careen proved sadly one-paced, the filly Fine

Romance of almost no account, and another filly, Crown and Sceptre, incapable of fulfilling her early promise to seize the Queen's first victory of the season at Chepstow in April. It was left to two four-year-olds to keep the royal records looking remotely respectable. Castle Rising, despite the susceptible legs which prompted the Queen to switch him from her West Ilsley stables to Ian Balding's, whose stables boast a therapeutic swimming pool, scored second and third places in May and June – the latter in the pattern race for the Queen's Vase at Royal Ascot – while Insular reached the frame three times between April and July, and may have done so again but for an interference on the course at Ascot in June. He was, however, unable to repeat his astounding record of four successive wins in 1983, and has not yet realised Lord Porchester's expectation that he would 'be a fun horse' for the 1984 Flat, nor Ian Balding's that he would get better as he gets older. There is, however, a possibility that 1985 will see him racing in the Queen Mother's colours over hurdles. Meanwhile, the Queen had entered three of her nine two-year-olds for races by the end of July, and the prospects for some rather more decisive royal success in 1985 seemed good. The two most promising were Bakers Dozen, which proved a game sprinter, finishing a six-furlong race at Newbury in an eye-popping burst of speed, and the filly Silver Dollar, another superb finisher at Ascot in June, landing first place and a useful £7,000 for the Queen. Silver Dollar immediately commanded odds of 20-1 for the 1985 Oaks for which her trainer Major Dick Hern confirmed she would be a prospect. It may, however, have given the Queen belated second thoughts about selling Circlet the previous autumn: Silver Dollar is one of her progeny!

Like most of the Queen's horses, Prince Philip's carriage-driving teams saw little outright success during the year, but nevertheless provided him with an interesting and highly competitive season in which at one time be seemed likely to overhaul his old rival George Bowman. He competed twice abroad: in September, he beat all his compatriots in the Swedish International, his overall fourth place comparing well with his subsequent performance in the Dutch International in April, when third place in the dressage and fourth in the cone-driving was marred by fifteenth place in the marathon, which left him twelfth overall. Nevertheless, even here he finished higher than the only other two British entries. At the end of April, he finished fifth in the horse-teams section at the Brighton carriage-driving championships, in which Prince Michael also took part for the first time, though without achieving a place in the pairs section. Then came some of the Duke of Edinburgh's best performances – second place at the Perth Driving Trials at Scone Palace in May, when he drove the Queen's Fell pony team from Balmoral on their first outing of the year; third place at the Sandringham carriage-driving trials in June; and second again at Holker Hall in Cumbria in July. These results, together with impressive performances at Floors Castle near Kelso in July, and at Lowther Castle the previous August, more than offset the dismay he might have felt at achieving only seventh place at the Royal Windsor Horse Show in May. They also contributed to the best news of the season, released early in July, that the Duke had won a place in the British team to compete in the World Driving Championships in Hungary in August.

One sport with which Prince Philip is rarely directly identified is football, but events in November reminded us that, like George V and George VI before him, he is Patron of his local football team – Windsor and Eton Football Club. An amateur club, Windsor and Eton achieved the rare distinction of qualifying for the FA Cup in October, reaching the second round proper in December. The Duke was invited to take his place in the directors' box that month for the match against Bournemouth, an invitation which he had to pass up because he was abroad at the time, though he sent a good luck message to the team. 'He always takes a close interest in the side's future,' said the club's manager, while its secetary added, 'He's a nice guy who really knows his football.' The Queen Mother, too, was praised for her cheerful tolerance of the game when, in pouring rain, she attended the Milk Cup Final at Wembley in March. Despite the bitterly cold weather, she did not cut and run when the full-time whistle blew, but stayed on for extra time and the presentations – all very much to the admiration of those who spend their own time convincing themselves that royalty is less able to stand up to the rigours expected of other mortals. 'Whoever was responsible for making the Queen Mother sit through three hours of the Milk Cup Soccer Final at this time of year in such atrocious conditions,' ran one hot protest, 'surely owes her an apology.' Coincidentally, the event came in the same month as the somewhat surprising revelation by Princess Anne, in a radio interview, that her husband was a keen football fan. 'It doesn't always meet with my approval,' she said – but that didn't stop Captain Phillips visiting White Hart Lane after his favourite team, Tottenham Hotspur, had beaten Anderlecht in the final of the UEFA Cup in May, to join them in a celebration which lasted well into the small hours! Princess Anne also talked in the same interview of her own attempts to master tennis when, in her teens, she was coached by the well known player turned commentator, Dan Maskell. She was thought to be capable of making Wimbledon standard, but she found herself 'temperamentally unsuited to the game' – it was 'too gladiatorial' for her. Not so, however, for Princess Michael of Kent, who plays at Queen's Club twice a week if possible – though ironically she pulled a leg muscle at one practice there during Wimbledon fortnight in June – nor for her nephew Lord Nicholas Windsor, who the previous August entered an under-14 tournament at Hunstanton in Norfolk, only to be beaten 6-0, 6-2 in the first round. The event chairman said that he had played well, and considering he had come up against one of the seeds in that round, had played a much more competitive game than the score suggested. Lord Nicholas was apparently undaunted: he stayed in England for more coaching while his family holidayed in Corfu the following month, and the Duke of Kent himself confirmed that his son would be playing at Hunstanton again next August.

The Duke of Edinburgh's continuing interest in the equestrian world took him, as President, to several meetings of the International Equestrian Federation, at which he steered the organisation authoritatively round several potential controversies. With the Olympics on everyone's mind, he addressed a meeting in Amsterdam in December on the dangers of commercialism, announcing that in future world or European championships, the sponsors' names would no longer be used as an integral part of the titles of the events. 'We take a very liberal view of sponsors and how they use their names,' he said, 'and we don't want to exclude sponsors, but some of them will ask for the moon, and there is a danger we will prostitute the sport. Championships are the only thing we are trying to protect, or we might end up with the Coca Cola Olympic Games.' He also expressed his concern about the use of illicit materials on horses' legs at shows, and asked that organisers be more vigilant in the future. Accusations of malpractice were aimed back at the Federation in April, when the Duke was called upon to defend its decision to hold international qualifying rounds throughout the winter, despite the attendant risks of encouraging the overjumping of horses. He denied that providing the facilities for competition necessarily implied connivance at horses being overused, but he admitted that he was 'very concerned about the amount of work that horses are given nowadays,' and said that an inquiry into the matter was in progress. Sponsorship also came up again, and the Duke trod his normal careful path between the need to fund events, and the desire to avoid undue commercial exploitation. 'Keeping horses is an expensive business,' he explained. 'I don't know how any show – except perhaps a local village one with no overheads – can conceivably operate without sponsors. There is a danger of some sponsors asking for more than their pound of flesh, but that is a subject of continual discussion.'

In view of the advanced warning he gave the Amsterdam meeting in December of his intention to quit as President, the International Equestrian Fund may well have weighed his pronouncements with special care, since they were to be among the last he would ever make officially on its behalf. The confusion into which his proposed resignation threw the Federation also projected into vivid relief the value of royal involvements generally, and the indispensibility of particular members of the Royal Family for particular jobs. The Duke's wide-ranging patronages of sport and other recreations are matched by the Queen's impeccable constitutional directness, diplomatic courtesy and ceremonial leadership; Prince Charles' concern for the disadvantaged is similarly complemented by his wife's busy, caring attitude to the young, the old, the sick and the handicapped; Princess Anne's stalwart preoccupation with those lucky enough to represent their country at the Olympics as well as to those hovering between life and death in the world's most undernourished corners is echoed by Princess Margaret's work for the NSPCC in its centenary year, and the support of the junior branches of the Royal Family for worthy national and international causes covering a wide spectrum of interests – social, architectural, medical and economic.

It is perfectly logical to argue that royalty is pragmatically superfluous in an age and society which prides itself on a tradition of democracy and egalitarism and this royal year has witnessed a very typical showing by those of republican persuasion. In September, Arthur Scargill spoke articulately about the type of Britain he would like to see, with a Royal Family being 'put to useful tasks in society'. By that he meant that Prince Philip would be slotted in as an adviser on naval affairs, and the Princess of Wales set to work modelling maternity wear. To this curious vision was added a more mundane one when, in October, the Mayor of Islington took down the Town Hall's portrait of the Queen, and replaced it with a copy of a statement of friendship between his town council and the new, if short-lived, Marxist government in Grenada. In February, another Labour-controlled council in the appropriately named town of Flint, vetoed the presentation of a gift for the Queen to mark her forthcoming visit, on the grounds that the money would be better spent elsewhere. And in July, the Queen found herself welcomed to Scotland by Edinburgh's Lord Provost who refused to wear the traditional scarlet robes – a ceremonial flourish which the Queen of all people would surely have appreciated – because he considered such things outmoded. How far instances like these represent personal insults, and how far they seriously plead in favour of abolishing a centuries-old constitutional establishment is always difficult to say without being accused of subjectivity. But both the Queen and her family know that, while they remain dedicated, concerned and hard working, the privileges which at times seem disproportionally lavish to those of commoner clay, need not be grudgingly afforded. The despairing reaction of the Canadians to the news of the postponement of the royal tour in July bears testimony to that, as does the more touching story of the East London man who died in March and left the whole of his meagre estate to his sovereign 'for her own use absolutely'. Perhaps the Queen followed the advice of one of her subjects on that occasion, and bought something to remember him by. Almost certainly in comparing this modest, devoted, and somewhat pathetic gesture with the occasional dart of anti-monarchist abuse, she will have appreciated the basic truth of the old Arab maxim: 'The dogs may bark, but the caravan rolls on.'

It was a happy start to the royal year for Prince and Princess Michael of Kent as they emerged from Westminster Cathedral at the end of July (left and below), their five-year-old marriage finally recognised and blessed by the Roman Catholic Church. The Prince and Princess attend Anglican and Catholic church services on alternate Sundays. The Queen was all smiles, too, when opening the Royal Society of Edinburgh's premises (below left), and holding a garden party at Holyroodhouse (right) on 29th June. The following day, she reviewed the Royal Scots Regiment there (opposite, below), with Princess Anne (bottom left). The Princess attended many of the regiment's celebrations in this, its 350th year, including an anniversary ball at Edinburgh's Assembly Rooms (below, far left).

Queen and Press in good humour at the *Glasgow Herald* offices on 1st July, 1983. The day's engagements – part of a busy annual Scottish tour – included a visit (right) to the Royal College of Physicians.

Approaching her eighty-third birthday, the Queen Mother looked to be enjoying life as never before. While her staff booked her engagements as far as two years ahead, she re-lived two familiar public duties in July. Surrounded by flowers on a damp day, she visited Camden and Islington on behalf of the London Gardens Society on the 6th. Two weeks later, she arrived (below) for the Royal Tournament in a blaze of military ceremonial.

Prince Andrew's visit to Newport, Rhode Island in mid-July, in support of Britain's America's Cup challenge, began with a reception at the Old Colony House. Smiles hid his concern as IRA protestors heckled his arrival. The crackle of a gun salute made him and his detective jump, before both realised their mistake and were convulsed with relieved laughter. The Prince was in Rhode Island as guest of Peter de Savary, whose efforts to secure the America's Cup for Britain were expensive, unsparing and, in the unhappy event, unsuccessful. The Cup went to Australia, though all that happened long after Prince Andrew had enjoyed an active and exciting trip.

It was only to be expected of a man about to embark on his fifth year in the Royal Navy that Prince Andrew found himself thoroughly at home on the motor launch *Lisanola*, from which he saw Britain's

Victory '83 being put through her paces during one of many practice runs. He had the good fortune to be invited aboard the yacht, and tried his hand at sailing her.

The central event of Prince Andrew's trip to Newport was to attend a ball as part of Britain's America's Cup festivities. It followed a dinner party at a local restaurant, attended by 120 distinguished guests, and it also sparked off excitement about the Prince's choice of partner for the occasion. 'Who are you taking to the ball?' he was asked. 'Myself,' he replied. 'You've heard of

blind dates, haven't you?' In the event he was accompanied by the mysterious lady in pink, whose name he refused to divulge as he passed ranks of photographers yelling for details that evening. Once inside, he and his companions split up and the Prince joined in the celebrations by dancing with Lana Paton (in blue), the girlfriend of Peter de Savary, whom he thanked afterwards for allowing him to enjoy her company. Tickets for the ball had cost $150, and de Savary had a garden landscaped in the grounds of the house, Beechwood, at a cost of around $100,000. Among the attractions inside were the band of the Brigade of Guards, Peter Duchin's orchestra, and the Sonatas Steel Band. After the ball, the entire complement of guests went outside to

watch Beating Retreat, and a huge firework display lit up the Newport sky that night. The remainder of Prince Andrew's official time during the weekend was taken up attending a mayoral reception, and a church service at the Trinity Church. Spare time was spent enjoying the perfect weather in de Savary's yacht *Calysma* and attending a cricket match (these pages) – one of the few examples of this British ritual ever staged in the United States. The four-day visit was followed by a private holiday in Canada – Prince Andrew's last fling before a brief rest at Balmoral, and the resumption of his naval duties. But both naval and official obligations would bring him back to the States twice more within the following year.

Relishing the traditional delights of August's Cowes Week, Prince Philip looked relaxed and in good humour, piloting *Yeoman XXI* (left), or snatching a moment's earnest conversation with his royal cousin and crew member, King Constantine of Greece (top). The King's teenage daughter, Princess Alexia was also there (right) as was Prince Edward, who attended both as learner (above) and as competitor.

If the Queen Mother's birthday doesn't quite have the status which offers her daughter the full ceremonial of Trooping the Colour, it is nevertheless an established part of the summer season. Even its ritual is becoming familiar: the assembly of a crowd of hundreds outside the doors of Clarence House, and the chorus of cheers and applause as a large-brimmed hat, bobbing into sight on an upper terrace, eventually reveals a beaming birthday girl (right), bright as a button, proud as Punch, half amused, half moved by the admiring audience below. The odd toddler (bottom picture) hogs the attention for a while – a small distraction compared with what follows

when the Queen Mother comes down to greet her well-wishers. In a reassuring breach of the generation gap, the braver children storm an unobtrusive police guard, and the luckier or more persistent ones reach their royal target with a volley of flowers, cards and chocolates (left, below left). The less fortunate (bottom) find the London bobby a willing intermediary. On this pleasant August morning, the crowds were rewarded by the sight of the Queen Mother's two daughters (below) and the Prince and Princess of Wales enjoying this informal atmosphere before the celebrant's final wave (right).

There was a promising start to a new royal venture early in August when Captain Mark Phillips opened Gatcombe Park (opposite page) for the first of, hopefully, an annual series of horse trials. The novelty of a day out on royal premises induced some 20,000 spectators, probably less interested in the competition than in the distinguished company, which included Prince and Princess Michael (below) and Jackie Stewart and his wife (right).

After a fortnight spent going separate ways, there was a royal reunion on 14th August, when the Queen led her family off *Britannia*'s barge to meet the Queen Mother at Scrabster. Prince Andrew sported a new and, in events, brief beard, while Princess Anne, on the eve of her 33rd birthday, carried her $2\frac{1}{2}$-

year-old daughter Zara ashore (right). The Queen Mother had travelled from the Castle of Mey, where the previous day she had attended a local horticultural show (left). The family came together again for the Braemar Games (above) early in September. As usual, the Prince and Princess of Wales, Princess Alexandra and Mr Angus Ogilvy joined the royal party.

Prince Charles, Princess Diana and Prince William made their own way to their Balmoral holiday, but even royal vacations are fragmented, and both the Prince and Princess undertook several official engagements from the Castle that summer. Princess Diana's brief, private visit to London fired new speculation, which took two months to subside, that she was pregnant, while 14-month-old Prince William contributed to the family's holiday excitement by escaping his nanny's attention and setting off the security alarms. Detectives within the Castle, and police squads without, were quick to react, if rather slower to appreciate the funny side.

Prince Andrew, still sporting the beard seen at Scrabster (left), visited BA's helicopter base at Aberdeen on 16th August. Princess Diana (overleaf) was at Coatbridge, Lanarkshire on 9th September.

(Previous page) a breezy welcome for the Princess at the MacIntyre Community of the Mentally Handicapped at Westoning Manor in Bedfordshire on 20th September. A month later, her cousins Viscount Linley and Lady Sarah Armstrong-Jones were at a Foyle's literary luncheon in London to help their father and stepmother (above) launch Lord Snowdon's new photographic book, *Sittings*.

The Queen was one of four godparents at the Bayswater baptism on 20th October of Princess Theodora, fourth child of King Constantine of Greece. His wife, Queen Anne-Marie, was joined by her sister Queen Margrethe of Denmark (in mauve), while sister-in-law Queen Sofia of Spain brought two of her children, Cristina and Felipe (top right). Prince Paul, Prince Nicholas and Princess Alexia of Greece (opposite, top) also attended.

Memories dominated early November. On the 2nd, the Queen unveiled Lord Mountbatten's statue at Horse Guards (top) before almost all the Royal Family (above, far left). The following week, the Queen Mother (opposite) again visited the Field of Remembrance at Westminster, and joined many relatives at the Cenotaph on Remembrance Day. (Overleaf) Princess Diana visited the deaf in Cumbria on 17th November (right) and, next day, the blind at Bristol (left).

The Queen's first State Visit to Kenya since independence began in a blaze of colour and shimmering heat on 10th November. Formal inspection of the guard of honour (opposite, top) was followed by a drive (opposite, below) to State House, where she spoke at that evening's banquet, hosted by President arap Moi (above).

A heavy day of engagements on 11th November included visits to Nairobi's Parliament Buildings (these pages) and to the capital's polytechnic. That evening, the Queen gave her own reciprocal banquet at the residence of the British Ambassador. It was her final evening in Nairobi, and she dressed stunningly for the occasion (right).

Kenya's Remembrance Day was observed on the original Armistice anniversary, 11th November, and the Queen and Prince Philip led Kenya's and the Commonwealth's tribute in a quiet, solemn ceremony in Nairobi. Her cluster of poppies and the black of her gloves, shoes and patterned dress offered the only similarities to the sombre garb of a Whitehall ceremony: Prince Philip's tropical rig looked strangely incongruous. This was not the only wreath the Queen laid that day: early in the morning she had placed a tribute of white lilies on the tomb of Jomo Kenyatta, the former President who had led his country to independence in 1963.

Buffalo at close range (right) failed to deter the Queen as, with marksman Richard Prickett (above) she toured the Treetops water hole where, almost 32 years before, she succeeded to the Throne. Both the Queen and the Prince seemed bemused by the drastic changes they saw.

There was no irregularity in the guard of honour which awaited the Queen as she landed at Bangladesh (above). If the uniforms were not ceremonial, that was only a reflection of the tight military rule which has governed the country since 1975. The regime is, nevertheless, quite popular, President Chowdhury (right) being a benign nominal leader, while General Ershad, with whom the Queen had talks as soon as she arrived (below and overleaf) allows a vociferous opposition. Just before the Queen landed, he promised a measured progress to democratic government.

The following morning, the gardens of Dhaka's Presidential Palace were strewn with petals (opposite, top) as the Queen and Prince Philip attended a civic reception. (Overleaf) the Queen at a State banquet on the evening on her arrival in Dhaka.

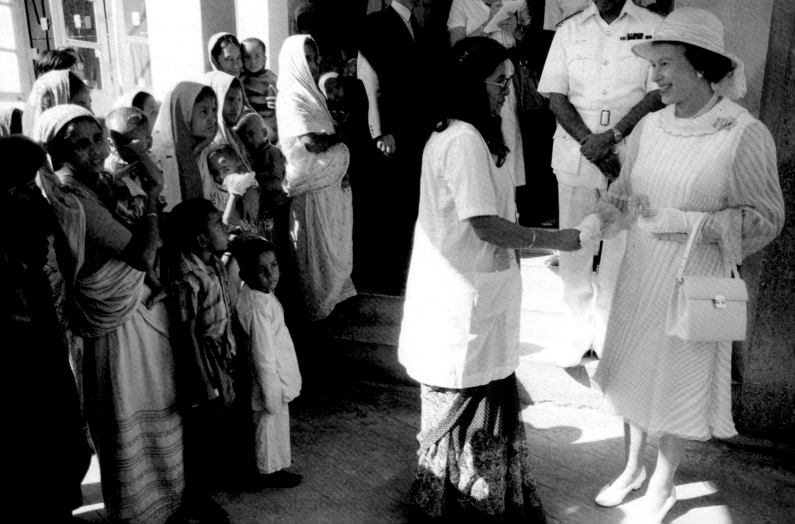

The traditional welcoming tributes were resumed the following day as the Queen, recently presented with the keys of Dhaka, headed a triumphal procession in the city (opposite, top). The festivity contrasted poignantly with the rather pathetic scenes at the child nutritional centre, run by the Save the Children Fund, where the Queen was presented with a single marigold which she loyally clutched during the whole of her tour of the wards (left). Flowers were clearly the day's theme, as even the bright blue and yellow train (right) which took her to Sripur was ablaze with them, while bouquets and other gifts were presented to her when she broke her journey at Bairagpur to meet villagers.

After a busy day for the Queen and Prince Philip – the Duke had spent most of the 16th November at Lakatoora visiting tea plantations and watching cultivation techniques – they were reunited in Dhaka for the final festivities of this first royal visit to Bangladesh since 1971. The British Ambassador's residence was the venue for the Queen's farewell banquet attended by the President (right), and by General

Ershad. The occasion was less formal than many: the Queen wore no Orders over her evening dress, opting instead for a neat, choker-type necklace in place of the more familiar royal jewellery. Afterwards, however, the Queen held a late evening reception in the garden of the residence, attended by some 200 additional guests.

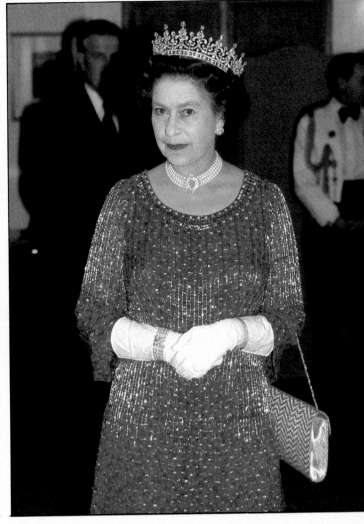

Her grandfather, King George V attended his Durbar here in 1911; her uncle was installed as Viceroy in 1947; her father was the country's last King-Emperor; and after twenty-three years the Queen herself was back in Delhi. In 1961 she had been greeted by President Nehru. Now his daughter, Mrs Indira Gandhi welcomed Her Majesty, who looked delighted to be visiting India again.

The massive, Lutyens-designed Hyderabad House, with its reminders of the British Raj, was the setting for some informal talks between the Queen and Mrs Ghandi, which were filmed for inclusion in the Queen's Christmas message a month later.

The Queen visited the fabled Red Fort in Delhi (left) and Mahatma Gandhi's tomb at Rajghat. Here she wore, in place of her own shoes, airline 'slipperettes'. (Above and right) a pre-lunch photocall with Mrs Gandhi at Hyderabad House. (Opposite, below) the Queen presenting the Order of Merit to Mother Theresa in Delhi the following day.

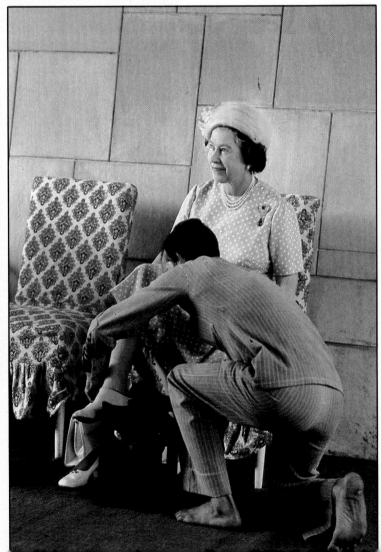

Highlight of the Queen's second day in India was her tour of St Thomas' School. Greeted by girls with incense trays (above), she visited the primary department (right) and then hopped into a palanquin carried by senior girls – dressed as male bearers – who performed a play called *The Awakening of Indian Womanhood.*

The third day of the royal tour took the Queen to the ancient tombs near the Golconda Fort where ladies of the family of the Nizam of Hyderabad welcomed her (top) into the magnificent gardens. So expansive was the setting that (left) the Queen needed binoculars to see everything

during her forty-minute visit. The Queen spent her 36th wedding anniversary next day without the Duke, who was at a game reserve to see tiger conservation programmes. After attending Sunday morning service, the Queen visited a village, Devara Yamzal near Hyderabad, to watch a pageant from a dais festooned with garlands and furnished with a brightly decorated throne.

The Queen in high spirits at
the military academy at Pune
– the Poona of British
Empire days. Prince Philip
(overleaf) seemed more
thoughtful.

(Previous pages) the Princess of Wales at Wantage on 2nd December (right) and visiting victims of the Harrods bomb explosion on the 19th. The approach of Prince William's second Christmas was marked by a photo session in the garden of his parents' London home, Kensington Palace.

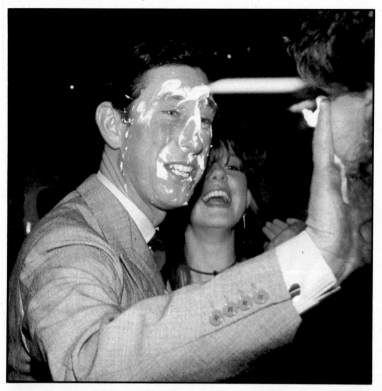

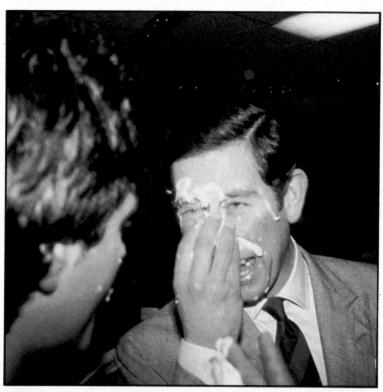

An even more engaging public performance on 20th December, when Prince Charles received a custard pie in the face at a West Indian community centre in Manchester. That evening the Prince, with Princess Diana (right), attended a charity Christmas concert at Manchester's Free Trade Hall.

Crown-Princess Marie-Aglae of Liechtenstein (left) accompanied the Prince and Princess of Wales on the Alpine slopes at the beginning of their skiing holiday on 8th January. The bargain struck between Prince

and Press was honoured and the royal couple eventually soared to the top of Hoch Eck (right and bottom) to begin a much appreciated private vacation.

Princess Michael at an NSPCC fund-raising gala, Stratford, on 5th February. She met a host of stars (top right), went on stage to select prize draw winners (top), met technicians and stage hands, and stayed until two in the morning. 'She was smashing!' enthused one organiser.

For the Princess of Wales' last public engagement before she visited Norway, she arrived (previous pages, left) at the Ritz Hotel in Piccadilly on 8th February, where she unveiled Michael Noakes' new portrait of Prince Charles. On 11th February, the Princess flew to Oslo, to be greeted by the Norwegian Royal Family with a bouquet of carnations (previous pages, right) which matched her warm blue woollen coat. That night she dressed in glowing scarlet (these pages) for the London City Ballet's gala performance of *Carmen*, and found time to accept a small child's posy (overleaf, left) during a tree-planting ceremony in the grounds of the British Embassy before she left next day. On 13th February, she announced her second pregnancy, and renewed public interest followed her everywhere – even on the brief holiday in Scotland which Prince Charles and his family snatched (overleaf, right) later that month.

The Queen with the Mayor of London (left) and Archbishop of Canterbury (below left) at a London church service on 16th February. Princess Diana toured Red Cross headquarters in London (bottom) on 22nd. The Duchess of Gloucester visited an army educational centre at Eltham (below) on 28th, while Princess Alice visited RAF Swinderby, Lincolnshire two days later.

A succession of royal gala
evenings brightened a gloomy
British winter. On 23rd
February, the Queen Mother
attended the Elgar commemorative concert at Westminster
Abbey (far left). She was at
the Odeon, Leicester Square,
for the premiere of *Champions*
eight days later (left), with
Princess Anne (opposite, top
centre). The Queen also
visited the Odeon (opposite,
top left) to see *The Dresser*
on 19th March. On 12th April,
the Duchess of Kent attended
the Amir of Bahrain's State
banquet in London (opposite,
top right), while a month
earlier, Prince and Princess
Michael (this page) had
attended a London Coliseum
performance of the opera
Gloriana. (Overleaf, right) a
chic Princess Diana at the
Genesis concert at Birmingham
in February and (left) drape-
suited for a March visit to a
North London health centre.

Back after a year's absence, the Queen visited Newmarket's annual stallion show in March, casting her expert eye over the day's entries.

Princess Anne at Peterborough's Shire Horse Show on 17th March (above), while there were more formal duties for the Queen (left) at Westminster Abbey's Commonwealth Day service on 12th March, and Prince Charles (top right), visiting *HMS President* on the Thames on the 14th. (Right) the Duchess of Kent at Thetford, Norfolk on 9th March.

Princess Michael revealed during the year that she had had to teach her husband to waltz. Her instruction seemed to have worked: at the Ponies of Britain Ball at Stamford on 16th March, the couple took the floor and gave the guests a lesson in the grand style.

The Queen and Prince Philip left London on 23rd March for a five-day State Visit to Jordan. Controversial for its political and security implications, the tour began cautiously, with a stop-over in Cyprus and a circuitous route avoiding Syria. But it was all smiles when the royal couple finally arrived (these pages) in Amman to be greeted by King Hussein, whose

sometimes precarious political relations with the West have never shaken his personal friendship with the British Royal Family. His regard for the Queen and Prince Philip was reflected in the resplendent banquet he and Queen Noor (far left) gave that first evening – a full State occasion, with every royal utterance scrupulously combed for political undertones. The Queen praised King Hussein's unceasing attempts to find a solution to the Palestinian problem, while the King addressed his country's cause to the 'sense of justice of the British people. We appreciate their courageous views and keenness to eliminate the mistakes of the past.'

After a procession to Amman's Martyrs' Memorial (opposite, top) the Queen spent a more relaxing time at King Hussein's stables, where his daughter Princess Alia runs a stud of over 100 pure-bred Arab horses. Though not quite like home for the Queen, it proved a close substitute.

King Hussein laid on perhaps the most unusual picnic the Queen has ever attended. By the shores of the Dead Sea, magnificent tents and richly-covered sofas contrasted starkly with the reminder – pointed out by the King (opposite page) – that Israel was only just across the water.

Everything and everyone was dwarfed by the dimensions of Petra, the ancient trading centre built by the Nabateans two thousand years ago. The Queen and Prince Philip, accompanied as they were almost everywhere on this tour by Hussein and his Queen, walked into the ruined city to capture the grandeur of its approaches.

Petra was heavily guarded (above) and cleared of most of its cave-dwelling families, though some inhabitants – including this New Zealand-born mother (top) – were presented to the Queen. This was her last sightseeing event of the tour, and the royal couple stayed at King Hussein's palace at Aqaba that night, leaving (left) next day.

There was a minimum of formality at Aqaba Airport as the Queen and Duke of Edinburgh took their leave of King Hussein and Queen Noor, seen (right) in a photograph officially released shortly before the tour began. The atmosphere was noticeably more relaxed than five days earlier, and the King's quiet relief when he subsequently gave an interview was barely concealed.

Until the royal aircraft (top) was out of sight security was strictly observed (opposite, below).

For the guests, a potentially dangerous tour was over; King Hussein's much earlier visit to Britain at last returned.

Princess Diana admitted the effects of morning sickness at Leicester in March (above), but at Stanmore the next day (right), seemed in good spirits. With the approach of Easter, no end of presents were being offered her – a knitted doll for her baby at Glastonbury (top right) and Easter eggs for Prince William at Stoke (left).

For the first time in 172 years women officers took part in the Sovereign's Parade at Sandhurst, where the Duchess of Kent took the Salute on 6th April. Just after the Queen's Jordanian visit, Queen Noor (above right) saw her nephew receive his commission.

With the Duke of Beaufort's death only two months before, Badminton Horse Trials in April inevitably lacked its usual festive air. But the Queen was there (far right), and Captain Mark Phillips (left) competed, though unsuccessfully, while his children Peter (right) and Zara (above) looked as mischievous as ever, and provided the public with some entertaining distractions.

Spring flowers for the Princess of Wales as she arrived at Wellington College at Crowthorne on 16th April, to hear the National Children's Orchestra in rehearsal. Though she is patron of the orchestra, she admitted that music was not her strong point at school. Prince William might do better, however, as his mother was presented with a quarter-size violin to take back for him. Next day, Princess Alexandra was presenting radio and television awards in London – to the delight of the BBC who bagged most of them. Jan Leeming, Frank Bough and David Coleman (opposite page) were proud recipients, while ITV's George Cole and Dennis Waterman (bottom left) made the most of their moment of glory.

The Queen discharged her annual Maundy obligations this year at one of the most attractive of small English cathedrals, when she distributed purses of specially-minted money to 58 men and 58 women at Southwell Minster, near Newark, on 19th April. Then she and Prince

Philip met ice-dancing royalty when Olympic champions Jayne Torvill and Christopher Dean were presented at a Nottingham Council reception. After the enormous surge of patriotism and pride which surrounded the young couple as they easily secured their gold medal at Sarajevo – an achievement watched by Princess Anne and on which the Queen personally telegraphed her congratulations – this was a most popular royal event.

Clouds with silver linings were the theme as the Queen trod between huge banks of golden tulips to open Liverpool's Garden Festival on 2nd May. Born out of a riot-torn Toxteth in 1981, the festival was housed on a long-derelict 125-acre site. The Queen toured the gardens on a miniature railway (as had George V and Queen Mary at Wembley sixty years before), visited the Japanese Garden and yellow submarine overlooking John Lennon's statue, met Liverpool's senior inhabitant – 106 years old – and nearly had her bouquet eaten by *Blue Peter*'s labrador, Goldie.

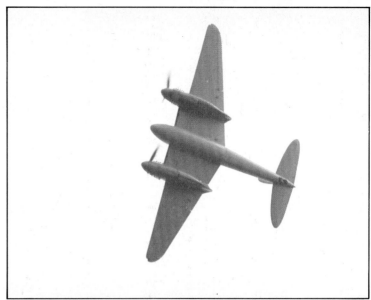

Not far from the Queen Mother's birthplace lies Salisbury Hall, a 17th-century stately home, with connections with Charles II and an aircraft museum which houses the legendary, wartime de Havilland Mosquito aircraft. On 4th May, the Queen Mother visited the museum to open a new hangar, inspected the original Mosquito prototype and watched its nostalgic flypast (top right) before taking tea at Nell Gwynne's Cottage.

Five regiments provided the music at the Hyde Park bandstand for a parade and service at which, on 6th May, the Combined Cavalry Old Comrades paid tribute to their war dead. The Association has the Duke of Kent for its patron, but it was Princess Anne who attended the ceremony and who laid a massive wreath at their memorial.

(Previous pages) the Duchess of Gloucester at London's Intercontinental Hotel, attending the All Pakistan Women's Association's Spring Feast on 10th May. That afternoon, the Queen Mother went to All Saints Church at Ascot to open its new church hall (these pages). She has no particular connection with the church, but that didn't stop her from enjoying a pleasantly informal afternoon, brightened by the singing of its forty-strong choir. Of course, they asked her to pose for a photograph, and the Queen Mother obliged, as she always does. And as she's also good at planting trees, she did that too.

A selection of Prince Charles' early season polo matches. (Above) playing at Windsor on 13th May for Ingwenya against Downey Fields in the final of the Rodney Moore Cup: Ingwenya won 4-2. (Left and top right) on the same day, playing for Windsor against Travelwise: Windsor lost 9-6½. (Opposite page, top left and top right) playing at Windsor on 19th May for Rajasthan Polo Club against Laurent Perrier. The Queen saw his team lose 7-3. (Right and far left) playing at Windsor on 24th May for Les Diables Bleus, beating Chopendoz 8-7 in front of the Princess of Wales. (Far right, and opposite, top centre) in the quarter finals of the Queen's Cup at Windsor on 3rd June, when his team, Les Diables Bleus, beat Piaget 10-7.

By most accounts the Royal Windsor Horse Show lacked the touch of extravagance usually associated with this prestigious annual event, but any occasion staged at Home Park, Windsor, within sight of the Queen's Berkshire home, and graced by royalty determined to enjoy their day's leisure, cannot be mediocre for long. So even the threat of indifferent weather could not put off the many spectators as the Queen sported her most comfortable, functional country clothes to tramp the ground where Prince Philip would be competing during the four-day event. As is often the case, the Duke's only surviving sister, Princess Sophie of Hanover (bottom left) belied her 70 years to brave a cold, breezy day in support of her brother, whose two-fold aim was to regain the Harrods International Driving Grand

Prix which he lost last year, and win a place in the British team for the World Driving Championships in Hungary in August. Princess Anne (above), Prince Edward and Prince Paul of Greece (top picture) were there to see Prince Philip take the lead after the first day's presentation and dressage (opposite page), despite a strict line taken by the judges, and a heart stopping

moment when his two leading horses suddenly took a dislike to each other. Prince Philip, who had suffered a number of spills earlier in the season when driving novice horses, seemed much more confident after his near victory the previous week at a Brighton carriage-driving event (in which Prince Michael also competed), and was in any case back with his familiar team of Cleveland bays/Oldenburg crosses, owned by the Queen. These days, it seems, no major equestrian event escapes the presence of Princess Anne's two children, and sure enough, Master Peter Phillips looked engrossed with the proceedings as, supervised by the Queen (opposite page), he put his pair of miniature binoculars to good use. But his quiet

behaviour didn't last and, before long, he was being firmly taken in hand by Princess Anne (above). Sister Zara seemed much more amenable, possibly because she was looking forward to her 3rd birthday for which, four days later, she would throw a small party for her young friends and relations. There was also an unexpected treat at Windsor when Prince Philip allowed both Peter and Zara to ride in his driving carriage. Typically, it was Peter who took the whip, and commanded the horses, while Zara had to be reassured by her mother. Meanwhile, Prince

Philip had two more stages to complete, and unfortunately he was to lose ground. Going for total accuracy in the marathon lost him precious time points, and he was not helped by a broken carriage cable after colliding with a branch just before the obstacle section. In the final analysis, he had dropped to seventh place, and the Queen found herself once again congratulating Tjeerd Velstra, last year's winner, on retaining the championship. But she could afford a smile (top, with King Constantine): her own private carriage won a coaching event, and Prince Philip still secured his passage to Hungary.

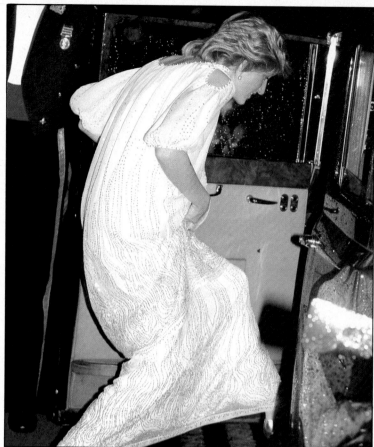

The Princess of Wales looking proudly pregnant (above) as she awaited her car after a banquet given by the President of the Royal Society of Arts, Sir Hugh Casson, (right) in Piccadilly on 14th May. Back in September, both the Princess and Sir Hugh had submitted their own portrait sketches of Prince William and Prince Charles respectively for a publication in aid of Mencap. The Princess wore white again, but this time with gold sequins, for the Royal Opera House Development Appeal concert six days later (top right and opposite).

The Queen at Cambridge on 16th May, where, touring the Grafton Shopping Centre, she received a teddy bear (top) for Prince William, then met Prince Edward at Jesus College (left) where he is a student.

Not one of the most success-ful days for Prince Charles, as he received the Queen's commiserations after his team lost a polo match by four goals at Smith's Lawn, Windsor on 19th May. The losing side was the Rajasthan Polo Club, for whom the Prince had agreed to play during their visit to Britain.

Few royals can resist
visiting the Chelsea Flower
Show, held this year on 21st
May. The Queen (above and
opposite, top left) attended
with Princess Margaret (right
and far left), another
regular visitor; the Duchess
of Gloucester (above)
accompanied Princess Alice;
and Princess Michael (left)

may have picked up a few tips for her new rose garden at Nether Lyppiatt. Royal husbands included Prince Charles, who took Princess Diana along, and Prince Michael, though Prince Philip had to cry off at the last moment to attend World Wildlife Fund meetings in Washington.

The Princess of Wales' visit to the Chelsea Flower Show was something of a surprise, partly because it came in the middle of a comparatively hectic spell, before her programme of public engagements tailed off as her confinement approached. At the time, rumours of royal twins were still rife and it was two months before Prince Charles scotched them when he met a mother of twins during a visit to East London.

Princess Michael looked every inch the Edwardian beauty in a classic, figure-hugging evening robe, and a choker which would have made even Queen Alexandra a trifle jealous. With Prince Michael, she was attending a gala performance at the London Coliseum on 22nd May of *Onegin*, by the late John Cranko, chosen by the London Festival Ballet to open its 1984 season.

(Top, and opposite page) a colourfully-dressed Princess Alexandra visiting Cranleigh School in Surrey on 23rd May, while on the same day the Princess of Wales was making her second visit to the Albany Trust in Deptford (left). She had to run the gauntlet of several political controversies, including a plea to help prevent the possible abolition of the GLC. She said she would speak to her father, before a crucial vote in the House of Lords. Two of Princess Anne's many engagements in May took her to RAF Lyneham (top left) on the 3rd, and to the Surrey County Show at Guildford on the 28th (above, left). But it was a quiet month for Princess Michael, seen (above) competing at the Amberley Horse Trials on 5th May.

The high-goal polo season brought Prince Charles to Windsor on 24th May. His team won 8-7, to the delight of Princess Diana, who now really seems to enjoy polo.

Filthy weather – even for eventing – attended the Windsor Horse Trials late in May but, suitably dressed, Princess Anne had the stomach to withstand all the climate could throw at her. She had, after all, helped design the course, and her husband was a competitor. Captain Phillips rewarded her loyalty, leading throughout and winning the entire event.

The Princess of Wales never seemed more sophisticated than during her visit to Chester and Warrington on 30th May. Her hosts treated her royally, renaming a hospital after her – the Countess of Chester Hospital – and asking her to join Prince Charles in pulling the cord to unveil a sculpture of the Mad Hatter's Tea Party. That didn't work, so they pulled the cover off the statue themselves, and Prince Charles then, in mock disgust, placed the redundant cord round the neck of a local official.

The Queen Mother began a three-day tour of the Channel Islands on 30th May. First port of call was Guernsey, which 'holds many happy memories for me, renewed through the living bonds which continue to link Guernsey and the Crown.' As everywhere in the islands, the Queen Mother, who first visited them with King George VI in the aftermath of liberation exactly thirty-nine years before, was a popular guest, and nowhere more so than on Sark, where the genteel way of island life seemed tailor-made for the Queen Mother's very individual style of carrying out her duties. She forsook the helicopter in which she had arrived (left) for a horse and carriage (above),

the traditional means of touring the island. That evening, the Royal Yacht *Britannia*, in which she had sailed to Guernsey, took her to Jersey, where she landed the next morning (far right). As on previous days, her engagement book was packed, but she smiled and chatted her way through the receptions, visits and those Channel Island specialities, the *vins d'honneur*. The Queen Mother has been known in years past to try her hand at snooker or billiards. When she visited the Maufant Youth Centre in Jersey, she graduated to the pool table (left), slamming in a ball to the delight of her hosts who had tactfully placed it where she could hardly miss! Such is the prerogative of Queens, as indeed a tour such as this is the prerogative of their subjects. Normally, at this time of year, the Queen

Mother does a round trip taking in the Cinque Ports, of which she is Lord Warden. But, with the D-Day anniversary close by, nothing could have been more appropriate as this all too rare return to what Churchill called 'our dear Channel Islands.'

A sixty-eight-man parachute drop (opposite, top) by soldiers who had fought in the Falklands provided a spectacular start to Prince Charles' visit on 5th June to Ranville in Normandy to commemorate D-Day with the Parachute Regiment. It was a day of pride for the veterans who marched past their Colonel-in-Chief (top) and of gratitude for the Prince, who laid a wreath where 2,500 servicemen lie buried in the town's military cemetery (above).

Two Queens, two Kings, two Presidents, a Grand-Duke and a Prime Minister assembled on Utah Beach on 6th June to commemorate the 40th anniversary of D-Day. It was one of the largest international gatherings of its kind, with ingenious aerial displays (opposite, top) and military and naval ceremonies embracing the

story of those countries who suffered German occupation, and those whose armies or resistance movements contributed to their liberation.

(Left) the Princess of Wales attended the premiere of *Indiana Jones and the Temple of Doom*, in Leicester Square on 11th June. Next day Prince William (previous pages) posed – though a little early – for his second birthday photocall at Kensington Palace. Mother, child and family came together again – on the parade ground (above) and on the Palace balcony (following pages) for Trooping the Colour on 16th June.

On 20th June, repeating her practice of two years before, the Princess of Wales left Ascot on the second day of the royal meeting to watch Prince Charles at polo practice at Guards' Club. He was due to play the next day – Prince William's birthday – for Windsor Park against Laurent Perrier in the quarter-finals of the Royal

Windsor Cup. His last-minute training proved justified. Windsor Park won, and eventually went on to the final, three days later, which they won 5-4 to take the Cup. The Queen was there to present it, as she presented the Archie David Cup after the following match that day (these pages), when her son joined a Windsor Park team consisting of two low handicappers, one of whom, Mark Austin (right), took Prince Charles' usual position of back. This time, however, Windsor Park received only consolation prizes from the Queen (below right) – they were beaten 5-2 by Dauntsey Squirrels.

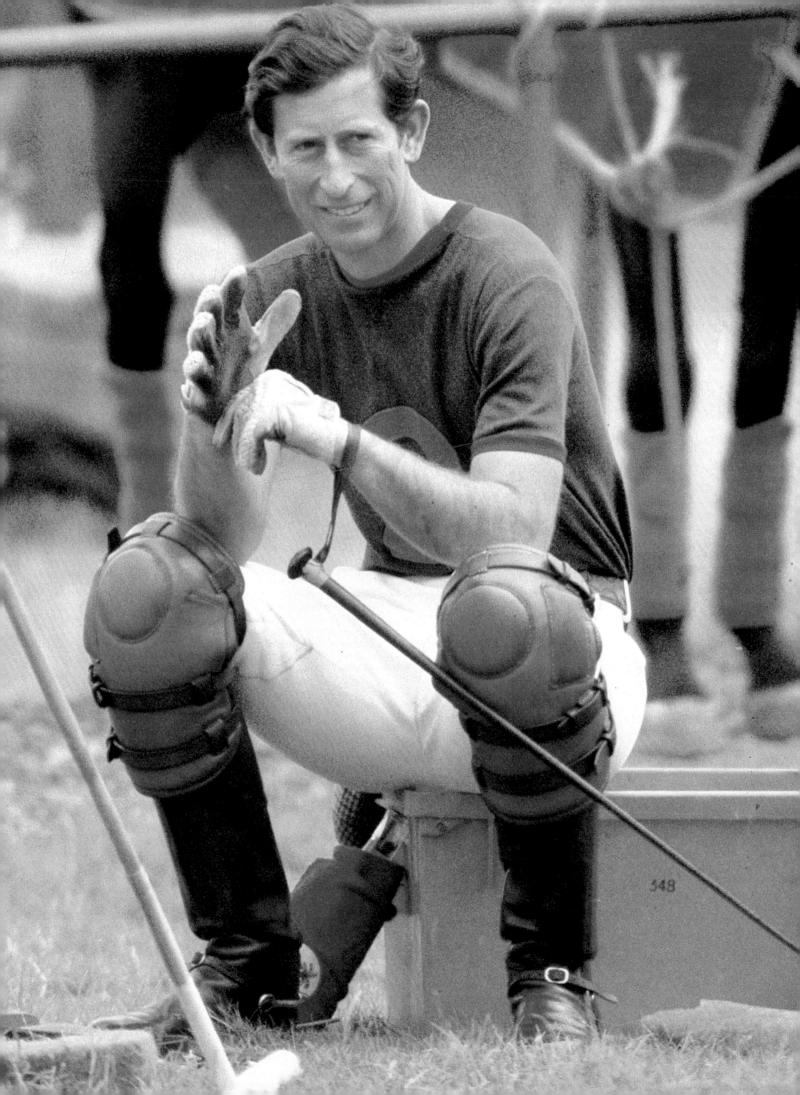

Looking fit and happy at one
of her last engagements
before the birth of her baby,
Princess Diana arrived with
Prince Charles at Odstock
Hospital near Salisbury, to
watch him open a new spinal
treatment centre. Instructors
and patients were thrilled
when she almost laid down by
the side of a pool to chat
with them, and to divulge not
only that Prince William can
swim too – with armbands –
but that she herself swam
thirty lengths at Highgrove
only a few days before.

The Princess of Wales took delivery of a new Ford Escort convertible late in Spring, and drove it to Cirencester on 28th June to watch Prince Charles play in the Warwickshire Cup. His team won, though narrowly, while his wife attracted the interest of spectators by her bright blue culottes and her healthy tan. It was only three days to her 23rd birthday, which she spent at yet another polo match, and which was celebrated by many tributes to the enormous contribution she had made in three years to the popularity of the monarchy.

Royal Diary

*The official engagements
of each member of the Royal Family
for a complete year
are listed on the following pages.
The engagements for
Prince and Princess Michael of Kent
are not official, but have been
included where they were public
or undertaken on behalf of a
public organisation.*

Engagements of THE QUEEN
August 1983-July 1984

August	3	Held three audiences, Buckingham Palace.
	4	Held one audience, Buckingham Palace.
		Embarked on the Royal Yacht *Britannia* at Southampton Docks, and sailed for the Western Isles.
	15	Disembarked from the Royal Yacht *Britannia* at Aberdeen, and drove to Balmoral Castle.
	21	Attended Divine Service, Crathie Parish Church.
	28	Attended Divine Service, Crathie Parish Church.
		Held a personal Investiture, Balmoral Castle.

September 3 Attended the Highland Games, Braemar, Deeside.
4 Attended Divine Service, Crathie Parish Church.
11 Attended Divine Service, Crathie Parish Church.
18 Attended Divine Service, Crathie Parish Church.
25 Attended Divine Service, Crathie Parish Church.

October 2 Attended Divine Service, Crathie Parish Church.
9 Attended Divine Service, Crathie Parish Church.
16 Attended Divine Service, Crathie Parish Church.
18 Opened and toured the Aberdeen Curling Rink.
Visited tenants' cottages of the Scottish Veterans Garden City Association, Gladstone Place, Dyce.
Left Dyce Airport for London, and arrived at Buckingham Palace.
Received the Prime Minister in audience, Buckingham Palace.
19 Held four audiences, Buckingham Palace.
Held a Council Meeting, Buckingham Palace.
Gave a luncheon party for the President of Mozambique, and invested him as a Knight Grand Cross of the Order of St Michael and St George.
Attended the Annual National Service for Seafarers, St Paul's Cathedral.
20 Held an Investiture, Buckingham Palace.
Held two audiences, Buckingham Palace.
Received the President of the French Republic, Buckingham Palace.
21 Opened the new Burrell Gallery and toured the collection, Burrell Museum, Pollok Park, Glasgow.
25 Held four audiences, Buckingham Palace.
Gave a luncheon party for the King and Queen of Tonga, Buckingham Palace.
Attended a dinner party given by the High Commissioner for India, Kensington Palace Gardens, London.
26 Gave a reception for delegates to the 22nd Annual Conference of the British Commonwealth Ex-Services League.
Received the Prime Minister in audience, Buckingham Palace.
27 Held three audiences, Buckingham Palace.
Opened and toured the Silver Jubilee Exhibition of Voluntary Service Overseas, Commonwealth Institute, London.
30 Held a personal Investiture, Windsor Castle.
31 Gave a reception to mark the 21st anniversary of Community Service Volunteers, Buckingham Palace.

November 1 Held an Investiture, Buckingham Palace.
Received the Prime Minister in audience, Buckingham Palace.
2 Unveiled the statue of Earl Mountbatten, Foreign Office Green, London.
Gave a luncheon party, Buckingham Palace.
Attended a reception to mark the Golden Jubilee of the Milk Marketing Board, Guildhall, London.
Attended a reception given by the Prime Minister, Banqueting House, Whitehall, London.
3 Held an Investiture, Buckingham Palace.

3	Held one audience, Buckingham Palace.
7	Attended the Royal Variety Performance, Theatre Royal, Drury Lane, London.
8	Held an Investiture, Buckingham Palace.
	Received the Foreign Secretary in audience, Buckingham Palace.
9	Left Heathrow Airport, London to begin State Visits to Kenya, Bangladesh and India.
10	Arrived at Jomo Kenyatta Airport, Kenya, and drove to State House.
	Attended a State banquet, State House, Nairobi.
11	Laid a wreath at the National Mausoleum, Nairobi.
	Toured the Kenya Parliament buildings, Nairobi.
	Attended a Press reception, State House, Nairobi.
	Visited Kenya Polytechnic, Nairobi.
	Attended the Remembrance Day ceremony, and laid a wreath, Commonwealth War Graves Commission cemetery, Nairobi.
	Took tea with Commonwealth High Commissioners and their wives, State House, Nairobi.
	Gave a State banquet for the President of Kenya, British High Commissioner's residence, Nairobi.
12	Visited Thika and toured two factories.
	Attended a luncheon at the Thika Sports Club.
	Watched a display of traditional dancing at Nyeri.
	Arrived at State Lodge, Sagana.
13	Visited Treetops Hotel, near Sagana.
	Attended a reception for the British Community in Kenya, Intercontinental Hotel, Nairobi.
	Attended a farewell ceremony, State House, Nairobi.
14	Left Nairobi Airport for Bangladesh.
	Arrived at Dhaka Airport, and drove to the Presidential guest house.
15	Laid a wreath and planted a tree at the Savar Memorial to war dead, Dhaka.
	Visited the President of Bangladesh at the Presidential residence, Dhaka.
	Attended a luncheon with the Commonwealth Heads of Mission.
	Attended an afternoon party for members of the British community in Bangladesh, High Commissioner's residence, Dhaka.
	Attended a State banquet, and watched a cultural show, at the official Presidential residence, Dhaka.
16	Visited the Save the Children Fund Child Nutrition Unit, Dhaka.
	Paid brief visits to the villages of Sripur and Bairagpur.
	Attended a civic reception, Presidential residence, Dhaka.
	Attended a Press reception, Presidential guest house, Dhaka.
	Gave a State banquet for the President of Bangladesh, British High Commissioner's residence, Dhaka.
17	Left Dhaka Airport for India.
	Arrived at Delhi Airport and drove to the Presidential residence.
	Visited the President of India.
	Attended a Commonwealth Press Union and Press reception, British High Commissioner's residence, New Delhi.
	Attended a State banquet at the Presidential residence.
18	Visited the Red Fort, New Delhi.
	Visited St Thomas' School, New Delhi.
	Laid a wreath at the National Memorial, Rajghat.
	Attended lunch at Hyderabad House with Mrs Gandhi.
	Planted a tree at the British High Commission compound, New Delhi.
	Laid a wreath on the Stone of Remembrance at the Commonwealth War Graves Commission cemetery, New Delhi.
	Watched an equestrian display by the President's bodyguard, New Delhi.
	Flew from New Delhi to Hyderabad.
19	Visited ICRISAT, and Bharat Heavy Electrical Research and Development Centre, Hyderabad.
	Visited the Qutab Shahi Tombs, and toured the Golconda Fort.
	Viewed an exhibition at the British Library, Hyderabad.
	Attended a banquet given by the Governor of Hyderabad, Maharajah's Palace.

	20	Attended Morning Service, Holy Trinity Church, Bolarum. Toured the village of Devara Yamzal.
	21	Flew from Hyderabad to Pune. Inspected and addressed a parade, National Defence Academy, Pune. Attended a Cadets' Mess lunch at the Academy. Flew to New Delhi, and attended a reception at the British High Commissioner's residence.
	22	Held several audiences with delegates of the Commonwealth Heads of Government Meeting, New Delhi. Attended a reception for the British Community in India, Presidential residence, New Delhi. Dined with the British High Commissioner at his residence, New Delhi.
	23	Attended the opening ceremony of the Commonwealth Heads of Government Meeting, New Delhi. Held several audiences with delegates to the Commonwealth Heads of Government Meeting, New Delhi. Gave a banquet for leaders of delegations to the Commonwealth Heads of Government Meeting, Hyderabad House, New Delhi.
	24	Held several audiences with delegates to the Commonwealth Heads of Government Meeting, New Delhi. Visited the Nehru Memorial Museum, Teen Murti House, New Delhi.
	25	Held audiences with delegates to the Commonwealth Heads of Government Meeting, New Delhi. Toured a Trade Fair at Pragati Maidan. Attended a reception for Ministers and officials of the Commonwealth Heads of Government Meeting, Hyderabad House, New Delhi.
	26	Left New Delhi Airport. Arrived at Heathrow Airport, London.
	28	Entertained the Prince and Princess of Liège to luncheon, Windsor Castle. Held an audience, Windsor Castle. Attended the presentation of King Leopold III of the Belgians' Garter Banner, St George's Chapel, Windsor Castle.
	30	Held an Investiture, Buckingham Palace.
December	1	Held four audiences, Buckingham Palace. Received an Address from the House of Commons, Buckingham Palace. Held an evening reception for the Diplomatic Corps, Buckingham Palace.
	6	Held an Investiture at Buckingham Palace.
	7	Received the Prime Minister in audience, Buckingham Palace. Attended a dinner given by the Officers of the Royal Tank Regiment, Merchant Taylors' Hall.
	8	Held four audiences, Buckingham Palace. Opened the new London South Western District Office of the Post Office, Nine Elms, London.
	9	Held four audiences, Buckingham Palace.
	12	Visited the Blues and Royals, Combermere Barracks, Windsor.
	13	Held four audiences, Buckingham Palace. Received the Prime Minister in audience, Buckingham Palace.
	14	Opened and toured Newham General Hospital, Plaistow, London. Opened St Barthlomew's Church and Centre, East Ham, London. Visited the Springboard Housing Association Flat complex, East Ham. Opened and toured the Passmore Edwards Museum Interpretative Centre, St Mary Magdalene Church, East Ham. Received the President of Lebanon, Buckingham Palace. Attended a gala concert, as Chief Patron of Motability, St James's Palace.
	15	Held four audiences, Buckingham Palace. Visited HM Customs and Excise, City of London.
	20	Held two audiences, Buckingham Palace. Held three personal Investitures, Buckingham Palace. Received the Prime Minister in audience, Buckingham Palace.
	22	Held a Council, Buckingham Palace. Held three personal Investitures, Buckingham Palace.

January	1	Attended Divine Service, Sandringham Church.
	8	Attended Divine Service, Sandringham Church.
	11	Visited Dersingham Youth and Community Centre, Norfolk.
	13	Held a personal Investiture, Sandringham.
	15	Attended Divine Service, Sandringham Church.
	22	Attended Divine Service, Sandringham Church.
		Presented The Queen's Gold Medal, King Edward VII School, King's Lynn.
	24	Visited RAF Marham, Norfolk, and toured the airfield's school and the Sandringham Centre.
		Held a personal Investiture, Sandringham.
	29	Attended Divine Service, St Lawrence's Church, Castle Rising, Norfolk.

February	5	Attended Divine Service, West Newton Parish Church Norfolk.
		Held two personal Investitures, Sandringham.
	6	Arrived at Buckingham Palace from Sandringham.
	7	Held three audiences, Buckingham Palace.
		Received the Prime Minister in audience, Buckingham Palace.
	8	Held two audiences, Buckingham Palace.
		Held a personal Investiture, Buckingham Palace.
		Held a Council, Buckingham Palace.
		Attended the funeral of the Duke of Beaufort, St Michael and All Angels Church, Badminton.
	9	Held two audiences, Buckingham Palace.
		Held a personal Investiture, Buckingham Palace.
	10	Held two audiences, Buckingham Palace.
		Held two personal Investitures, Buckingham Palace.
	12	Held a personal Investiture, Windsor Castle.
	14	Held an Investiture, Buckingham Palace.
		Held an audience, Buckingham Palace.
		Gave a luncheon party, Buckingham Palace.
	15	Held three audiences, Buckingham Palace.
		Held a personal Investiture, Buckingham Palace.
		Received the Prime Minister in audience, Buckingham Palace.
	16	Attended the diamond jubilee service of the British Leprosy Relief Association, All-Hallows-by-the-Tower, London.
	17	Held two audiences, Buckingham Palace.
		Held a personal Investiture, Buckingham Palace.
		Received the Prime Minister of New Zealand, entertaining him and his wife to luncheon.
	19	Held a personal Investiture, Windsor Castle.
	21	Held an Investiture, Buckingham Palace.
		Received the Prime Minister in audience, Buckingham Palace.
	22	Held two audiences, Buckingham Palace.
		Attended a luncheon at the Bank of England, City of London.
	23	Held two audiences, Buckingham Palace.
		Entertained the President of Italy to luncheon, Buckingham Palace.
		Visited the *Genius of Venice* exhibition, Royal Academy of Arts, London.
	24	Held two audiences, Buckingham Palace.
		Held a personal Investiture, Buckingham Palace.
		Entertained the Crown Prince of Saudi-Arabia to luncheon, Buckingham Palace.
	26	Held a personal Investiture, Windsor Castle.
	28	Held an Investiture, Buckingham Palace.
	29	Held two audiences, Buckingham Palace.
		Held two personal Investitures, Buckingham Palace.

March	1	Held three audiences, Buckingham Palace.
	6	Held an Investiture, Buckingham Palace.
		Entertained the Crown Prince, Crown Princess and Prince Naruhito of Japan to luncheon, Buckingham Palace.
		Received the Prime Minister in audience, Buckingham Palace.

7	Held an audience, Buckingham Palace.
	Gave a reception for the Corps of Commissionaires, Buckingham Palace.
	Received and replied to an Address from the House of Commons, Buckingham Palace.
8	Visited the annual Stallion Show of the National Light Horse Breeding Society, Newmarket.
12	Attended the Commonwealth Day Observance Service, Westminster Abbey.
	Attended a Commonwealth Day reception, Marlborough House.
	Received the Chancellor of the Exchequer in audience, Buckingham Palace.
13	Held an Investiture, Buckingham Palace.
	Held an audience, Buckingham Palace.
	Received the Prime Minister in audience, Buckingham Palace.
14	Received the President of the Gambia, Buckingham Palace.
	Held two audiences, Buckingham Palace.
	Held a Council, Buckingham Palace.
	Picked the Lists of High Sheriffs for England and Wales, Buckingham Palace.
	Held a luncheon party, Buckingham Palace.
15	Held four audiences, Buckingham Palace.
	Held a personal Investiture, Buckingham Palace.
	Left London for Clwyd.
16	Toured the Territorial Army Centre of the 3rd Battalion, Royal Welch Fusiliers, Colwyn Bay.
	Visited Colwyn Bay Civic Centre.
	Attended a thanksgiving service, St Asaph Cathedral.
	Toured and lunched at Ruthin School.
	Opened Delyn House, Flint.
18	Entertained the Governor-General of Canada to luncheon, Buckingham Palace.
19	Attended the Royal Film Performance, *The Dresser*, Odeon Theatre, Leicester Square, London.
20	Held an Investiture, Buckingham Palace.
	Held two personal Investitures, Buckingham Palace.
21	Attended a service marking the centenary of St Columba's Church of Scotland, Pont Street, London.
	Attended a reception, St Columba's Church Hall.
	Gave a reception for winners of the Queen's Awards for Export and Technology in 1983, Buckingham Palace.
22	Held a personal Investiture, Buckingham Palace.
	Held three audiences, Buckingham Palace.
	Attended a performance of *Starlight Express*, Apollo Theatre, Victoria.
23	Held an audience, Buckingham Palace.
25	Left Heathrow Airport, London and arrived at Cyprus en route for Jordan.
26	Arrived at Marka airport, Amman to be welcomed by the King and Queen of Jordan.
	Visited Queen Zein at Zahran Palace, Amman.
	Attended a reception for embassy staff and members of the British community in Jordan, British Ambassador's residence, Amman.
	Gave a reception for members of the Press, British Ambassador's residence.
	Attended a State banquet given by the King and Queen of Jordan, Basman Palace, Amman.
27	Attended a ceremony at the Tree of Life, Martyrs' Memorial, Amman.
	Toured section of the Al-Hussein Medical Centre, Amman.
	Visited the Royal Stables, Amman.
	Visited the Al-Hussein Rehabilitation Society, Amman.
	Gave a banquet for the King and Queen of Jordan, British Ambassador's residence, Amman.
	Gave a reception, Basman Palace, Amman.
28	Visited Zedirfai Farm, Jordan Valley.
	Attended a picnic lunch by the Dead Sea.
	Visited the Marine Centre, Aqaba.
29	Toured the cave city of Petra.
30	Left Aqaba airport for London, and arrived at Heathrow Airport.
April	2	Entertained the President of Israel to luncheon, Windsor Castle.
	4	Visited the Life Guards, Combermere Barracks, Windsor.

	4	Attended the Royal Statistical Society's sesquicentenary reception, Banqueting House, Whitehall, London.
	6	Visited the Queen's Flight, RAF Benson, Oxfordshire.
	9	Opened the Joint European Torus, Culham, Oxfordshire.
	10	Welcomed the Amir of Bahrain at the beginning of his State Visit, Royal Pavilion, Home Park, Windsor, and accompanied him to Windsor Castle.
		Invested the Amir of Bahrain with the Order of the Bath, Windsor Castle.
		Gave a State banquet for the Amir of Bahrain, Windsor Castle.
	11	Visited Madame Tussaud's exhibition with the Amir of Bahrain, Windsor Station.
		Held a Council, Windsor Castle.
	12	Entertained at a State banquet by the Amir of Bahrain, Dorchester Hotel, London.
	16	Entertained the Secretary General of NATO to luncheon, Windsor Castle.
	18	Visited King Edward VII Hospital, Windsor.
		Visited the Lady Gomer Berry Nurses' Home, Windsor.
	19	Distributed the Royal Maundy, Southwell Minster, Nottinghamshire.
		Entertained to luncheon by Nottingham City Council, Council House, Nottingham.
	25	Received the Garter Insignia of the late Duke of Beaufort, Windsor Castle.
		Attended the Presentation of the late Duke of Beaufort's Garter banner, St George's Chapel, Windsor.
May	1	Held two audiences, Buckingham Palace.
		Received the Prime Minister in audience, Buckingham Palace.
		Left Euston Station for Liverpool.
	2	Opened and toured the International Garden Festival, Liverpool.
		Opened and toured the Queen Elizabeth II Law Courts, Derby Square, Liverpool.
	4	Visited the 1st Battalion, The Royal Welch Fusiliers, Battlesbury Barracks, Warminster, Wiltshire.
	8	Opened the Thames Barrier, London.
		Received the Prime Minister in audience, Buckingham Palace.
	9	Held three audiences, Buckingham Palace.
		Attended a London Philharmonic Orchestra charity concert, Barbican, London.
	10	Held a personal Investiture, Buckingham Palace.
	15	Held two audiences, Buckingham Palace.
		Received the Prime Minister in audience, Buckingham Palace.
	16	Opened and toured the Information Technology Centre, Cambridge.
		Opened and toured the Grafton Shopping Centre, Cambridge.
		Visited Emmanuel College and lunched with the Vice-Chancellor of Cambridge University.
		Visited Jesus College, Cambridge.
	17	Held two audiences, Buckingham Palace.
		Opened and toured St Joseph's Hospice, Hackney.
		Gave a reception, Buckingham Palace.
	18	Held an audience, Buckingham Palace.
		Held a Council, Buckingham Palace.
	21	Visited the Chelsea Flower Show, Royal Hospital, Chelsea.
	22	Left Heathrow Airport, London for West Germany, and arrived at Essen Airport.
		Attended a reception and private dinner party, 26th Field Regiment Officers' Mess, Napier Barracks.
	23	Reviewed the Royal Artillery by Range Rover, Napier Barracks.
		Opened an indoor riding school and watched a disabled children's riding display, Dortmund.
		Attended a regimental Sergeant Majors' reception and lunch, 22nd Armoured Division Sergeants' Mess, Dortmund.
		Viewed displays of regimental military equipment and activities.
		Attended a regimental garden party.
		Attended a regimental reception and dinner, Officers' Mess.
	24	Left Essen Airport and arrived at RAF Wietzenbruch.
		Visited the Rathaus, Celle.
		Watched a battle group attack demonstration and freefall display, Scheuen Training Area.

	24	Started a Royal Green Jackets charity race to London, Scheuen Training Area.

24 Started a Royal Green Jackets charity race to London, Scheuen Training Area.
Attended a regimental reception and all-ranks luncheon, Scheuen Training Area.
Visited an exhibition of regimental life, Trenchard Barracks, Celle.
Attended a garden party, Trenchard Barracks.
Attended a regimental dinner, Officers' Mess, Trenchard Barracks.

25 Left RAF Wietzenbruch for Balmoral via Heathrow and Dyce Airports.

30 Opened and toured a new terminal, Birmingham International Airport.
Attended a reception and luncheon, Airside Suite, Birmingham Airport.
Visited the *Expo '84* exhibition, National Exhibition Centre, Birmingham.

31 Held two audiences, Buckingham Palace.
Attended the Chartered Institute of Building's sesquicentenary reception, St James's Palace.

June 1 Held two audiences, Buckingham Palace.
Received a bouquet from the Gardeners' Company to commemorate her Coronation, Buckingham Palace.

4 Received the Prime Minister in audience, Buckingham Palace.

5 Held an audience, Buckingham Palace.
Entertained President and Mrs Reagan to luncheon, Buckingham Palace.
Visited Southwick House, *HMS Dryad*, Havant, Hampshire.
Embarked on the Royal Yacht *Britannia* and sailed for France.

6 Visited Caen as part of the D-Day commemorations, and attended a civic reception at the Hôtel de Ville.
Laid a wreath at the Commonwealth War Graves Commission cemetery, Bayeux.
Attended a commemorative D-Day ceremony, Utah Beach.
Attended a military ceremony, Canadian cemetery, Beny-Rivières.
Visited the D-Day museum, Arromanches.
Reviewed a parade of veterans and a Battle of Britain memorial fly-past, Arromanches.
Left Normandy and arrived at Heathrow Airport, London.

7 Held three audiences, Buckingham Palace.
Entertained the Prime Minister of Canada to luncheon, Buckingham Palace.
Attended the 2nd Battalion Coldstream Guards' garden party, Burtons Court, London.

8 Presented awards and trophies during a day's visit to the South of England Show, Ardingly, Sussex.

9 Gave a dinner party for Heads of State and delegates attending the Economic Summit in London, Buckingham Palace.

12 Held a personal Investiture, Buckingham Palace.
Held two audiences, Buckingham Palace.
Entertained the Governor-General of Canada to luncheon, Buckingham Palace.
Received the Prime Minister in audience, Buckingham Palace.

13 Visited RAF Cottesmore, Leicestershire.
Visited Cottesmore Primary School.
Opened the Families Club, RAF Cottesmore.

14 Held three audiences, Buckingham Palace.
Visited the British Council headquarters, Spring Gardens, London.
Attended Beating Retreat, Horse Guards Parade, London.

15 Held an audience, Buckingham Palace.

16 Took the Salute at the Queen's Birthday Parade, Horse Guards Parade, London.

17 Attended the National Light Horse Breeding Society's centenary display, Great Park, Windsor.

18 Visited the Royal Highland Show, Ingliston, Edinburgh, and presented the Highland Cattle Society's centenary trophy.

19 Attended Ascot Races.

20 Received members of the South African Legion Battlefield Pilgrimage Party, Windsor Castle.
Attended Ascot Races.

21 Attended Ascot Races.

22 Attended Ascot Races.

25 Received the President of Sri Lanka, Buckingham Palace.

	25	Held a Council, Buckingham Palace.
	26	Opened and toured the Women's Institute's exhibition *Life and Leisure '84*, Olympia, London.
		Received the President of Costa Rica, Buckingham Palace.
		Opened and toured the Crown Estates Commissioners' new office development, Millbank, London.
		Left Waterloo Station for Dorset.
	27	Visited the Royal Marines, Hamworthy, Poole, Dorset.
	28	Held four personal Investitures, Buckingham Palace.
		Held an audience, Buckingham Palace.

July 1 Held a personal Investiture, Buckingham Palace.
2 Toured the exhibition centre and computer suite, and opened a new library extension, Napier College, Edinburgh.
Arrived at the Palace of Holyroodhouse.
Attended a reception marking the 200th anniversary of the Society of Solicitors, Parliament House, Edinburgh.
3 Attended an Order of the Thistle installation service, St Giles' Cathedral, Edinburgh.
Gave a luncheon party for the Knights of the Thistle, Palace of Holyroodhouse.
Visited the Royal Scottish Geographical Society's centenary exhibition, Randolph Crescent, Edinburgh.
Gave a dinner party, Palace of Holyroodhouse.
4 Visited the Scottish Veterans' residence, Whitefoord House, Edinburgh.
Visited Queensberry House Hospital, Edinburgh.
Held a personal Investiture, Palace of Holyroodhouse.
Held two audiences, Palace of Holyroodhouse.
Presented the Queen's Prize to the winner of the Royal Company of Archers' annual shooting event, Palace of Holyroodhouse.
Gave a garden party, Palace of Holyroodhouse.
5 Opened Fairbairn Court for the Bield Housing Association, Greenlaw, Berwickshire.
Visited Henderson Park, Coldstream.
Opened Hamish Morison Ltd's new hatchery, Duns, Berwickshire.
Lunched and attended Sports Week activities, Berwickshire High School.
Toured a complex of grain dryers and stores, Craigswalls, Berwickshire.
Visited Eyemouth Harbour.
Opened the Royal British Legion's sheltered housing development, Swan Court, Eyemouth.
Opened Eyemouth and District Disabled Centre.
6 Visited Fairmile Nursing Home, Edinburgh.
Visited the 1st Battalion The Argyll and Sutherland Highlanders, Redford Barracks, Edinburgh.
Attended a reception given by Her Majesty's Chaplains in Scotland, Abden House, Edinburgh
7 Left the Palace of Holyroodhouse and returned to London.
8 Held a personal Investiture, Windsor Castle.
9 Entertained at dinner by the Canadian High Commissioner, 12 Upper Brook St, London.
10 Held four audiences, Buckingham Palace.
Held a personal Investiture, Buckingham Palace.
Gave a garden party, Buckingham Palace.
11 Held four audiences, Buckingham Palace.
Held a personal Investiture, Buckingham Palace.
12 Attended a service of the Order of St Michael and St George, St Paul's Cathedral, London.
Gave a garden party, Buckingham Palace.
13 Held four audiences, Buckingham Palace.
Held a personal Investiture, Buckingham Palace.
17 Held three audiences, Buckingham Palace.
Gave a garden party, Buckingham Palace.
18 Held four audiences, Buckingham Palace.
Held a personal Investiture, Buckingham Palace.
27 Held four audiences, Buckingham Palace.

	27	Held a personal Investiture, Buckingham Palace.
	29	Held three personal Investitures, Windsor Castle.
	31	Held an Investiture, Buckingham Palace.
		Held a Council, Buckingham Palace.
		Held an audience, Buckingham Palace.
		Held two personal Investitures, Buckingham Palace.
		Attended a performance of *Arabella*, Glyndebourne.

Engagements of **THE DUKE OF EDINBURGH**
August 1983-July 1984

August	1	Attended a Royal Ocean Racing Club reception, The Prospect, Cowes, Isle of Wight.
		Attended a Royal London Yacht Club reception, Cowes.
		Attended the Royal Yacht Squadron's Ball, Cowes Castle.
	2	Disembarked from the Royal Yacht *Britannia* at Cowes.
	8	Embarked on the Royal Yacht *Britannia, en route* for Balmoral.
	13	Disembarked from the Royal Yacht *Britannia*, and travelled to Balmoral Castle.

September	3	Attended the Highland Games, Braemar, Deeside.

October	5	Left RAF Marham to attend four days of meetings as President of the International Equestrian Federation in Zurich, Switzerland.
	9	Left Heathrow Airport, London for Hong Kong via Bombay.
	10	Arrived at Hong Kong.
		Attended a dinner with those connected with World Wildlife Fund Hong Kong, the Prince Philip Dental Hospital and the Duke of Edinburgh's Award Scheme, Government House, Hong Kong.
	11	Toured the Nature Reserve and visited the headquarters of the Education and Conservation Centre, Mai Po Marshes.
		Toured the Stokes Camp and unveiled a plaque to rename it 'The Duke of Edinburgh Training Camp.'
		Visited the Hong Kong Zoological and Botanical Gardens.
		Attended a reception for service unit officers, Government House.
		Attended the Panda Dinner and Ball, Hilton Hotel.
	12	Left Hong Kong for Thailand, and arrived at Bangkok.
		Received in audience by the King of Thailand, Chitlada Palace, Bangkok.
		Attended a dinner with the Thai Association for the Conservation of Wildlife committee, Peninsular Hotel, Bangkok.
	13	Held an audience with the Thai Minister of Agriculture and conservation officials, Oriental Hotel, Bangkok.
		Held a Press conference, Library Room, Oriental Hotel.
		Received an honorary Doctorate of Philosophy in Forestry, Kasetsart University, Bangkok.
		Entertained at luncheon by the Prime Minister of Thailand, Government House, Bangkok.
		Attended a reception with members of the British community in Thailand, British Ambassador's residence.
		Attended a reception, slide show and banquet, Oriental Hotel, Bangkok.
	14	Left Don Muang airport, Bangkok for Malaysia and arrived at Kuala Lumpur.
		Attended a meeting with the Malaysian Prime Minister and the Minister of the Environment.
		Gave a Press conference, High Commissioner's residence, Kuala Lumpur.
		Attended a reception and President's banquet, Hilton Hotel.
	15	Visited the Ampang Forest Reserve.
		Met WWF-Malaysia staff and received on its behalf a word processor from the Hong Kong and Shanghai Banking Corporation, WWF offices, Kuala Lumpur.
		Attended a sponsors' luncheon, Lake Club, Kuala Lumpur.
		Recorded a television interview, RTM Angkasapuri studios.
	16	Left Subang airport, Kuala Lumpur for India, and arrived at Bombay via Port Blair and Madras.

	17	Left Bombay for Jordan, and arrived at Amman via Muscat and Bahrain.
		Attended a dinner given by the Crown Prince and Princess of Jordan, Amman.
	18	Witnessed the release of wild oryx into a reserve, Azraq Park.
		Visited an animal and plant exhibition, Shomari.
		Toured wetland reserves by helicopter.
		Visited the desert castles of Qasr El-Amra and Harranah.
		Attended a luncheon given by the Crown Prince and Princess of Jordan.
		Attended a reception for the British community in Jordan, British Ambassador's residence, Amman.
		Attended a dinner given by the King and Queen of Jordan, Royal Palace, Amman.
	19	Toured the Jordan Valley by helicopter.
		Watched a polo match between the Royal Jordanian Polo Club and the British Army Cyprus Polo Association, Amman.
		Attended a Scottish Ballet performance, Jordanian National Theater, Amman.
	20	Left Amman and arrived at London Airport via Rhodes and Rome.
	24	Presided at the opening, and two sessions, of the 22nd Annual Conference of the British Commonwealth Ex-Services League, Windsor Castle.
		Hosted a British Commonwealth Ex-Services League Reception, Holiday Inn, Slough, Buckinghamshire.
	25	Visited the exhibition *Albert, His Life and Work*, Royal College of Art, Kensington, London.
		Attended a dinner party given by the High Commissioner for India, Kensington Palace Gardens, London.
	26	Gave a reception for delegates to the 22nd Annual Conference of the British Commonwealth Ex-Services League, Buckingham Palace.
		Chaired the Annual General Meeting, and attended a reception, of the Royal Institute of Navigation, Royal Geographical Society, Kensington Gore, London.
		Attended the trophies and awards dinner of the Guild of Air Pilots and Air Navigators, Mansion House, London.
	27	Presided at a meeting of judges of the the *Dawn to Dusk* Tiger Club Competition, Buckingham Palace.
		Attended a Trinity House luncheon for the Lord Mayor of London, Trinity House, London.
		Presided at a meeting of the Westminster Abbey Trustees, Westminster Abbey, London.
	31	Gave a reception to mark the 21st anniversary of Community Service Volunteers, Buckingham Palace.
November	1	Presented the President's Certificates for the National Playing Fields Association, Buckingham Palace.
		Presented the Prince Philip Award for the Plastics and Rubber Institute, Buckingham Palace.
		Presented prizes and chaired a meeting of the English Language Committee, Buckingham Palace.
		Opened an extension for the disabled, Home for Aged Jews, Nightingale House, London.
		Gave a reception for the London Federation of Boys Clubs, Buckingham Palace.
	2	Attended the unveiling by the Queen of the statue of Earl Mountbatten, Foreign Office Green, London.
		Gave a luncheon party, Buckingham Palace.
		Attended a reception to mark the Golden Jubilee of the Milk Marketing Board, Guildhall.
		Attended a reception given by the Prime Minister, Banqueting House, Whitehall, London.
	6	Left London for Gland, Switzerland, to attend meetings of the World Wildlife Fund International and the International Union for Conservation of Nature and Natural Resources.
	10	Arrived Jomo Kenyatta Airport, and drove to State House, Nairobi.
		Attended a State banquet, State House, Nairobi.
	11	Attended the wreath-laying by the Queen at the National Mausoleum, Nairobi.
		Toured the Parliament buildings, Nairobi.
		Attended a Press reception, State House, Nairobi.
		Attended a lunch given by the National Museum of Kenya, Nairobi.
		Visited the Kenya Polytechnic, Nairobi.
		Attended the Remembrance Day ceremony at the Commonwealth War Graves Commission

11	cemetery, Nairobi.
	Attended a tea party with Commonwealth High Commissioners and their wives, State House, Nairobi.
	Gave a State banquet for the President of Kenya, British High Commissioner's residence, Nairobi.
12	Attended a luncheon at the Isaac Walton Inn, Embu.
	Visited the Thuchi/Nkubu Road project.
	Arrived at State Lodge, Sagana.
13	Visited Treetops Hotel, near Sagana.
	Attended a reception for the British Community in Kenya, Intercontinental Hotel, Nairobi.
	Attended farewell ceremonies, State House, Nairobi.
14	Left Jomo Kenyatta Airport for Bangladesh.
	Arrived at Dhaka Airport, and drove to the Presidential guest house.
15	Attended the wreath-laying ceremony at the Savar Memorial to war dead, Dhaka.
	Visited the President of Bangladesh, State House, Dhaka.
	Attended a luncheon given by the Federal Chambers of Commerce, Sonagaon Hotel.
	Attended an afternoon party for members of the British community in Bangladesh, High Commissioner's residence, Dhaka.
	Attended a State banquet and cultural show, State House, Dhaka.
16	Met local planters and British Overseas Development Administration officials, Lakatoora Golf Club.
	Toured the Lakatoora Tea Garden and inspected cultivation and harvesting.
	Watched a cultural programme, Malnichera Rest House.
	Attended a civic reception, State House, Dhaka.
	Attended a Press reception, Presidential guest house, Dhaka.
	Attended the Queen's State Banquet for the President of Bangladesh, British High Commissioner's residence, Dhaka.
17	Left Dhaka Airport for India.
	Arrived at Delhi Airport and drove to the Presidential residence.
	Attended a Commonwealth Press Union reception, British High Commissioner's residence, New Delhi.
	Attended a State banquet, Presidential residence, New Delhi.
18	Visited the Red Fort, New Delhi.
	Toured the British School, New Delhi.
	Attended the wreath-laying by the Queen at the National Memorial, Rajghat.
	Attended a luncheon at Hyderabad House, New Delhi, given by Mrs Gandhi.
	Visited the British High Commission Compound, New Delhi.
	Attended the wreath-laying at the Stone of Remembrance, Commonwealth War Graves Commission cemetery, New Delhi.
	Watched an equestrian display by the President's bodyguard, New Delhi.
	Flew from New Delhi to Hyderabad.
19	Visited ICRISAT and Bharat Heavy Electrical Research and Development Centre.
	Left Hyderabad for Gondia, and arrived at Kanha Forest Lodge.
20	Visited Kanha Game Reserve and lunched at Kanha Forest Lodge.
	Flew back to Hyderabad to rejoin the Queen.
21	Attended the Royal Parade and March Past, National Defence Academy, Pune.
	Attended the Cadets' Mess luncheon at the Academy.
	Attended a reception at the British High Commissioner's residence, New Delhi.
22	Laid the foundation stone of a new building, Indian Ex-Services League offices, New Delhi.
	Attended the 10th anniversary function for Project Tiger, FICCI Auditorium.
	Inaugurated a Project Tiger exhibition, National Museum of Natural History, New Delhi.
	Visited the Ecology Gallery of the National Museum of Natural History, New Delhi.
	Attended a buffet luncheon with members of FICCI and the Chamber of Commerce, Maurya Sheraton Hotel, New Delhi.
	Visited the Computer Centre, laboratories and the campus of the Indian Institute of Technology, New Delhi.
	Attended a reception for the British Community in New Delhi, Presidential guest house.

	22	Attended a dinner with the British High Commissioner, at his residence in New Delhi.
	23	Attended a ministerial luncheon in connection with Project Tiger, Taj Hotel, New Delhi.
		Presented Duke of Edinburgh's Gold Awards, British High Commissioner's residence.
		Attended the banquet given by the Queen for leaders of delegations to the Commonwealth Heads of Government Meeting, Hyderabad House, New Delhi.
	24	Visited the Gir lion sanctuary, Keshod.
		Attended a World Wildlife Fund dinner, Oberoi Towers Hotel, Bombay.
	25	Attended a meeting of the Duke of Edinburgh's Study Conference, Royal Palace, Bombay.
		Met members of the Deputy High Commission and British Council staff, Royal Palace, Bombay.
		Attended a meeting of conservationists and naturalists, Godrej Bahavan.
		Attended a lunch given by the Governor of Maharashtra, Bombay.
		Attended a reception for Commonwealth Heads of Government, Ministers and officials, Hyderabad House, New Delhi.
	26	Left New Delhi Airport, and arrived at Heathrow Airport, London.
	28	Entertained the Prince and Princess of Liège, to luncheon, Windsor Castle.
		Attended the presentation of King Leopold III of the Belgians' Garter Banner, St George's Chapel, Windsor.
	29	Gave a reception for the American Express Group Board, St James's Palace.
		Attended the Central Council of Physical Recreation Sponsors of Sports Dinner, Hyde Park Hotel, London.
	30	Attended a meeting of the Royal Academy Trustees, Buckingham Palace.
		Attended a reception for the Duke of Edinburgh's Award Gold Standard winners, St James's Palace.
		Attended the Ambassador of Sweden's Dinner, Portland Place, London.
December	1	Attended a meeting of the National Maritime Museum Trustees, Greenwich, London.
		Attended a reception for the Jewish Friends of the Westminster Abbey Trust, Westminster Abbey, London.
		Held an evening reception for the Diplomatic Corps, Buckingham Palace.
	2	Attended a reception for the Duke of Edinburgh's Award Gold Standard winners, St James's Palace, London.
	4	Travelled to Amsterdam to preside at meetings of the International Equestrian Federation.
	13	Presented the MacRobert Award for the Fellowship of Engineering, Buckingham Palace.
		Presented Design Management Awards at the Design Management Symposium.
		Presented the Albert Medal at a Royal Society of Arts dinner, London.
	14	Gave a reception for Friends of the Duke of Edinburgh's Award Scheme, Buckingham Palace.
		Attended the Margaret Pike Memorial Trust Supper, Commonwealth Institute, Kensington.
		Left London for Cumbria.
	15	Opened a marketing office block, and toured the premises of British Sidac Limited, Wigton, Cumbria.
		Visited St Cuthbert's Boys Club, Wigton.
		Attended a Restoration Appeal service, Carlisle Cathedral.
		Opened the Kinmont Barn senior citizens meeting place, Carlisle.
	20	Attended a National Playing Fields Association meeting, City of London.
		Attended a gala performance of *Aladdin*, Shaftesbury Theatre, London.
February	6	Launched the Norfolk Outward Bound Association, King's Lynn.
		Presided at a Cambridge University Press dinner, St John's College, Cambridge.
	7	Visited the University of Cambridge.
	8	Visited the University of Cambridge.
		Visited Trivector Commerce Ltd, Sandy, Bedfordshire.
	9	Selected the Duke of Edinburgh's Designer's Prize for 1984, Design Centre, Haymarket, London.
		Chaired a meeting of the Royal Society of Art's Committee for the Environment, Buckingham Palace.
		Chaired a Fellowship of Engineering meeting and attended a Fellowship dinner, Institute of

9	Civil Engineers, London.
10	Visited ERA Technology Ltd, Leatherhead, Surrey.
13	Attended the Windsor Rugby Football Club's Post Minders' Dinner, Windsor.
14	Left Heathrow Airport London, for Switzerland.
15	Attended meetings of World Wildlife Fund International, Gland, Switzerland.
16	Received the *Hör Zu* 'Golden Camera' award, West Berlin.
17	Visited the headquarters of the World Wildlife Fund Netherland, Zeist.
	Arrived at Heathrow Airport, London from the Netherlands.
20	Attended the President's Dinner, Naval and Military Club, Piccadilly, London.
21	Attended a meeting between Trinity House and the Council of British Shipping, Trinity House, London.
	Attended a booksellers' reception given by Hamish Hamilton Ltd, Stationers' Hall, London.
	Attended a Duke of Edinburgh's Award appeal dinner, Royal Artillery Mess, Woolwich.
22	Held an audience, Buckingham Palace.
	Attended a luncheon at the Bank of England, City of London.
	Attended two receptions for Duke of Edinburgh Award Gold Standard achievers, St James's Palace.
	Attended the première of the film *Chance of a Lifetime*, Britannic House, Moor Lane, London.
23	Attended the *Genius of Venice* exhibition, Royal Academy of Arts, London.
24	Toured John Smith's Brewery, Tadcaster, North Yorkshire.
	Opened an extension to the Mountbatten Non-Invasive Heart Unit, Killingbeck Hospital, Leeds.
	Toured the factory of Rose Forgrove, Leeds.
	Visited Lucas Aerospace, Bradford, and opened its new factory.
	Attended the Variety Club's *Women of the Year* dinner, Queen's Hotel, Leeds.
27	Gave a reception for the Lord's Taverners Patron's Club, St James's Palace.
28	Attended a reception given by the European-Atlantic Group, St Ermin's Hotel, London.
29	Visited the Baltic Exchange, City of London.
	Attended a reception to launch a Folio Edition of Jonathon Kingdon's *African Mammal Drawings*, Wellcome Trust, London.
	Visited the Intelligence and Security Group (Volunteers), Artillery House, London.

March	1	Presided at a Royal Mint Advisory Committee meeting, Buckingham Palace.
		Attended two receptions for Duke of Edinburgh Award Gold Standard achievers, St James's Palace.
		Attended a Woodroffe's Luncheon, Cavalry and Guards Club, Piccadilly, London.
		Dined with the Royal Marines Officers' Dinner Club, Lincoln's Inn, London.
	2	Visited Hardys & Hansons plc and toured their brewery, Nottingham.
		Visited East Midlands Television Centre, Nottingham.
		Opened a science laboratory building during a tour of Nottingham High School.
	6	Attended a dinner given by the Society of Merchants Trading to the Continent, Savoy Hotel, London.
	7	Visited the United Kingdom Land Forces headquarters, Wilton, Wiltshire.
		Attended a National Council for Voluntary Organisations reception, Drapers' Hall, London.
		Attended a dinner given by the Institute of Mathematics for past presidents, Cavendish Hotel, London.
	8	Visited the National Light Horse Breeding Society's annual Stallion Show, Newmarket.
	9	Delivered the first annual Chancellor's Lecture, Edinburgh University.
	12	Attended the Commonwealth Day Observance Service, Westminster Abbey.
		Attended a Commonwealth Day reception, Marlborough House.
		Attended a dinner in aid of the Museum of Army Flying, Fishmongers' Hall, London.
	13	Visited London Docklands.
		Opened and toured Broadway Shopping Centre, Bexleyheath, Kent.
		Attended a dinner for the retiring President of the British Heart Foundation, White's Club, London.
	14	Presented the Royal Society of Arts 1983 Pollution Abatement Technology Awards, John Adam Street, London.

	15	Attended two receptions for achievers of the Duke of Edinburgh Award Gold Standard, St James's Palace.
		Chaired a meeting of the Award Scheme Trustees, Buckingham Palace.
	16	Toured the new Territorial Army Centre of the 3rd Battalion, Royal Welch Fusiliers, Colwyn Bay.
		Visited Colwyn Bay Civic Centre.
		Attended a thanksgiving service, St Asaph's Cathedral.
		Toured and lunched at Ruthin School.
		Visited Delyn House, Flint.
	18	Entertained the Governor-General of Canada to luncheon, Buckingham Palace.
		Attended a meeting of the Egham and Thorpe Royal Agricultural and Horticultural Association, Great Fosters Hotel, Egham, Surrey.
	19	Attended the Royal Film Performance, *The Dresser*, Odeon Theatre, Leicester Square, London.
	20	Chaired the annual general meeting of the Central Council of Physical Recreation, Fishmongers' Hall, London.
		Visited the Paediatric Research Unit, Guy's Hospital Medical School, London.
		Visited Chelsea Boys' Club.
		Visited St Andrew's Club, Old Pye Street, Westminster.
		Attended a Moët & Chandon dinner, Grosvenor Crescent, London.
	21	Launched the International Plants Conservation Programme, Royal Botanic Gardens, Kew.
		Gave a reception for winners of the Queen's Awards for Export and Technology in 1983, Buckingham Palace.
	22	Attended a National Maritime Museum trustees' meeting, Greenwich.
		Presented the Lord's Taverners' Trophy to Essex C.C.C., Buckingham Palace.
		Attended a performance of *Starlight Express*, Apollo Theatre, Victoria.
	23	Represented the Queen at the Memorial Service for the Duke of Beaufort, Guards Chapel, London.
	25	Left Heathrow Airport, London and arrived at Cyprus en route for Jordan.
	26	Arrived at Marka airport, Amman, to be welcomed by the King and Queen of Jordan.
		Visited Queen Zein at Zahran Palace, Amman.
		Attended a reception for embassy staff and members of the British community in Jordan, British Ambassador's residence, Amman.
		Gave a reception for members of the Press, British Ambassador's residence, Amman.
		Attended a State banquet given by the King and Queen of Jordan, Basman Palace, Amman.
	27	Attended a ceremony at the Tree of Life, Martyrs' Memorial, Amman.
		Toured sections of the Al-Hussein Medical Centre, Amman.
		Visited the Royal Stables, Amman.
		Toured the University of Jordan, Amman.
		Visited the British Council, Amman.
		Gave a banquet for the King and Queen of Jordan, British Ambassador's residence, Amman.
	28	Visited Zedirfai Farm, Jordan Valley.
		Attended a picnic lunch by the Dead Sea.
		Visited the Marine Centre, Aqaba.
	29	Toured the cave city of Petra.
	30	Left Aqaba airport for London, and arrived at Heathrow Airport.
April	2	Entertained the President of Israel to luncheon, Windsor Castle.
	4	Attended the Royal Society's sesquicentenary reception, Banqueting House, Whitehall, London.
		Presided at a Court Luncheon of the Honourable Company of Master Mariners, *HQS Wellington*, London.
	6	Visited The Queen's Flight, RAF Benson, Oxfordshire.
	9	Attended the opening by the Queen of the Joint European Torus, Culham, Oxfordshire.
	10	Welcomed the Amir of Bahrain on his State Visit to Britain, Royal Pavilion, Home Park, Windsor, and accompanied him to Windsor Castle.
		Gave a State banquet for the Amir of Bahrain, Windsor Castle.
		Visited Woods of Windsor Ltd, at Colnbrook and Windsor.
	11	Visited Madame Tussaud's exhibition with the Amir of Bahrain, Windsor Station.

11	Attended a meeting of The Prince Philip Trust Fund trustees, Windsor Castle.
12	Entertained at a State banquet given by the Amir of Bahrain, Dorchester Hotel, London.
16	Entertained the Secretary-General of NATO to luncheon, Windsor Castle.
18	Visited King Edward VII Hospital, Windsor.
	Visited the Lady Gomer Berry Nurses' Home, Windsor.
19	Attended the Maundy Service, Southwell Minster, Nottinghamshire.
	Entertained at luncheon by Nottingham City Council, Council House, Nottingham.
22	Left Heathrow Airport London for Sweden.
23	Attended the finals of the Volvo Showjumping World Cup, Gothenburg.
	Left Gothenburg for London and returned to Windsor Castle.
25	Attended the Presentation of the late Duke of Beaufort's Garter banner, St George's Chapel, Windsor.
27	Chaired the annual St George's House lecture, St George's Chapel, Windsor.
30	Attended a Fellowship of Engineering anniversary dinner, Guildhall, London.

May	1	Held two audiences, Buckingham Palace.
		Attended the 1984 Design Council awards ceremony, RAF Museum, Hendon.
		Attended an anniversary dinner given by Lloyd's of London Press Ltd, Guildhall, London.
		Left Euston Station for Liverpool.
	2	Attended the opening by the Queen of the International Garden Festival, Liverpool.
		Attended the opening by the Queen of the Queen Elizabeth II Law Courts, Derby Square, Liverpool.
		Left Speke Airport, Liverpool for Austria, and arrived at Vienna.
	3	Held a Press conference, Press Club Concordia, Vienna.
		Attended a business and political luncheon, British Ambassador's residence, Vienna.
		Toured the Hainburg riverine forest.
		Attended a performance of *Aida*, Opera House, Vienna.
		Attended a dinner given by *Erste Allgemeine Versicherung*, Hotel Sacher, Vienna.
	4	Toured wetlands at Larnge Lacke.
		Left Vienna for Heathrow Airport, London and drove to Windsor.
	5	Attended the Old Comrades Dinner of the Queen's Royal Irish Hussars, Lord's Tavern, London.
	8	Attended the opening by the Queen of the Thames Barrier, London.
		Attended a dinner given by Lord and Lady Ampthill in aid of cancer research, Chelsea, London.
	9	Attended a Variety Club and Outward Bound Trust luncheon, Hilton Hotel, London.
		Attended the St George's House Council Meeting, St George's House, Windsor.
	14	Attended the centenary dinner of the North East Coast Institutions of Engineers and Shipbuilders, Civic Centre, Newcastle-upon-Tyne.
	15	Opened the International Conference on Marine Propulsion, Civic Centre, Newcastle-upon-Tyne.
		Presented the 1984 Templeton Foundation Prize for Progress in Religion, Buckingham Palace.
		Opened the Topolski exhibition *Memoir of a Century*, Concert Hall Approach, London.
		Attended a Westminster Abbey Trust and Council of Donors meeting, Westminster Abbey.
		Attended Lord Zuckerman's retirement dinner, Zoological Society, Zoo Restaurant, London.
	16	Attended the opening by the Queen of the Information Technology Centre, Cambridge.
		Attended the opening by the Queen of the Grafton Shopping Centre, Cambridge.
		Visited Emmanuel College and lunched with the Vice-Chancellor of Cambridge University.
		Visited Jesus College, Cambridge.
	17	Attended a service of dedication of the Order of the British Empire, St Paul's Cathedral.
		Presided at the National Playing Fields Association annual general meeting, St Ermin's Hotel, London.
		Gave a reception, Buckingham Palace.
	18	Left Heathrow Airport, London for the U.S.A. via Prestwick, Reykjavik and Sondrestrom.
	19	Arrived in Washington D.C. from Sondrestrom via Goose Bay and Bedford.
		Gave a Press interview, Embassy Row Hotel, Washington.
		Attended a dinner for donors to the World Wildlife Fund, 1803 Kalorama Square, Washington.
	20	Attended a World Wildlife Fund Executive Committee meeting, Embassy Row Hotel,

	20	Washington.
		Attended a World Wildlife Fund Board of Trustees meeting and luncheon, Embassy Row Hotel, Washington.
		Attended a tennis event and reception for donors, sponsors and celebrities, Swedish Ambassador's residence, Washington.
		Gave two Press interviews, Embassy Row Hotel, Washington.
		Attended *An Evening with World Wildlife Fund-U.S.,* Smithsonian Institute, Washington
	21	Attended a meeting of World Wildlife Fund-International Council, National Geographic Society, Washington.
		Attended a luncheon with President Reagan, White House, Washington.
		Attended a National Wildlife Federation reception and received its 1983 Conservation Award, Embassy Row Hotel, Washington.
		Attended a barbecue at the home of Vice-President Bush, Washington.
	22	Toured an exhibition of art donated to the World Wildlife Fund, National Geographic Society, Washington.
		Attended the continued International Council meeting, National Geographic Society.
		Gave a Press conference announcing a campaign for the protection of endangered species, Embassy Row Hotel, Washington.
		Visited the offices of World Wildlife Fund-U.S., Washington.
		Attended the second session of the World Wildlife Fund Board of Trustees meeting, Embassy Row Hotel, Washington.
		Attended a reception and dinner for major World Wildlife Fund donors, British Embassy, Washington.
	23	Left Washington for Scotland, via Sept-Iles, Goose Bay and Sondrestrom.
	24	Arrived at Perth from Sondrestrom via Reykjavik and drove to Scone.
	29	Toured Whitecross Industrial Estate, Tideswell, Derbyshire.
		Opened the Old College, Market Square, Tideswell.
		Toured the Eccles Fold housing development for the elderly, Chapel-en-le-Frith, Derbyshire.
	30	Attended the opening by the Queen of a new terminal, Birmingham Airport.
		Attended a reception and luncheon, Airside Suite, Birmingham Airport.
		Visited the *Expo '84* exhibition, National Exhibition Centre, Birmingham.
		Attended a meeting of the Smeatonian Society of Civil Engineers, Institution of Civil Engineers, Great George Street, London.
	31	Introduced the symposium *Advances in Animal Conservation,* Zoological Society's meeting rooms, Regent's Park, London.
		Attended the Chartered Institute of Building's sesquicentenary reception, St James's Palace.
June	4	Presided at the anniversary dinner for Younger Brethren, Trinity House, London.
	5	Attended the Annual Court, Trinity House, London.
		Entertained President and Mrs Reagan to luncheon, Buckingham Palace.
		Visited Southwick House, *HMS Dryad,* Havant, Hampshire.
		Embarked on the Royal Yacht *Britannia* and sailed for France.
	6	Visited Caen, Normandy.
		Laid a wreath at the Commonwealth War Graves Commission cemetery, Bayeux.
		Attended an Allied D-Day ceremony, Utah Beach.
		Attended a commemorative ceremony at the Commonwealth War Graves Commission cemetery, Beny-sur-Mer.
		Attended a D-Day Canadian military ceremony, Beny-Riviéres.
		Visited the D-Day museum, Arromanches.
		Attended the Queen's review of a veterans parade and a flypast, Arromanches.
	7	Attended a meeting of the National Maritime Museum trustees, Greenwich.
		Attended the 2nd Battalion Coldstream Guards garden party, Burton Court, London.
	8	Presented new colours to the 1st Battalion The Duke of Edinburgh's Royal Regiment, Howe Barracks, Canterbury.
	9	Took the salute at the second rehearsal of Trooping the Colour, Horse Guards Parade, London.
		Gave a dinner party for Heads of State and delegates attending the London Economic Summit, Buckingham Palace.

12	Entertained the Governor-General of Canada to luncheon, Buckingham Palace.
	Attended a Scholarship Fund Appeal garden party, Inner Temple, London.
13	Attended a Cambridge University Press garden party, Cambridge.
	Attended a dinner marking the 700th anniversary of the founding of Peterhouse College, Cambridge.
14	Conferred honorary degrees, Cambridge University.
	Took the Salute at Beating Retreat, Horse Guards Parade, London.
15	Presented athletics trophies and plaques, Buckingham Palace.
	Presented the London City & Guilds 1984 Prince Philip Medal, Buckingham Palace.
	Attended the City & Guilds of London Institute's luncheon, Connaught Rooms, London.
16	Attended the Queen's Birthday Parade, Horse Guards Parade, London.
17	Attended the National Light Horse Breeding Society's centenary display, Great Park, Windsor.
18	Visited the Royal Highland Show, Ingliston, Edinburgh.
	Visited Rannoch School, Tayside.
19	Attended Ascot Races.
20	Received members of the South African Legion Battlefield Pilgrimage Party, Windsor Castle.
	Attended Ascot Races.
21	Attended Ascot Races.
22	Attended Ascot Races.
25	Attended a reception in connection with the restoration of the Prince Christian Victor statue and the King George V memorial, Castle Hotel, Windsor.
	Attended a gala evening in aid of the Prince Philip Trust Fund, Blazers, Windsor.
26	Attended Meridian Day festivities, Greenwich Park.
	Attended the opening by the Queen of the Crown Estates Commissioners' new office development, Millbank, London.
	Left Waterloo Station for Dorset.
27	Visited the Royal Marines, Hamworthy, Poole, Dorset.

July

2	Visited Napier College, Edinburgh and attended the opening of its new library extension by the Queen.
	Arrived at the Palace of Holyroodhouse.
	Attended a reception marking the 200th anniversary of the Society of Solicitors, Parliament House, Edinburgh.
3	Visited the Royal Scottish Academy's summer exhibition, Edinburgh.
	Attended an Order of the Thistle installation service, St Giles' Cathedral, Edinburgh.
	Gave a luncheon party for Knights of the Thistle, Palace of Holyroodhouse.
	Attended a reception for Gold Standard achievers of the Duke of Edinburgh's Award, Palace of Holyroodhouse.
	Gave a dinner party, Palace of Holyroodhouse.
4	Visited the Scottish Veterans' residence, Whitefoord House, Edinburgh.
	Visited Queensberry House Hospital, Edinburgh.
	Gave a garden party, Palace of Holyroodhouse.
	Attended the Scottish Baroque Ensemble's 15th anniversary concert, Queen's Hall, Edinburgh.
5	Visited Bield Housing Association's Fairbairn Court, Greenlaw, Berwickshire.
	Visited Henderson Park, Coldstream.
	Attended the opening by the Queen of Hamish Morison Ltd's new hatchery, Duns.
	Visited Berwickshire High School and watched Sports Week events.
	Toured a grain-storing and drying complex, Craigswalls, Berwickshire.
	Visited Eyemouth Harbour.
	Attended the opening by the Queen of Swan Court sheltered housing scheme, Eyemouth.
	Visited Eyemouth and District Disabled Centre.
	Left the Palace of Holyroodhouse.
9	Entertained at dinner by the Canadian High Commissioner, 12 Upper Brook St, London.
	Gave a garden party, Buckingham Palace.
11	Opened O'Grady Court for the National Association of Housing Associations, West Ealing.
	Attended the Tyne-Tees *Face the Press* luncheon, Hyde Park Hotel, London.

	11	Held two audiences, Buckingham Palace.
		Attended a service in connection with the restoration of Westminster Abbey, London.
	12	Gave a garden party, Buckingham Palace.
	25	Left Heathrow Airport, London and arrived at Sondrestrom, Greenland via Prestwick and Reykjavik.
	26	Left Sondrestrom and arrived at Thompson, Manitoba via Frobisher and Churchill.
		Presented awards to gold standard achievers in the Duke of Edinburgh Award Scheme, Thompson.
	27	Left Thompson and arrived at Pasadina, via Salt Lake City.
	28	Attended a public veterinary inspection for the Los Angeles Olympics.
		Attended the opening ceremony of the Olympic Games, Coliseum, Los Angeles.
	29	Attended the three-day event dressage, Santa Anita.
		Attended a barbecue for equestrian visitors to Los Angeles, The Arboretum.
	30	Attended the three-day event dressage, Santa Anita.
	31	Attended a cocktail party and dinner, Fairbanks Ranch Clubhouse, St Malo Beach.

Engagements of **THE PRINCE OF WALES**
August 1983-July 1984

August	3	Opened and toured the new National Spinal Injuries Centre, Stoke Mandeville Hospital, Aylesbury, Buckinghamshire.
	28	Held an audience, Kensington Palace.
		Opened the 11th World Petroleum Congress, Royal Albert Hall, London.
September	3	Attended the Highland Games, Braemar, Deeside.
	21	Attended the Dairy Farming Event, National Agricultural Centre, Stoneleigh, Warwickshire.
		Attended a Prince's Trust Musical Concert, Royal Albert Hall, London.
October	2	Visited the Princess Louise Scottish Hospital, Bishopton, Renfrewshire.
		Attended a Royal Scottish Gala Variety Performance, Kings Theatre, Glasgow.
	5	Attended a British Film Institute Banquet, Guildhall, London.
	6	Attended a Welsh Guards luncheon, Officers' Mess, St James's Palace, London.
		Held two audiences, Kensington Palace.
		Attended a Barry Manilow Concert, Royal Festival Hall, London.
	13	Opened a new Holiday Home for the Multiple Sclerosis Society, Grantown-on-Spey, Moray.
		Visited Grant House for the elderly, Grantown-on-Spey, Moray.
	24	Attended a performance of *Hay Fever*, Queens Theatre, London.
	25	Held an audience, Kensington Palace.
	26	Attended the Friends of Covent Garden Chairman's luncheon, Stamford House, London.
	27	Visited Project Fullemploy, Great Eastern Street, London.
		Attended a British Aerospace dinner, RAF Bentley Priory, Stanmore, Middlesex.
	30	Began a three-day working visit to the Isles of Scilly.
November	2	Attended the unveiling by the Queen of the statue of Earl Mountbatten, Foreign Office Green, London.
		Attended a Royal College of Music Centenary Appeal Auction, Christie's, King Street, London.
		Attended a reception given by the Prime Minister, Banqueting Hall, Whitehall, London.
	3	Attended the Chiefs of Staff Meeting, Ministry of Defence, London.
		Attended the International Council of United World Colleges Chairman's dinner, Stafford Hotel, London.
	7	Attended a concert by Placido Domingo, Royal Festival Hall, London.
	8	Held an audience, Kensington Palace.
	9	Attended the dedication of the Falkland Islands Campaign Memorial, Guards Chapel, London.
		Attended the 10th anniversary dinner of Independent Local Radio, Mansion House, London.
	10	Presided at a meeting of the Prince's Council, Duchy of Cornwall Office, Buckingham Gate, London.

	12	Attended the Royal British Legion Festival of Remembrance, Royal Albert Hall, London.

12 Attended the Royal British Legion Festival of Remembrance, Royal Albert Hall, London.

13 Laid a wreath at the Cenotaph on behalf of the Queen, Remembrance Day ceremony, Whitehall, London.
Attended a Remembrance Day service, Guards' Chapel, London.
Laid a wreath at the Guards' Memorial, Horseguards, London.

15 Visited the Central District of the Duchy of Cornwall, and toured Duchy property in Plymouth and Dartmoor.
Attended a Duchy of Cornwall Central District Dinner, Manor House Hotel, Moretonhampstead.

16 Attended a meeting of the Duchy of Cornwall Wildlife and Landscape Advisory Group, Western District.
Attended a reception for representatives of Trade and Industry in Cornwall.

17 Met the Chairman and Trustees of the South Atlantic Fund, Kensington Palace.
Gave a reception for the Royal Jubilee Trusts and the Prince's Trust, Kensington Palace.

18 Held a Council on behalf of the Queen, Clarence House.

21 Visited Glamorgan Heritage Coast Committee Project, Mid-Glamorgan.
Visited Atlantic College, St Donat's, Wales.

22 Received winners of the Prince of Wales' Award for Rural Crafts, Kensington Palace.
Gave a luncheon party for industrialists concerned with the employment of disabled people, Kensington Palace.

23 Visited the IBM Factory, Greenock, Renfrewshire.
Attended a Council for National Academic Awards ceremony, McEwan's Hall, Edinburgh.

24 Visited the Waltham Forest Asian Centre Walthamstomw, London.
Saw an exhibition by John Ward, Maas Gallery, London.
Entertained at dinner by the High Commissioner for Canada, Upper Brook Street, London.

25 Visited the headquarters of the Prince of Wales' Division, Whittington Barracks, Lichfield, Staffordshire.
Opened the British Racing School, Newmarket, Cambridgeshire.

29 Presided at a Royal Jubilee Trusts Administrative Council meeting, Buckingham Palace.
Attended the Red Dragon Ball, Grosvenor House, London.

30 Attended a Canterbury Cathedral Appeal Fund Trustees' meeting, Canterbury.
Attended a Mary Rose Trust reception, Lloyds, London.

December 1 Attended a Commonwealth Development Corporation meeting, Hill Street, London.
Held an audience, Buckingham Palace.
Attended the Queen's evening reception for the Diplomatic Corps, Buckingham Palace.

2 Held an audience, Kensington Palace.

5 Attended a concert by the English Chamber Orchestra, State Apartments, Kensington Palace.

7 Opened Moorside Community School, Newcastle-upon-Tyne.
Visited Washington Waterfowl Park, near Sunderland.
Opened HM Coastguards Maritime Rescue Coordination Centre, Tynemouth.
Attended a Welsh National Opera performance of *Carmen*, Dominion Theatre, London.

13 Held two audiences, Kensington Palace.
Visited the Dobson Exhibition, National Portrait Gallery, London.
Gave a reception marking the publication of the Dartmoor Report concerning the Duchy of Cornwall, Kensington Palace.

14 Visited the exhibition *Albert, his Life and Work*, Royal College of Art, Kensington.
Visited old age pensioners in the Manor of Kennington, London.

15 Gave a reception in aid of the Prince of Wales' Award for Industrial Innovation and Production, Kensington Palace.

16 Held two audiences, Kensington Palace.

18 Attended a Friends of Covent Garden Christmas Party, Royal Opera House, Covent Garden, London.

19 Visited Westminster Hospital, London.
Visited St Thomas's Hospital, London.

20 Opened the Low Energy Factory during a visit to J.E.L. Energy Conservation Services Limited, Stockport, Greater Manchester.

	20	Visited the West Indian Sports and Social Club and Community Centre, Manchester.
		Attended the Malcolm Sargent Cancer Fund Carol Concert, Free Trade Hall, Manchester.
January	24	Embarked, at Portland Naval Base, on *HMS Glasgow*.
	26	Disembarked from *HMS Glasgow* at Glasgow.
	31	Visited a Zimbabwean sculptor's exhibition, Piccadilly, London.
February	1	Held two audiences, Kensington Palace.
		Visited the exhibition *Genius of Venice*, Royal Academy of Arts, London.
	2	Visited the 1st Battalion, the Welsh Guards, Pirbright, Surrey.
	7	Visited the National Hospital, Queen Square, London.
		Held two audiences, Kensington Palace.
	8	Attended the funeral of the Duke of Beaufort, Badminton.
		Chaired a seminar on Low Input Systems of Agriculture, Kensington Palace.
		Attended a reception given by the 2nd King Edward VII's Own Goorkhas, Ritz Hotel, London.
	9	Held an audience, Kensington Palace.
	10	Embarked on *HMS Walkerton*, Liverpool.
	14	Visited the Police Staff College, Bramshill, Hampshire.
		Gave a reception for The Prince's Trust, Kensington Palace.
	15	Visited Jaguar Cars Ltd, Allesley, Coventry.
	16	Attended the launch of the Farming and Wildlife Trust, Royal Society of Arts, London.
	21	Left Heathrow Airport, London, for Brunei.
	22	Arrived at Brunei, to be received by the Sultan.
		Attended an audience with the Sultan, New Istana.
	23	Attended an Independence Day National Assembly, National Stadium.
		Attended a buffet lunch, British High Commissioner's Residence.
		Toured the Churchill Museum.
		Attended a State Banquet, New Istana.
	24	Attended a military parade, Padang.
		Toured a missile gunboat, Muara Base.
		Visited an engineering hangar, Muara Base.
		Toured the gymnasium and swimming pool, Muara Base.
	25	Flew over Brunei Liquid Natural Gas Plant and oilfields.
		Visited Brunei Shell Petroleum headquarters Seria.
		Visited the 6th Gurkha Rifles, Tuker Lines, Seria, and lunched at the Officers' Mess.
		Left Brunei Airport for London, via Bahrain.
	26	Arrived back at Heathrow Airport, London.
	28	Visited the Information Technology Centre, Barnstaple, Devon.
		Named the National Environmental Research Council's ship *RRS Charles Darwin*, Appledore, Devon.
		Visited the North Devon Maritime Museum, Appledore, Devon.
	29	Visited Task Undertakings Ltd, Birmingham.
		Attended a concert given by Genesis, National Exhibition Centre, Birmingham.
March	1	Inaugurated a Bottle Bank, Kensington Palace.
	2	Visited H.M. Institution, Castle Huntly, Longforgan, Dundee.
	6	Presided at a meeting of The Prince's Council, Buckingham Gate, London.
		Entertained The Prince's Council members to luncheon, Kensington Palace.
		Attended a Jewish Welfare Board dinner, Guildhall, London.
	7	Visited the Inner London Probation Service headquarters, Great Peter Street, London.
		Visited Sherborne House Centre, Decima Street, London.
		Held an audience, Kensington Palace.
	8	Attended the annual luncheon of the Governors and members of the Royal Association of British Dairy Farmers, Hatfield House, Hertfordshire.
	9	Visited the Fire Service College, Moreton-in-Marsh, Gloucestershire.
		Visited the Sue Ryder Home, Leckhampton Court, Gloucestershire.
	13	Gave a luncheon in connection with his Advisory Group on Disability, Kensington Palace.
		Presided at a committee meeting of the Royal Jubilee Trusts, Kensington Palace.

14	Attended the Royal Naval Film Corporation's annual general meeting and luncheon, on board *HMS Resident*, King's Reach, London.
15	Visited the factory of Westall Richardson Ltd, Sheffield.
	Visited St Luke's Hospice, Eccleshall, Sheffield.
	Attended a reception given by the Lord Mayor of Sheffield, Town Hall.
	Attended a performance of *Tosca*, Crucible Theatre, Sheffield.
16	Held an audience, Kensington Palace.
18	Left London for Tanzania.
19	Arrived at Dar-es-Salaam.
	Attended a briefing at the Commonwealth Development Corporation Office.
	Visited the House of Arts, Dar-es-Salaam.
	Attended a reception at the British High Commission.
	Laid a wreath at the Dar-es-Salaam Commonwealth War Graves Commission cemetery.
	Visited the President of Tanzania.
	Attended a dinner given by the Tanzanian President, State House, Dar-es-Salaam.
20	Left Dar-es-Salaam for Njombe.
	Toured the Commonwealth Development Estate at Njombe.
	Attended a reception for road construction staff, Hagafiro.
21	Left Njombe for Zambia, and arrived at Lusaka.
	Visited the President of Zambia.
	Attended a reception at the British High Commission, Lusaka.
22	Visited a Commonwealth Development Corporation sugar estate, Kaleya.
	Toured a fish farm, Nakambala.
	Attended a dinner given by the Zambian President, State House, Lusaka.
23	Toured a copper mine, Kasompe.
	Visited a museum, Livingstone.
	Visited the Victoria Falls.
	Attended a reception given by the Central Committee of Southern Province, Livingstone.
24	Left Livingstone for Zimbabwe and arrived at Harare.
	Entertained to luncheon by the President of Zimbabwe, State House, Harare.
	Visited the Henderson Agricultural Research Station, Mazowe.
	Attended a Government reception, Harare.
25	Visited the Great Zimbabwe ruins, Masvingo.
	Attended a reception at the British High Commission, Harare.
	Attended a dinner with the Prime Minister of Zimbabwe.
26	Toured a cattle station, Donnington Farm, near Harare.
	Visited Chibero Agricultural College.
	Left Harare for Botswana and arrived at Gaborone.
	Attended a dinner given by the President of Botswana, State House, Gaborone.
27	Visited the Gaborone Dam.
	Toured Gaborone Secondary School.
	Attended a reception, State House, Gaborone.
	Attended a reception, British High Commission, Gaborone.
28	Visited a burial ground, Serowi, and attended a village reception.
	Visited a diamond mine, Orapa.
	Toured a museum, Gaborone.
29	Visited the Botswana Meat Corporation abattoir, Lobatse.
	Toured a Commonwealth Development Corporation ranch, Molopo.
30	Travelled to the Chobe River for a four-day private holiday.

April	4	Arrived at Gatwick Airport from Botswana.
	10	Met the Amir of Bahrain at the beginning of his State Visit, Windsor Castle.
		Attended the State banquet for the Amir of Bahrain, Windsor Castle.
	11	Held two audiences, Kensington Palace.
	24	Visited Home Farm, Stoke Climsland, Duchy of Cornwall.
	26	Attended an agricultural briefing, National Institute of Agricultural Engineering, Silsoe, Bedfordshire.

	26	Gave a reception marking the British Council's fiftieth anniversary, Kensington Palace.
		Attended the International Council of United World Colleges Chairman's Dinner, Athenaeum, Pall Mall, London.
	27	Presented The Prince of Wales' awards for Industrial Innovation and Production, Kensington Palace.

May

	1	Opened a new archaeology gallery, University Museum of Archaeology and Anthropology, Cambridge.
		Opened the new area office of ICFC, and visited industrial units, Cambridge Science Park.
	2	Held two audiences, Kensington Palace.
		Attended a Royal Warrant Holders' Association reception, Hilton Hotel, London.
	3	Opened MacEwen Court sheltered housing development, Inverness.
		Visited the National Trust for Scotland's Visitors' Centre, Culloden.
	9	Opened Dinorwig Power Station. Llanberis, Gwynedd.
	11	Held three audiences, Kensington Palace.
	14	Attended a banquet at the Royal Academy of Arts, Piccadilly, London.
	16	Visited the Royal Forestry Society's Thoresby Estate, Nottinghamshire.
	17	Visited the Jorvik Viking Centre and Coppergate development, York.
		Attended a reception given by the Queen, Buckingham Palace.
	20	Attended a Royal Opera House fund-raising concert, Royal Opera House, Covent Garden, London.
	21	Visited the Chelsea Flower Show, Royal Hospital, Chelsea.
		Attended a concert given by the Bach Choir and English Chamber Orchestra, Royal Festival Hall, London.
	22	Attended a concert in aid of the Royal College of Music Centenary Appeal, Exbury, Hampshire.
	23	Visited HM Prison, Wormwood Scrubs, London.
		Visited the Pre-Raphaelite exhibition, Tate Gallery, London.
	24	Visited the Royal Ordnance Survey headquarters, Southampton.
		Visited the Royal Commission of Historical Monuments office, Southampton.
		Attended Grand Day dinner, Gray's Inn, London.
	25	Attended an *HMS Kelly* reunion dinner, *HMS President*, Kings Reach, London.
	29	Opened Street Farm workshops, Doughton, Tetbury, Gloucestershire.
		Attended a meeting of the Duchy of Cornwall's Wildlife and Landscape Advisory Group, Newton St Loe, Bath.
	30	Visited the Town Hall, Chester.
		Toured the general wing of the West Cheshire Hospital, Chester.
		Visited the Golden Square Shopping Centre, Warrington.
		Attended a gala sesquicentenary evening and presented the Royal Gold Medal for Architecture, for the Royal Institute of British Architects, Hampton Court Palace.
	31	Held two audiences, Kensington Palace.

June

	2	Attended a dinner in aid of United World Colleges and the Mary Rose Trust, Sutton Place, Guildford.
	4	Attended a performance of *L'Elisir d'Amore*, Royal Opera House, Covent Garden, London.
	5	Visited the Game Conservancy headquarters, Fordingbridge, Hampshire.
		Attended an Allied landings commemorative ceremony, Ranville, Normandy.
		Attended a Development Commission anniversary reception, St James's Palace.
	6	Visited the Western District of the Duchy of Cornwall.
	7	Visited the Royal Cornwall Show, Wadebridge.
	8	Held two audiences, Kensington Palace.
		Attended a rock gala, Royal Albert Hall, London.
	9	Attended a dinner given by the Queen for Heads of State and delegates attending the London Economic Summit, Buckingham Palace.
	11	Attended the film première *Indiana Jones and the Temple of Doom*, Empire Theatre, Leicester Square, London.
	13	Visited Cranfield Institute of Technology, Bedford.

14	Visited the Chelsea Physic Garden, London.
15	Visited RAF Brawdy, Wales.
	Attended the Gordon Highlanders' annual regimental dinner, Caledonian Club, London.
16	Attended the Queen's Birthday parade, Horse Guards Parade, London.
19	Opened the new headquarters of the Transport Department's Accidents Investigations Branch, Royal Aircraft Establishment, Farnborough, Hampshire.
21	Opened the Library extension, St David's University College, Lampeter.
	Visited Lampeter Town Hall for charter centenary celebrations.
	Visited Boverton Farm, Glamorgan, Duchy of Cornwall Eastern District.
26	Held an audience, Kensington Palace.
	Attended a meeting of the steering committee of the Prince of Wales' Award for Industrial Innovation and Production, Engineering Council, Canberra House, London.
27	Visited the Douglas Arter Centre for multihandicapped young people, Salisbury.
	Opened and toured the Duke of Cornwall Spinal Treatment Centre, Odstock Hospital, Salisbury.
	Attended a meeting of the Duchy of Cornwall's Advisory Group on Archaeology, Fordington, Dorchester.
28	Visited woodlands, Eastern District, Duchy of Cornwall.
29	Attended the memorial service for Sir John Betjeman, Westminster Abbey.

July	3	Attended an Order of the Thistle installation service, St Giles' Cathedral, Edinburgh.
		Attended the Queen's luncheon for Knights of the Thistle, Palace of Holyroodhouse.
	5	Attended a Neil Diamond concert, National Exhibition Centre, Birmingham.
	9	Opened the *Mary Rose* exhibition, H.M. Naval Base, Portsmouth.
	10	Attended the Queen's garden party, Buckingham Palace.
	11	Left Heathrow Airport, London for West Germany.
	12	Visited the 1st Battalion The Royal Regiment of Wales, Stornoway Barracks, Lemgo.
		Visited the 1st Battalion The Gordon Highlanders, Barossa Barracks, Hemer, and Iserlohn.
	13	Visited RAF Laarbruch.
		Left West Germany for England and arrived at Birmingham International Airport.
		Attended the Chindits Old Comrades Association reunion, Gamecock Barracks, Nuneaton, Warwickshire.
	17	Presided at a meeting of the Prince's Council, Buckingham Gate.
		Attended the Queen's garden party, Buckingham Palace.
	18	Visited Toynbee Hall, East London, and opened the new Glower and Dean Estate.
		Gave a reception in connection with the Prince of Wales' Award for Industrial Innovation and Production, Kensington Palace.
	19	Attended a colloquium on conventional medicine and complementary therapies, Royal Society of Medicine, London.
	20	Visited The Prince's Trust camp, Badbury Rings, Wimborne, Dorset.
	22	Opened the 7th World Wheelchair Games, Ludwig Guttman Sports Centre, Stoke Mandeville, Buckinghamshire.
	23	Began a four-day visit to the Eastern District of the Duchy of Cornwall.
	26	Attended a performance of the Royal Tournament, Earl's Court, London.
	27	Held two audiences, Kensington Palace.

Engagements of **THE PRINCESS OF WALES**
August 1983-July 1984

August	3	Attended the opening by the Prince of Wales of the National Spinal Injuries Centre, Stoke Mandeville Hospital, Aylesbury, Buckinghamshire.
September	3	Attended the Highland Games, Braemar, Deeside.
	7	Visited the James Keiller factory, Dundee.
	9	Visited the Coatbridge Training Workshop, and the Coatbridge Projects, Coatbridge, Lanarkshire.

	20	Visited the MacIntyre Community of Mentally Handicapped Children and Adults, Westoning Manor, Bedfordshire.
	21	Attended a Prince's Trust Musical Concert, Royal Albert Hall, London.
October	2	Visited the Princess Louise Scottish Hospital, Bishopton, Renfrewshire.
		Attended a Royal Scottish Gala Variety Performance, Kings Theatre, Glasgow.
	6	Attended a Welsh Guards luncheon, Officers' Mess, St James's Palace, London.
		Attended a Barry Manilow Concert, Royal Festival Hall, London.
	24	Attended a Performance of *Hay Fever*, Queen's Theatre, London.
	26	Received a copy of *Stories for a Prince*, published in aid of the Royal National Institute for the Blind, Café Royal, Regent Street, London.
	27	Opened the West Indian Parents Family Centre, Brixton, London.
November	1	Opened and toured a new block at the London Chest Hospital, Bethnal Green, London.
	2	Attended the unveiling by the Queen of the statue of Earl Mountbatten, Foreign Office Green, London.
		Presented prizes to winners of the Pre-School Playgroups Association's Build a House Project, Kensington Palace.
		Attended a reception given by the Prime Minister, Banqueting House, Whitehall, London.
	7	Attended a concert by Placido Domingo, Royal Festival Hall, London.
	9	Attended the dedication of the Falkland Islands Campaign Memorial, Guards Chapel, London.
		Attended the 10th Anniversary dinner of Independent Local Radio, Mansion House, London.
	12	Attended the Royal British Legion Festival of Remembrance, Royal Albert Hall, London.
	13	Attended the Remembrance Day ceremony, Cenotaph, Whitehall, London.
	15	Attended the Duchy of Cornwall Central District dinner, Manor House Hotel, Moretonhampstead.
	16	Visited the Mount Edgcumbe Hospice, St Austell, Cornwall.
	17	Visited the British Deaf Association's Headquarters, Carlisle, Cumbria.
	18	Visited the Maytrees Home for the Blind, Bristol.
	21	Visited Atlantic College, St Donat's, Wales.
		Visited the Cardiff Community Dance project, Cardiff.
	24	Visited Waltham Forest Asian Centre, Walthamstow, London.
		Entertained at dinner by the High Commissioner for Canada, Upper Brook Street, London.
	25	Attended the opening by the Prince of Wales of the British Racing School, Newmarket, Cambridgeshire.
	29	Attended a National Rubella Council reception, Lancaster House, London.
		Attended the Red Dragon Ball, Grosvenor House Hotel, London.
December	1	Attended a rehearsal of the London City Ballet, Festival Ballet House, London.
		Attended the Queen's evening reception for the Diplomatic Corps, Buckingham Palace.
	2	Opened the Wantage Adult Training Centre, Oxfordshire.
	6	Opened the Park Lane Fair, Park Lane Hotel, Piccadilly, London.
	7	Visited Queen Elizabeth II Silver Jubilee Activity Centre, Burseldon, Hampshire.
		Attended a Welsh National Opera performance of *Carmen*, Dominion Theatre, London.
	14	Visited the exhibition *Albert, his Life and Work*, Royal College of Art, Kensington, London.
		Visited old age pensioners in the Manor of Kennington, London.
	18	Attended the Friends of Covent Garden Christmas Party, Royal Opera House, Covent Garden, London.
	19	Visited Westminster Hospital, London.
		Visited St Thomas's Hospital, London.
	20	Opened a new Extra Care Centre, Abbeyfield Downing House, Withington, Manchester.
		Attended the Malcolm Sargent Cancer Fund Carol Concert, Free Trade Hall, Manchester.
January	24	Attended a Grocers' Company reception, Grocers' Hall, London.
February	1	Visited the exhibition *Genius of Venice*, Royal Academy of Arts, London.
	8	Attended the funeral of the Duke of Beaufort, Badminton.

	8	Attended a reception given by the 2nd King Edward VII's Own Goorkhas, Ritz Hotel, London.
	11	Left Heathrow Airport London for Norway.
		Attended the London City Ballet's performance of *Carmen*, Konserthaus, Oslo.
	12	Left Oslo and returned to London.
	15	Visited Jaguar Cars Ltd, Allesley, Coventry.
	21	Visited the Royal Marsden Hospital, Sutton, Surrey.
	22	Visited the British Red Cross Society's national headquarters, Grosvenor Crescent, London.
	29	Visited St Mary's Hospice, Selly Park, Birmingham.
		Attended a concert given by Genesis, National Exhibition Centre, Birmingham.
March	6	Attended a Jewish Welfare Board dinner, Guildhall, London.
	7	Visited the Lisson Grove Health Centre, London.
	13	Visited the Rheumatology Unit, Hammersmith Hospital, London.
	15	Visited the factory of Westall Richardson Ltd, Sheffield.
		Visited St Luke's Hospice, Eccleshall, Sheffield.
		Attended the Lord Mayor of Sheffield's reception, Town Hall, Sheffield.
	20	Visited *Woman's Own* magazine, Waterloo, London.
	22	Visited T.W. Kempton Ltd, Burleys Way, Leicester.
		Visited Charnwood Mencap Society, Loughborough.
	23	Opened the Royal National Orthopaedic Hospital's new spinal injuries unit, Stanmore, Middlesex.
	27	Opened and toured new rehearsal studios for the Welsh National Opera, Cardiff.
	29	Visited the Metropolitan Police Training Centre, Hendon, London.
April	3	Visited the Workface Centre, Glastonbury.
	5	Visited the factory of Royal Doulton tableware, Burslem, Stoke-on-Trent.
	10	Met the Amir of Bahrain at the beginning of his State Visit, Windsor Castle.
		Attended the State banquet for the Amir of Bahrain, Windsor Castle.
	11	Visited British Airways and the British Airports Authority, Heathrow Airport, London.
	16	Attended a rehearsal of the National Children's Orchestra, Wellington College, Berkshire.
May	2	Attended a Royal Warrant Holders' reception, Hilton Hotel, Park Lane, London.
	8	Accepted the honorary Fellowship of the Royal College of Physicians and Surgeons of Glasgow.
	14	Attended a banquet at the Royal Society of Arts, Piccadilly, London.
	17	Attended a reception given by the Queen, Buckingham Palace.
	20	Attended a Royal Opera House fund-raising concert, Royal Opera House, Covent Garden, London.
	21	Visited the Chelsea Flower Show, Royal Hospital, Chelsea.
		Attended a concert given by the Bach Choir and English Chamber Orchestra, Royal Festival Hall, London.
	23	Visited The Albany, Douglas Way, London SE8.
	29	Attended the opening by the Prince of Wales of the Street Farm workshops. Doughton, Tetbury, Gloucestershire.
	30	Visited the Town Hall, Chester.
		Toured the general wing of the West Cheshire Hospital, Chester.
		Visited Golden Square Shopping Centre, Warrington.
June	2	Attended a dinner in aid of United World Colleges and the Mary Rose Trust, Sutton Place, Guildford.
	6	Opened Callard and Bowser Group's new factory and head office, Waterton, South Glamorgan.
	8	Attended a rock gala, Royal Albert Hall, London.
	11	Attended the film première of *Indiana Jones and the Temple of Doom*, Empire Theatre, Leicester Square, London.
	16	Witnessed the Queen's Birthday Parade, Horse Guards Parade, London.
	27	Visited the Douglas Arter Centre for multihandicapped young people, Salisbury.

	27	Attended the opening by the Prince of Wales of the Duke of Cornwall Spinal Treatment Centre, Odstock, Salisbury.
July	5	Attended a Neil Diamond concert, National Exhibition Centre, Birmingham.
	24	Opened the Harris Birthright Research Unit for foetal medicine, King's College Hospital, London.
	26	Attended a performance of the Royal Tournament, Earl's Court, London.

Engagements of **PRINCE ANDREW**
August 1983-July 1984

August	15	Disembarked from the Royal Yacht *Britannia*, Aberdeen, and drove to Balmoral Castle.
	16	Visited British Airways Helicopters Base, Aberdeen.
September	17	Visited RAF Finningley, on Battle of Britain at Home Day.
		Presented the King's Cup Air Race Awards, RAF Finningley.
October	6	Attended the Victoria Cross and George Cross Association reunion dinner, Café Royal, Regent Street, London.
	14	Presented the Royal Aero Club Annual Awards, RAF Museum, Hendon.
November	2	Attended the unveiling by the Queen of the statue of Earl Mountbatten, Foreign Office Green, London.
		Attended a reception given by the Prime Minister, Banqueting House, Whitehall, London.
	12	Attended the Royal British Legion Festival of Remembrance, Royal Albert Hall, London.
	13	Laid a wreath at the Cenotaph, Remembrance Day ceremony, Whitehall, London.
December	14	Attended the charity première of *Never Say Never Again*, Warner Theatre, Leicester Square, London.
February	11	Attended the Tiger Club's annual dinner, and presented awards, Hilton Hotel, Gatwick.
April	1	Left RAF Brize Norton and arrived at Wideawake Airfield, Ascension.
		Boarded *HMS Herald* for St Helena.
	5	Arrived at St Helena and attended welcoming ceremonies at the Castle.
		Visited exhibitions in Jamestown.
		Attended an open-air children's concert, Jamestown.
		Attended a carnival, Jamestown.
		Attended a reception at the Castle, Jamestown.
	6	Toured St Helena island by car.
		Visited Longwood House, Napoleon's exile home, St Helena.
		Presented prizes at an inter-district sports event, Francis Plain.
		Embarked on *HMS Herald* and sailed for Ascension.
	9	Arrived at Ascension and was welcomed at Georgetown pierhead.
		Toured Georgetown by car.
		Met residents of the village of Two Boats.
		Visited Ascension school.
	10	Toured airhead and new construction work, RAF Travellers Hill.
		Left Ascension by aircraft, and arrived RAF Brize Norton.
	15	Left Heathrow Airport for Los Angeles via San Francisco.
		Welcomed at the Beverly Wilshire Hotel, Los Angeles.
		Attended an informal supper with the American Committee for Gordonstoun School Golden Jubilee, Los Angeles.
	16	Attended a *Britain Comes to Beverly Hills* breakfast, Beverly Wilshire Hotel.
		Toured local shops and inspected displays of British goods, Los Angeles.
		Toured the McDonnell Douglas Corporation's plant, Long Beach.

	16	Viewed the Spruce Goose Exhibition, Long Beach.
		Visited the British Consulate-General Offices, Los Angeles.
		Attended a reception and dinner party with Gordonstoun School students, Beverly Wilshire Hotel.
	17	Toured the M-G-M/United Artists film studios, Thalberg Building.
		Attended a reception given by the Mayor of Los Angeles, City Hall.
		Toured the Plaza and Cultural Centre, Los Angeles.
		Attended a Mexican-style lunch, Art Gallery, Los Angeles.
		Toured the Watts Labour Community Action Committee's housing project, and visited a completed development, Los Angeles.
	18	Visited a helicopter ground trainer, Naval Air Station, San Diego.
		Attended a luncheon on *U.S.S. Constellation*.
		Visited the Aeronautical Museum, Balboa Park, San Diego.
		Toured the Museum of Photographic Arts, San Diego.
		Attended a reception given by Lord Grade, Beverly Wilshire Hotel, Los Angeles.
		Attended a British Olympic Association dinner and entertainment, Beverly Wilshire Hotel.
	19	Toured projects at the Jet Propulsion Laboratory, Pasadena.
		Toured the Seismological Laboratory, Pasadena.
		Attended a luncheon with students at the Athenaeum Club, Pasadena.
		Left Los Angeles for London.
	20	Arrived at Heathrow Airport, London, and drove to Windsor.
	27	Attended the annual St George's House Lecture, St George's Chapel, Windsor.
May	3	Opened the photographic exhibition *Lives of the Saints*, Commonwealth Institute, Kensington.
	4	Attended the Royal Yachtsman's Reunion Dinner, Guildhall, Portsmouth.
	11	Received the Livery of the Guild of Air Pilots and Air Navigators, Eccleston Street, London.
June	9	Attended a dinner party given by the Queen for Heads of State and delegates attending the London Economic Summit, Buckingham Palace.
	24	Attended the British Helicopter Championships and presented prizes, Castle Ashby, Northamptonshire.
July	24	Took the Salute, Royal Tournament, Earl's Court, London.

Engagements of **PRINCE EDWARD**
August 1983- July 1984

August	15	Disembarked from the Royal Yacht *Britannia*, Aberdeen, and drove to Balmoral Castle.
September	3	Attended the Highland Games, Braemar, Deeside.
November	2	Attended the unveiling by the Queen of the statue of Earl Mountbatten, Foreign Office Green, London.
		Attended a reception given by the Prime Minister, Banqueting House, Whitehall, London.
December	13	Represented the Queen at the State Funeral of Sir Keith Holyoake, former New Zealand Prime Minister, St Paul's Cathedral, Wellington, New Zealand.
June	14	Attended Beating Retreat, Horse Guards Parade, London.

Engagements of **PRINCESS ANNE**
August 1983-July 1984

August 2 Attended the Admiral's Cup Trophy Race, Christchurch Bay, Hampshire.
8 Embarked on the Royal Yacht *Britannia*.
15 Disembarked from the Royal Yacht *Britannia*, Aberdeen, and drove to Balmoral Castle.
24 Opened the Thamesdown Housing Association's Elderly Persons' Dwelling, and toured the Sheltered Development and Disabled Persons Unit, Park Farm, Swindon.
29 Attended the Korea National Dance Company's Gala Performance, Queen Elizabeth Hall, London.

September 5 Opened the British Equine Veterinary Association's Congress, York University.
7 Attended a National Olympic Committee Meeting, International Students' House, London.
13 Attended the launch of the 'Round England Run', Grosvenor House Hotel, London.
Attended a Farriers Company Court Meeting and was installed as Upper Warden of the Company, Innholders Hall, London.
Attended a Farriers Company installation service, St Michael Paternoster Royal Church, College Hill, London.
Attended a Farriers Company dinner, Innholders Hall, London.
16 Opened and toured Clifford Dairies' new bottling plant, Bracknell, Berkshire.
Opened the National Exhibition of Children's Art, Mall Galleries, London.
19 Opened and toured Castle Wholesale and Distribution Centre, Glasgow.
Named the locomotive *Sir William Burrell*, Glasgow Central Station.
Entertained at luncheon by the Lord Provost of Glasgow, City Chambers, Glasgow.
Opened and toured the West of Scotland Science Park, Glasgow.
Opened and toured a new adventure playground for handicapped children, Linn Park, Glasgow.
20 Visited the Moray Group of the Riding for the Disabled Association, Drumbain, Rothes.
Opened a new club room for the Caithness Group of the Riding for the Disabled Association, Halkirk.
21 Held two audiences, Buckingham Palace.
22 Dined with officers of the Balmoral Royal Guard, and the Royal Scots, Victoria Barracks, Ballater, Deeside.
27 Visited the Woolverston new housing scheme for the elderly, Winchester, Hampshire.
Entertained at luncheon on board the *Solent Enterprise*.
Opened Southampton Grain Silos Limited's new building.
Visited Magnet Enterprises' training workshop for the unemployed.
28 Visited the 3rd Volunteer Battalion, Worcestershire and Sherwood Foresters' Regiment, Sennybridge.
29 Visited the Chelsea Group of the Riding for the Disabled Association, Royal Mews, Buckingham Palace.
Attended a Carmen's Company Ladies' Court Dinner, Innholders Hall, London.
30 Opened and toured the Wavin Plastics Limited factory complex, Chippenham, Wiltshire.
Attended a National Union of Townswomen's Guild Federation Dinner, City Hall, Cardiff.

October 1 Visited the 35th Signal Regiment, St George's Barracks, Sutton Coldfield.
Attended the 35th Signal Regiment Dinner and Officers' Mess Ball, City of Birmingham Council House.
3 Attended the Horse of the Year Show Gala Night, Wembley Arena, London.
4 Opened a new food hall, Harrods Limited, Knightsbridge, London.
Opened and toured the Arthur Ackermann and Son Bicentenary Exhibition, Old Bond Street, London.
Attended a Carmen's Company luncheon, and received a Land Rover for the Save the Children Fund, Guildhall, London.
Attended a Gieves and Hawkes Anniversary Fashion Show, Malvern, Hereford and Worcester.
5 Visited Bristol Grammar School, and opened the new teaching block.
Dined with Royal Artillery Officers, Woolwich, London.

	6	Attended Save the Children Fund Meetings, Queen Elizabeth Hall, London.
	24	Attended the Hackney Horse Society Centenary Dinner, Saddlers Hall, London.
	25	Attended the launch of the Westminster Children's Hospital Bone Marrow Unit Appeal, Dorchester Hotel, London.
		Visited Queen Mary College, Mile End Road, London.
	26	Attended a St John Musical Society Concert, Exeter Cathedral, Devon.
		Attended a St John Ambulance and Nursing Cadets' reception, County Hall, Exeter.
	27	Attended the Family Welfare Association's Celebrity Luncheon, Intercontinental Hotel, London.
	29	Visited the Devonport Child Care Project, Plymouth, Devon.
		Attended a Save the Children Gala Concert, Exeter University, Devon.
	31	Attended the National Union of Townswomen's Guilds' Hallowe'en Fayre, Ruislip, Middlesex.
		Attended the White Ensign Association's Dinner, Guildhall, London.
November	2	Attended the unveiling by the Queen of the statue of Earl Mountbatten, Foreign Office Green, London.
		Attended a reception given by the Prime Minister, Banqueting House, Whitehall, London.
		Opened the new Department of Nursing Studies, Chelsea College, London.
		Attended the première of *Oliver Twist*, Classic Cinema, Haymarket, London.
		Attended a Save the Children Fund Dinner, Claridge's Hotel, London.
	3	Opened and toured Princess Anne House, for the Northampton Junior Chamber, Waldington Court, Northamptonshire.
		Opened and toured the new factory of Magnetopulse Limited, Northampton.
		Visited the Royal Theatre, Northampton.
		Opened and toured the Police Headquarters' new extension, Wootton Hall, Northampton.
		Attended the British Olympic Appeal reception, Barclays Bank, Lombard Street, London.
	4	Attended a Road Haulage Association luncheon, and received a Land Rover for the Save the Children Fund, Grand Hotel, Bristol.
		Visited Monkton Combe Junior School, Combe Down, Bath and opened the new law building.
	7	Opened and toured the Home Farm Trust's new home, Milton, Oxfordshire.
		Attended the Euromoney reception, Banqueting Hall, Whitehall, London.
	10	Attended a charity reception and dinner, Royal Artillery Mess, Woolwich, London.
	12	Attended the Royal British Legion Festival of Remembrance, Royal Albert Hall, London.
	13	Attended the Remembrance Day ceremony, Cenotaph, Whitehall, London.
	14	Attended a Riding for the Disabled Association dinner, Bristol.
	15	Attended the Riding for the Disabled Association's Annual General Meeting and Conference, Grand Hotel, Bristol.
		Attended the Royal Counties Veterinary Association's banquet, Castle Hotel, Windsor.
	17	Visited the Hyde Park group of the Riding for the Disabled Association, Knightsbridge Barracks, London.
	18	Held two audiences, Gatcombe Park House.
		Attended a performance of *The Great Waltz*, Bristol Hippodrome.
	21	Attended a Governmental presentation on micro-electronics education, Grand Hotel, Bristol.
		Visited the Bristol Telecommunications Business Centre.
		Presented awards for business sponsorship of the arts, Savoy Hotel, London.
		Attended a dinner given by the 14th/20th King's Hussars, Cavalry and Guards' Club, London.
	22	Attended the awards presentation to nurses of the Hospitals for Sick Children, Guildhall, London.
	23	Attended a Royal Corps of Signals Institution lecture, Royal Commonwealth Society, London.
	24	Attended the Foundation Day celebrations, Institute of Education, Bedford Way, London.
	25	Attended a Young Farmers Club's Annual General Meeting, Alnwick Castle, Northumberland.
	28	Toured the Pilton Centre, Edinburgh.
		Opened and toured Harmeny School, Edinburgh.
		Opened Knightsbridge adventure playground, Livingston, West Lothian.
		Received a play bus for handicapped children, Glasgow.

December	1	Attended King's College Glasgow Commemoration Week celebrations, University of London.
		Attended the Queen's evening reception for the Diplomatic Corps, Buckingham Palace.
	7	Attended a reception to launch the 1984 Royal Tournament, St James's Palace, London.
		Attended the St John gala ball, Intercontinental Hotel, London.
	8	Visited Benenden School, Cranbrook, Kent.
		Attended a reception to launch the Charing Cross Medical Research Centre Appeal, St James's Palace, London.
	9	Visited the School of Signals, Blandford Camp, Dorset.
	14	Attended the Arab Gala Dinner, Savoy Hotel, London.
	15	Accepted a motor car from the Ford Motor Company, Save the Children Fund Headquarters, London.
	20	Attended the Christmas Celebrations, Westminster Cathedral, London.
	21	Attended the Save the Children Fund Annual Carol Concert, Royal Albert Hall, London.
January	6	Attended a British Olympic Association reception, Town Hall, King's Lynn, Norfolk.
	23	Left Gatwick Airport, London and arrived at Houston Airport, Texas, U.S.A.
		Attended a British Olympic Association buffet supper, Courtlandt Place, Houston.
	24	Visited Texas Heart Institute, St. Luke's Episcopalian Hospital, Houston.
		Sailed down the Houston Ship Channel.
		Toured Armand Bayou Nature Reserve.
		Attended a British Olympic Association reception, Four Seasons Hotel, Houston.
		Attended a British Olympic Association dinner, Exxon Building, Houston.
	25	Toured Ashton Villa and watched a slide-show, Galveston.
		Inspected restoration work on the *Elissa*, Galveston.
		Attended luncheon, Wentletrap Hotel, Galveston.
		Visited the French Quarter, New Orleans.
		Attended a dinner at the residence of James Coleman Senior, New Orleans.
	26	Visited riding stables, Santa Rosa, New Orleans.
		Toured the Evergreen Plantation.
		Inspected the Windsor Court collection of British art, Gallier Hall, New Orleans.
		Attended dinner, Rex Room, Antoine's, New Orleans.
	27	Watched farming activities, Turnbow Ranch, Brenham.
		Visited the Scattered Oaks Ranch, near Brenham.
		Left for Houston, and returned to Britain.
	28	Arrived at Gatwick Airport, London, from the U.S.A.
	30	Presented awards for the National Design Competition for Electronic Devices to Help the Disabled, Institution of Electrical Engineers, London.
February	1	Attended the Farriers Company's Court Ladies' Dinner, Innholders Hall, London.
	7	Attended a Lord Mayor's luncheon, Old Bailey, London.
		Visited the Yugoslav Ambassador to Britain, Hyde Park Gate, London.
		Attended a reception for the Westminster Medical School Research Trust, Speaker's House, London.
		Visited Independent Television News, ITN House, Wells Street, London.
	8	Attended the funeral of the Duke of Beaufort, Badminton.
		Attended the Warwickshire Gang Show gala evening, Royal Shakespeare Theatre, Stratford-upon-Avon.
	11	Left RAF Lyneham for Yugoslavia and arrived at Sarajevo Airport.
		Attended a reception for the British Winter Olympics team, Sarajevo.
		Attended a dinner, Holiday Inn, Sarajevo.
	12	Visited the President of the Olympic Organising Committee.
		Called on the President of Bosnia-Hercegovina.
		Watched Olympic speed-skating, luge and ice-dancing competitions.
		Visited the Winter Olympic Village, Sarajevo.
		Attended a dinner at the Restaurant Palata.
	13	Watched speed-skating, giant slalom and bobsleigh competitions.
		Watched the British bobsleigh team in training.

13   Attended a supper at the Olympic Village, Sarajevo.
      Watched ice-hockey matches, Zetra.
14   Watched biathlon and ice-dancing competitions, Zetra.
15   Left Sarajevo for Morocco.
      Toured Khemisset Save the Children Fund School, near Rabat.
      Visited the Moroccan Royal Family, Royal Palace, Rabat.
      Attended the British Ambassador's dinner, Ambassador's Residence, Rabat.
16   Left Rabat for the Gambia, and arrived at Banjul Airport.
      Attended a reception for members of the British community in Banjul, High Commissioner's
      Residence.
17   Visited Medical Research Council Laboratories, Fajars.
      Received the keys of the City of Banjul.
      Called on the President of the Gambia.
      Toured the Port of Banjul.
      Toured GPMB Oil Mill, Benton Bridge.
      Attended a presidential reception for Independence Day, State House, Banjul.
18   Attended the Gambia's Independence Day parade, MacCarthy Square, Banjul.
      Sailed, attended dinner and spent the night on board the *M.V. Lady Chilel Jawara*, Bintang.
19   Arrived at Carrols Wharf and disembarked.
      Visited Charmen.
      Toured a sub-dispensary, village garden and health worker's compound at Buduk.
      Visited a village well at Ker Jibel.
      Toured the Kuntaur Health Centre.
      Visited a village well and school at Galleh Manda.
      Visited a leprosy camp at Allatentu.
      Attended a luncheon with Save the Children Fund staff at Bansang.
      Attended a briefing on Primary Health Care and SCF work, Bansang.
      Attended a briefing on a schistosomiasis research project, at a field station at Basse
      Santa Su.
20   Toured the Basse Health Centre.
      Toured a hospital at Bansang.
      Visited a health worker at Kerewan-Samba-Sirra.
      Visited a village well and met health workers at Madina Umfally.
      Toured a health centre at Kudang.
      Attended a dinner with the crew of the Queen's Flight, Lamar Restaurant, Banjul.
21   Left Banjul Airport for Upper Volta.
      Arrived at Ouagadougou Airport and drove to the Residence of the U.S. Ambassador in
      Upper Volta.
      Called on the Upper Volta's Minister of Health.
      Visited the office of the President of Upper Volta.
      Attended tea and a briefing on SCF projects.
      Attended a reception for members of the British community in Upper Volta, Hotel Silmande,
      Ouagadougou.
      Attended a dinner given by the British Ambassador, Hotel Silmande.
22   Toured the hospital at Gorom Gorom.
      Visited the Gorom Gorom village pharmacy.
      Visited the food store, school and the village health worker at Jonja.
      Lunched at the Jonja Village Catholic Mission Guest House.
      Toured Dori Hospital.
      Visited the Save the Children Fund Nutrition Centre.
      Attended a supper at the house of the Director of SCF United States.
23   Visited Sebba SCF Team House.
      Toured the clinic and village school at Sebba.
      Attended a dinner at the Residence of the U.S. Ambassador, Ouagadougou.
24 · Attended a reception, U.S. Embassy, Ouagadougou.
      Left Ouagadougou for Britain via the Gambia.
25   Arrived at Gatwick Airport from Banjul.

29 Attended the launch at the Townswomen's Guilds' Save the Children Fund Child Nutrition Unit, Connaught Rooms, London.
Visited the Royal College of Veterinary Surgeons, Belgrave Square, London.
Attended a performance of *The Mikado*, Old Vic Theatre, London.
Attended a reception given by the Stratford, Ontario Theatre Company, Savoy Hotel, London.

March 1 Attended the première of the film *Champions*, Odeon, Leicester Square, London.
2 Attended a dinner at the University College Women's Dining Club, Gower Street, London.
4 Attended the Children's Royal Variety Performance, Her Majesty's Theatre, Haymarket, London.
6 Visited the Red Cross Camp for Disabled People, Weymouth.
Toured the Royal British Legion's new headquarters, Dorchester.
8 Attended the Riding for the Disabled Association's luncheon, Saddlers' Hall, London.
Visited the British School of Osteopathy, Suffolk Street, London.
14 Visited the WRVS handicraft exhibition, Shire Hall, Gloucester.
Attended a University of London presentation ceremony, Royal Albert Hall, London.
Attended a London University ecumenical service, Westminster Abbey.
15 Presented the Ritz Charity Trophy, Cheltenham Racecourse.
17 Attended the National Shire Horse Show, East of England Showground, Peterborough.
19 Opened the Portland Hospital for Women and Children, Great Portland Street, London.
Presented the BAFTA Craft Awards, Piccadilly, London.
24 Visited Downside School, Stratton-on-the-Fosse, Bath.
25 Presented the BAFTA awards, Grosvenor House Hotel, London.
26 Attended the Conference of Farriers, Royal Veterinary College, Camden Town.
29 Held an audience as Counsellor of State on behalf of the Queen, Buckingham Palace.
Attended the Doctor of the Year luncheon, Savoy Hotel, London.
Attended the Prime Minister's reception for the British Winter Olympics team, 10 Downing Street.
Attended the *Horse and Hound* centenary dinner, Porter Tun Room, The Brewery, Chiswell Street, London.
30 Attended the Mayoral Ball, Chippenham, Wiltshire.

April 3 Toured and opened the BEPI factory, Galashiels, Borders.
Opened Galashiels Swimming Pool.
Toured the factory of Claridge Mills Ltd.
Entertained at luncheon by the Duke of Buccleuch, Bowhill.
Visited the Town Hall, Market Place, Selkirk.
Opened Eschie Court at the Eildon Housing Association Development.
Attended a British Olympic Appeal gala dinner, Civic Centre, Newcastle-upon-Tyne.
4 Visited Hugh Mackay plc, Durham.
Attended the Dunelm Federation of Townswomen's Guilds luncheon, Durham Castle.
10 Attended a State banquet for the Amir of Bahrain, Windsor Castle.
16 Attended the London Friends of St Loye's College banquet, Mansion House, London.
17 Attended a dinner in aid of the Cambridgeshire British Olympic Appeal, Trinity College, Cambridge.
18 Entertained at luncheon by the Sail Training Association, Packington Hall, Coventry.
Visited the Shelforce Project, Erdington, Birmingham.
Toured the British Road Services Driving School, Erdington.
Attended a concert for the British Olympic Association, Queensway Hall, Dunstable, Bedfordshire.
25 Opened Taunton Deane Borough Council's development of flats for the elderly, Taunton, Somerset.
Visited the Wellington Library Exhibition, Wellington, Somerset.
27 Opened the Samaritan Centre, Swindon, Wiltshire.
Attended luncheon given by the Swindon and District Samaritans Premises Appeal, Crest Hotel, Stratton St Margaret.
Dined with the London University Students' Association, London Hospital Medical College.

	30	Opened and toured the Bowater Corporation's new factory, Norwich.
		Attended a gala concert, Town Hall, Cheltenham.
May	1	Received a Save the Children Fund Land Rover from BL, and met winners of *The Sunday Times* competition, Solihull.
		Visited Royal Holloway College, Egham, Surrey.
		Attended the British Sports Ball, Grosvenor House Hotel, London.
	2	Attended the Royal British Legion (Women's Section) conference, Opera House, Blackpool.
	3	Visited and presented standards to No. 47 and No. 70 Squadrons, RAF Lyneham.
		Attended a Carmen's Company court meeting and dinner, Draper's Hall, London and was admitted to the Company as an Honorary Assistant.
	4	Presented Dettol Youth Caring Awards, Pebble Mill, Birmingham.
		Attended the livery dinner of the Farriers' Company, Mansion House, London.
	5	Attended St Swithun's School centenary celebrations, Winchester.
		Attended a British Olympic Appeal fundraising reception, Winchester Castle.
	6	Attended a Combined Cavalry Old Comrades parade and memorial service, Hyde Park, London.
		Attended a luncheon with the 14th/20th King's Hussars Association, Intercontinental Hotel, London.
	8	Opened and toured the *Aids to Living* exhibition for the handicapped and elderly, Weston-super-Mare.
		Visited an exhibition of St John Ambulance history, Woodspring Museum, Weston-super-Mare.
	9	Attended a London University presentation ceremony, Royal Albert Hall, London.
		Attended London University's ecumenical service, St Paul's Cathedral.
	10	Opened the Northern and Shell Building, Mill Harbour, Isle of Dogs.
		Attended the presentation ceremony for Union Honorary Life Members, London University.
		Attended a charity greyhound race meeting, White City, London.
	11	Attended the Royal Lymington Cup Match Racing Championships, Hampshire.
		Attended a charity première of *West Side Story*, Her Majesty's Theatre, London.
	14	Opened the Cobbes Meadow Group indoor riding school for the disabled, St Augustine's Hospital, Chartham, Kent.
		Opened and toured Lympne Place for the Home Farm Trust, Hythe, Kent.
		Attended a charity gala evening by Givenchy, Guildhall, London.
	15	Visited Bejam's 200th store, Woodley, Berkshire.
		Opened and toured the Wilde Theatre, South Hill Park, Bracknell, Berkshire.
	16	Visited the Riding for the Disabled Association's Broadlands Group, Broadlands Riding School, Medstead, Hampshire.
		Attended a British Nordic Ski Team reception, Royal Aldershot Officers' Club.
	17	Opened and toured the Beverley Consolidated Charities Almshouses, North Humberside.
		Visited the Tunstall Telecom Group, North Humberside.
		Opened Whitley Lodge, Whitley Bridge, North Yorkshire.
		Attended a reception given by the Queen, Buckingham Palace.
	18	Visited St Thomas Cantilupe Church Primary School, Hereford.
		Visited Hereford Cathedral.
		Attended a fund-raising dinner for the British Olympic Association, Crest Hotel, Hambrook, Avon.
	21	Opened the Fire International '84 conference, Metropole Hotel, Birmingham.
		Opened and toured the Fire International '84 exhibition, National Exhibition Centre, Birmingham.
		Opened and toured Russells Hall Hospital, Dudley.
	23	Attended the Royal Yachting Association's Olympic Regatta, Weymouth Bay, Dorset.
	28	Attended the Surrey County Show, Guildford.
	30	Unveiled the painting *D-Day*, National Army Museum, Chelsea.
June	7	Attended the Royal Yachting Association's Olympic Ball, Savoy Hotel, London.
	8	Took the Queen's Review, RAF College, Cranwell, Lincolnshire.
		Attended the Institute of London Underwriters centenary reception, Guildhall, London.

	9	Attended a dinner given by the Queen for Heads of State and delegates attending the London Economic Summit, Buckingham Palace.
	11	Opened and toured Exeter University's new main library.
		Opened and toured HM Coastguard Maritime Rescue Sub-Centre, Brixham, Devon.
	12	Opened and toured Mold Community Hospital, Clwyd.
		Visited the Save the Children Fund shop, Mold.
		Opened and toured the Clwyd Special Riding Centre, Llanfynydd, Wrexham.
	13	Visited *HMS St Vincent*, Kensington.
		Visited the Queen Elizabeth's Foundation for the Disabled's unit, Banstead Place, Surrey.
		Attended a British Olympic Association gala concert, Barbican Centre, London.
	14	Opened and toured the new headquarters of the National Farmers' Union Mutual and Avon Insurance Society, Stratford-upon-Avon.
		Opened and toured the restored Municipal Almshouses, Stratford-upon-Avon.
		Attended the Royal International Horse Show, National Exhibition Centre, Birmingham.
	15	Visited Essex Agricultural Show, Chelmsford.
		Held an audience, Buckingham Palace.
	16	Witnessed the Queen's Birthday Parade, Horse Guards Parade, London.
	19	Opened and toured Ladymead House for the elderly, Bath.
		Visited the Royal United Hospital, Bath, and opened the Ornamental Garden.
		Opened and toured Chandos House, St John's Hospital, Bath.
	20	Visited the Junior Regiment, Royal Signals, Ousten, Northumberland.
	21	Visited the Cumbria Groups of Riding for the Disabled, Mirehouse and Keswick.
		Visited the North Manchester Group of Riding for the Disabled, Bury, Lancashire.
	22	Opened the new wing of the Bournemouth YWCA building.
		Visited Plessey Ltd, Christchurch, Dorset.
		Watched the Ptarmigan System Trials, Westdown Camp, Tisbury, Wiltshire.
	25	Attended a luncheon of the Farriers Company, House of Commons.
		Attended a Farriers Company Court meeting, Innholders Hall, London.
		Attended a London Schools Horse Society reception, Martini Terrace, Haymarket, London.
	26	Visited RDS Farm Electronics, Nailsworth, Gloucestershire, and opened a new extension.
	27	Attended a luncheon given by the Scottish Federations of the National Union of Townswomen's Guilds, Glasgow.
		Attended a British Council anniversary concert and reception, Royal Festival Hall, London.
	28	Attended Wye College commemorative celebrations, Ashford, Kent.
	29	Visited RAF Brize Norton.
	30	Attended the Princess Anne Award ceremony and fete for the Save the Children Fund, Leeds Castle, Maidstone, Kent.
		Attended a Farriers Company reception, Guildhall, London.
July	2	Visited the Drum Riding Centre for the Disabled Trust, Gilmerton, Edinburgh.
	3	Visited Strathcarron Hospice, Denny, Stirlingshire.
		Attended a luncheon party given by the Queen for Knights of the Thistle, Palace of Holyroodhouse.
		Visited The Royal Scots Museum and Club, and opened a new regimental shop, Edinburgh Castle.
		Attended a dinner party given by the Queen, Palace of Holyroodhouse.
	4	Visited the Scottish Veterans' residence, Whitefoord House, Edinburgh.
		Attended the Townswomen's Guilds, Edinburgh Lothian Federation's coffee morning, Central Hall, Edinburgh.
		Attended the Queen's garden party, Palace of Holyroodhouse.
	5	Opened and toured ACT Computers Ltd, Glenrothes.
		Opened the 3rd Twin Town Olympiad, Warout Stadium, Glenrothes.
		Left the Palace of Holyroodhouse for London.
		Attended a Son et Lumière in aid of the Save the Children Fund, Hampton Court Palace.
	6	Attended the British School of Osteopathy's annual awards presentation, Institute of Civil Engineers, London.
		Attended a St John's Ambulance and Nursing Cadets reception, Ewen Manor, Gloucestershire.

7	Left Gatwick Airport, London for the United States and arrived in Los Angeles.
	Attended a dinner party for the Music Centre Opera Association and the Royal Opera, Beverly Wilshire Hotel, Los Angeles.
8	Attended morning service, American Seaman's Church Institute, Los Angeles.
	Attended a press reception, British Consul-General's residence, Los Angeles.
	Visited Para Los Ninos Centre for Abused Hispanic Children, Los Angeles.
	Attended a reception and dinner given by the Music Centre Opera Association and the American Friends of Covent Garden, Los Angeles Music Centre.
9	Toured recording studios, Capitol Records building, Los Angeles.
	Inspected a videotext project and inaugurated the Los Angeles Olympic experiment, KTTV television station.
	Toured an art exhibition and silver collection, Los Angeles County Museum of Art.
	Visited the British store promotion, Bullocks Wilshire Department Store, Los Angeles.
	Attended a supper, Los Angeles Music Centre.
	Attended a performance of *Turandot*, Los Angeles Music Centre.
10	Visited the Academy of Motion Picture Arts and Sciences, Los Angeles.
	Watched filming in progress, Alfred Hitchcock Theater, Universal Studios.
	Visited the British section of Filmex, Picwood Theater.
	Presented BAFTA American awards and watched a film, Academy of Motion Picture Arts and Sciences.
	Attended a dinner, Chaden's Restaurant, Los Angeles.
11	Left Los Angeles for Atlanta, Georgia.
	Attended a British Olympic Association reception, Swan House, Atlanta.
	Attended a British Olympic Association dinner, World Trade Club, Atlanta.
12	Visited Marconi Avionics, Atlanta.
	Toured a new development at Laing's Properties, Lakeside, Atlanta.
	Left Atlanta and arrived Raleigh and Durham, North Carolina.
	Attended a dinner given by the Governor of North Carolina, Raleigh.
13	Attended the inaugural ceremony for America's 400th birthday celebrations, Manteo, Roanoke Island, North Carolina.
	Attended a reception, Elizabethan Gardens, Manteo.
	Left Manteo for London.
14	Arrived at Gatwick Airport from the United States.
	Visited the Women's Transport Service, The Paddock, Kensington Gardens, London.
16	Visited Riding for the Disabled Association holiday activities, Ivy Todd Farm, Ashdon, Essex.
	Attended the Berkeley Square Ball, London.
17	Attended the Queen's garden party, Buckingham Palace.
	Took the Salute at the Royal Tournament, Earl's Court, London.
18	Left Heathrow Airport, London for West Germany and arrived at RAF Gutersloh.
	Visited the 3rd and 22nd Signal Regiments, Senne Ranges, Bielefeld.
	Attended a reception and presentation Rathaus, Lippstadt.
	Attended a regimental dinner, Officers' Mess.
19	Continued her visit to the 3rd and 22nd Signal Regiments, Senne Ranges.
	Left RAF Gutersloh and arrived at RAF Lyneham for Gatcombe Park.
21	Attended the England v New Zealand one-day cricket international, Gloucestershire C.C. ground, Bristol.
23	Entertained to luncheon by the United States Ambassador, Winfield House, Regent's Park, London.
24	Opened the International Doll's Houses exhibition, Longleat House, Wiltshire.
26	Presented prizes at the Army Dog Trials, Royal Army Veterinary Corps Centre, Melton Mowbray, Leicestershire.
27	Left Gatwick Airport, London for the United States to attend the 1984 Olympics in Los Angeles.

Engagements of **THE QUEEN MOTHER**
August 1983-July 1984

August	17	Held a personal Investiture on behalf of the Queen, Clarence House.
	24	Visited the Pier Arts Centre, Stromness, Orkney.
		Attended a service of dedication, St Magnus Cathedral, Kirkwall, Orkney.

September 3 Attended the Highland Games, Braemar, Deeside.
13 Opened Servite House, Dundee.
Visited the Black Watch Memorial Home, Dunalistair.
25 Attended a 750th Anniversary Service, Dunblane Cathedral.

October 12 Opened the Queen Mother Library, University of Aberdeen.
Received an honorary degree of Doctor of Laws, University of Aberdeen.
Attended the Graduation luncheon, Elphinstone Hall, University of Aberdeen.
19 Visited the Fyfe-Jamieson Maternity Home, Forfar.
Attended an Edinburgh Angus Club reception, Glamis Castle.
27 Attended the Boys Brigade Centenary Service of Thanksgiving, St Paul's Cathedral, London.

November 2 Attended the unveiling by the Queen of the statue of Earl Mountbatten, Foreign Office Green, London.
Attended a reception given by the Prime Minister, Banqueting House, Whitehall, London.
Visited Queen Mary's London Needlework Guild, St James's Palace, London.
3 Attended a Special Forces Club reception, Imperial War Museum, London.
8 Attended a performance of *Blondel*, Old Vic, London.
10 Planted a cross in the Royal British Legion Field of Remembrance, St Margaret's Church, Westminster.
Attended a Careers of Women reception at the University of London Institute of Education.
12 Attended the Royal British Legion Festival of Remembrance, Royal Albert Hall, London.
13 Attended the Remembrance Day ceremony, Cenotaph, Whitehall, London.
Attended a service marking the 25th anniversary of the rebuilding of the City Temple, London.
15 Held three audiences on behalf of the Queen, Buckingham Palace.
Attended a reception given by the Queen's Own Hussars, St James's Palace, London.
17 Opened the Abbotswood Housing Project, Potters Bar.
Opened Elizabeth House for the Elderly, Welwyn Garden City.
18 Held a Council on behalf of the Queen, Clarence House.
22 Held three audiences and two personal Investitures on behalf of the Queen, Buckingham Palace.
Presented certificates and awards, Royal College of Music, London.
23 Attended luncheon at New Scotland Yard, London.
Attended a reception given by the East Grinstead Research Trust, New Zealand House, London.
24 Held two audiences, Clarence House.
Visited the Westminster Children's Society, Hyde Park Barracks, London.
Attended a reception given by the King's Regiment, Duke of York's Headquarters, Chelsea.
29 Attended a reception given by the Black Watch Association, Duke of York's Headquarters, Chelsea.
30 Opened the Royal College of Nursing headquarters, Cavendish Square.
Attended the Salmon and Trout Association's dinner, Fishmongers Hall, London.

December 1 Attended a concert given by the Ulster Orchestra, St John's Church, Smith Square, London.
6 Visited the Royal Smithfield Show, Earl's Court, London.
7 Held two audiences, Clarence House.
Dined with the Benchers of Middle Temple, London.
8 Attended an Army Board dinner, Royal Hospital, Chelsea.
14 Attended a reception given at the London Library.

January	11	Attended a King's Lynn Preservation Trust reception, Thoresby College, King's Lynn, Norfolk.
February	8	Attended the funeral of the Duke of Beaufort, Badminton.
	9	Visited the Adelaide Community Association's Swiss Cottage Community Centre, London.
	16	Visited the Hepburn Stanley Blind Aid Society, St Columba's Church of Scotland, London.
	20	Attended a Royal Horticultural Society dinner, Vincent Square, London.
	23	Attended a concert commemorating the 50th anniversary of Sir Edward Elgar's death, Westminster Abbey.
March	1	Attended the première of the film *Champions*, Odeon, Leicester Square, London.
	4	Attended a Thanksgiving Service for the King George VI and Queen Elizabeth foundation of St Catharine's, Chapel Royal, Windsor Great Park.
	8	Attended luncheon given by the Douglas Bader Foundation Trustees, Ritz Hotel, London.
	16	Visited the British Military Hospital, Munster, West Germany.
	17	Attended the Irish Guards' St Patrick's Day Parade, Oxford Barracks, Munster.
	20	Attended a musical reception on behalf of the Aldeburgh Foundation, St James's Palace.
	21	Attended a Royal Army Medical Corps dinner, Millbank, London.
	22	Received the presidents of Queen Mary's London Needlework Guild, St James's Palace.
	25	Attended the Milk Cup Final, Wembley Stadium.
	26	Attended the Schools' Music Association's *Youth Makes Music* concert, Royal Festival Hall, London.
	28	Unveiled a memorial to Sir Noel Coward, Westminster Abbey.
	29	Held an audience as Counsellor of State on behalf of the Queen, Buckingham Palace.
April	3	Attended a dinner given by the former captain of *HMS Ark Royal*, Admiralty House, London.
	5	Opened the Lew Cohen Leukaemia Research Unit, Faculty of Clinical Sciences, University College, London.
	6	Opened a new paddock complex, Kempton Park Racecourse.
	10	Received the Amir of Bahrain on the first day of his State Visit, Royal Lodge, Windsor.
		Attended the State banquet for the Amir of Bahrain, Windsor Castle.
	17	Visited the Shaftesbury Homes and 'Arethusa' Venture Centre, Lower Upnor, Kent.
		Opened restored almhouses of the Sir John Hawkins Hospital, Chatham, Kent.
	25	Attended the Presentation of the late Duke of Beaufort's Garter Banner, St George's Chapel, Windsor.
	26	Visited the British Racing Museum, Newmarket.
May	2	Attended a dinner given by the London Scottish Regiment, Caledonian Club, London.
	3	Attended a London University reception, Bedford College, London.
	4	Opened a new hangar during the Silver Jubilee celebrations of the De Havilland Aircraft Museum, Salisbury Hall, Hatfield, Hertfordshire.
	9	Visited the National Trust headquarters, Queen Anne's Gate, London.
	10	Held an audience, Clarence House.
		Opened All Saints' Church Hall, Ascot.
	15	Presented gallantry awards at the RNLI's annual meeting, Royal Festival Hall, London.
	24	Opened the Maritime Museum, Aberdeen.
	29	Left Portsmouth on the Royal Yacht *Britannia* for the Channel Islands.
	30	Unveiled a plaque, Town Church, St Peter Port, Guernsey.
		Visited King Edward VII Hospital, St Peter Port.
		Attended a States reception, Beau Sejour Leisure Centre.
		Toured the island of Guernsey.
		Attended a Boy Scouts and Girl Guides rally, and opened the new Girl Guides headquarters, St Andrews.
	31	Visited Alderney and Sark.
		Gave a reception, Royal Yacht *Britannia*.
June	1	Attended a centenary service of the Jersey Lifeboat Station, St Helier, Jersey.

	1	Opened Maufant Youth Centre, St Helier.
		Attended a States of Jersey reception, Grainville School.
		Toured the island of Jersey.
		Gave a dinner party, Royal Yacht *Britannia*.
	2	Arrived at Portsmouth in the Royal Yacht *Britannia* from Jersey.
		Opened St George's Court for the Church of England Soldiers', Sailors' and Airmen Clubs, Southsea.
		Gave a reception, Royal Yacht *Britannia*.
	3	Attended a D-Day anniversary service, Portsmouth Cathedral.
		Opened the D-Day Museum, Portsmouth.
	5	Unveiled a Blue Plaque to General de Gaulle, 4 Carlton Gardens, London.
	6	Attended Epsom Races.
	7	Visited an exhibition of embroidery, Royal School of Needlework, London.
		Opened a reconstructed hospice unit, Hospital of St John and St Elizabeth, St John's Wood, London.
	8	Opened Stewart House, London University's Schools Examination Department.
	9	Attended a dinner given by the Queen for Heads of State and delegates attending the London Economic Summit, Buckingham Palace.
	16	Witnessed the Queen's Birthday Parade, Horse Guards Parade, London.
	26	Visited the Royal Foundation of St Katherine, Ratcliffe.
	27	Attended the Friends of St Paul's festival service, St Paul's Cathedral, London.
	28	Opened the Guinness Trust's Lord Gage Centre, Newham, London.
	29	Entertained at luncheon by the Governor and Directors of the Bank of England, City of London.
	30	Attended the Royal British Legion Scotland (Women's Section) sixtieth anniversary conference, University of Aberdeen.
July	3	Attended a service marking the fiftieth anniversary of Marie Curie's death, Westminster Abbey.
		Attended a Royal Academy Trust reception, St James's Palace.
	4	Held an audience, Clarence House.
		Visited gardens in Lambeth, Southwark and the City of London.
	5	Attended an International Students' Trust garden party, Park Crescent Gardens, London.
	10	Visited Wolfson House, a home of the Jewish Welfare Board, Green Lanes, North London.
		Attended a Courtauld Institute of Art Fund Trust reception, Somerset House, London.
	11	Held two audiences, Clarence House.
		Visited the Queen Elizabeth Foundation for the Disabled, and opened Springbok House girls' hostel, Leatherhead, Surrey.
	12	Attended the topping-out ceremony for the new Lloyds of London building, City of London.
		Attended The Royal Yeomanry's reception, Westminster.
	13	Attended St James's Church tercentenary service, Piccadilly, London.
	14	Opened the Physiotherapy Department, Queen Victoria Memorial Hospital, Welwyn, Hertfordshire.
	17	Attended the Queen's garden party, Buckingham Palace.
	27	Attended the memorial service for Lord Adam Gordon, Chapel Royal, St James's Palace.

Engagements of **PRINCESS MARGARET**
August 1983-July 1984

August	20	Visited Walker's Bakery, Aberlour, Banffshire.
		Visited Macallan Distillery, Allarburn Creamery, and Johnston's Woollen Mills, Elgin.
		Visited Elgin Horticultural Society's Flower Show, Town Hall, Elgin.
		Attended a ball, RAF Kinloss.
	21	Attended an Elgin Rotary Club Gala, Cooper's Park, Elgin.
September	7	Presented the Queen's Award for Export and Technology to Gaeltec Limited, Dunvegan, Ross

	7	and Cromarty.

	7	and Cromarty. Visited Mackinnon Memorial Hospital, Broadford, Ross and Cromarty.
	12	Attended a Royal Ballet Gala Performance, Sadler's Wells Theatre, London.
	16	Left Heathrow Airport, London and arrived, via Antigua, at St Kitts. Drove to Government House, St Kitts.
	17	Toured the Fortifications, Brimstone Hill, St Kitts. Attended a reception given by the Governor, Government House, St Kitts. Attended an official dinner on board *HMS Berwick*, off St Kitts.
	18	Opened Sandy Point School, St Kitts. Attended the Premier's luncheon for guests attending the independence celebrations, St Kitts. Attended a dinner, Government House, St Kitts. Attended a State service, Warner Park, St Kitts. Presided at the independence ceremonies at Warner Park.
	19	Left St Kitts and arrived at Nevis. Attended the swearing-in ceremony of the Deputy Governor General and Deputy Premier. Visited Government House, Nevis. Attended the Deputy Prime Minister's luncheon, Nevis. Visited medical wards at Nevis Hospital. Opened the new 6th form school building, Nevis. Toured the Nelson Museum, Morning Star, Nevis. Left Nevis and returned to Government House, St Kitts. Attended a dinner on the Royal Fleet Auxiliary *Green Rover*.
	20	Left St Kitts for St Vincent, and a holiday on Mustique.
October	10	Attended a Girl Guides' Association reception, Mercers Hall, London.
	12	Visited the Intelligence Centre, Ashford, Kent.
	19	Attended a luncheon given by the Queen for the President of Mozambique, Buckingham Palace.
	20	Visited the Horder Centre for Arthritics, Crowborough, East Sussex.
	26	Visited the Commonwealth Countries League Fair, Commonwealth Institute, London. Opened the National Society for the Prevention of Cruelty to Children Special Unit, Plymouth, Devon. Attended a gala performance of *Annie*, Theatre Royal, Plymouth.
	27	Held a reception for the National Society for the Prevention of Cruelty to Children, Kensington Palace, London.
	31	Attended a Royal Anglian Regiment reception, Blenheim Camp, Bury St Edmunds, Suffolk.
November	1	Attended a service commemorating the 25th anniversary of Consecration, St Mary's Church, Newington, London.
	2	Attended the unveiling by the Queen of the statue of Earl Mountbatten, Foreign Office Green, London. Attended a reception given by the Prime Minister, Banqueting House, Whitehall, London.
	9	Opened the new premises of Elbeo Limited, Sutton in Ashfield, Nottinghamshire. Visited the Sutton Centre, Sutton in Ashfield. Attended a gala performance of *Coriolanus*, Nottingham Playhouse.
	10	Attended a reception given by Queen Alexandra's Royal Army Nursing Corps, Royal Hospital, Chelsea.
	15	Held three audiences on behalf of the Queen, Buckingham Palace. Attended the Grand Day dinner, Lincoln's Inn, London.
	16	Attended a reception given by the Mayor of Kensington and Chelsea, Kensington.
	17	Visited the Royal Ballet School, White Lodge, Richmond, Surrey. Attended a Staff Association ball in aid of the NSPCC, Grosvenor House Hotel, London.
	22	Held three audiences on behalf of the Queen, Buckingham Palace.
	23	Attended a Royal College of Nursing reception, Kensington Exhibition Centre, London.
	24	Attended a Barnardo's luncheon, Savoy Hotel, London.
	25	Attended a Royal Scottish Society for the Prevention of Cruelty to Children reception, Edinburgh.

	26	Attended the Scottish Association of Youth Clubs Conference, Loch Lomond Centre, Dunbartonshire.
	28	Attended the Westminster Ball, Hilton Hotel, London.
December	12	Attended a reception given by the Council of the Royal Warrant Holders' Association, New Zealand House, London.
	13	Held two audiences, Kensington Palace.
		Attended a gala performance of *Cinderella*, National Theatre, London.
	14	Visited the Day Centre, Ely, West Cardiff.
		Visited the office of Barnardo's, Cardiff.
		Attended a gala performance of *Humpty Dumpty*, New Theatre, Cardiff.
January	3	Received the first donation to the Centenary Appeal of the NSPCC, Kensington Palace.
	25	Visited the Order of St John Headquarters, Grosvenor Crescent, London.
February	1	Visited the Greater Manchester Probation Service's exhibition, County Hall, Manchester.
		Entertained at luncheon by the Greater Manchester Probation Committee.
		Opened the Harvey and Ann Rhodes Selcare Centre, Oldham, Lancashire.
March	20	Attended a concert in aid of a Royal Society for the Protection of Birds campaign, Royal Albert Hall, London.
	22	Attended a service of thanksgiving and dedication, Chelmsford Cathedral.
	23	Attended the Memorial Service for the Duke of Beaufort, Guards Chapel, London.
	27	Visited Queen Alexandra's Royal Army Nursing Corps, Aldershot.
		Attended an Alexandra Day Service, All Saints Royal Garrison Church, Aldershot.
		Attended a reception and luncheon given by the QARANC, Training Centre, Aldershot.
April	2	Attended the Duke of Westminster's reception for the National Society for the Prevention of Cruelty to Children, Berkeley Hotel, London.
	3	Attended a performance by Sadler's Wells Ballet, and presented ballet awards, Sadler's Wells Theatre, London.
	5	Inspected the Benfleet Tidal Barrier, Benfleet Creek, Essex.
		Inspected the Sea Defences at Tewkes Creek, Canvey Island.
		Visited Prouts Boatbuilders, Small Gains Creek, Canvey Island.
		Visited Waterside Farm Sports Centre, Canvey Island.
	10	Met the Amir of Bahrain at the beginning of his State Visit, Windsor Castle.
		Attended a State banquet for the Amir of Bahrain, Windsor Castle.
	11	Attended a reception marking a meeting of the Workgroup of European Nurse Researchers, Banqueting Hall, Whitehall, London.
	12	Attended a Scottish Ballet gala performance, Her Majesty's Theatre, Aberdeen.
	13	Presided at the Scottish Children's League annual general meeting, Haddo House, Aberdeen.
	15	Attended a charity gala·variety performance, Congress Theatre, Eastbourne.
	27	Visited Robinson College, University of Cambridge.
		Visited Clare Hall, University of Cambridge.
		Toured the University School of Clinical Medicine, Cambridge.
		Visited the new headquarters of the Cambridge University Press.
		Visited King's College Chapel, Cambridge.
	29	Attended a service, Little St Mary's Church, Cambridge.
		Attended a reception, Peterhouse Church, Cambridge.
	30	Opened Cooper Vision Optics Ltd's new laboratory and offices, Southampton.
May	2	Attended an Air League reception, New Zealand House, London.
	3	Opened the Parkinson's Disease Society Research Centre, Denmark Hill, London.
	9	Visited the Viyella Mill, Pleasley Vale, Mansfield.
		Visited William Hollins and Co. Ltd's offices and design centre, Somercotes.
	11	Attended a luncheon, City Chambers, Edinburgh.
		Presided at the annual general meeting of the Royal Scottish Society for Prevention of

	11	Cruelty to Children, Edinburgh.
	12	Held a reception for the Royal Scottish Society for Prevention of Cruelty to Children, Holyroodhouse.
	15	Visited *RMS St Helena*, Avonmouth Docks.
		Attended the opening of the *Wedgwood in London* exhibition, Wigmore Street, London.
	16	Attended the NSPCC's annual general meeting, Queen Elizabeth Hall, London.
	17	Visited the Joint Air Reconnaissance Intelligence Centre, RAF Brampton, Cambridgeshire.
		Attended a reception given by the Queen, Buckingham Palace.
	18	Visited the restored Castle Gates Library, Shrewsbury.
		Visited Shrewsbury School.
		Visited Brownlow Community Centre, Whitchurch, Shropshire.
	21	Visited the Chelsea Flower Show, Royal Hospital, Chelsea.
	22	Attended the Girl Guides' Association's annual general meeting, Mansion House, London.
	23	Opened the exhibition of Court Dress, Kensington Palace.
		Attended the Hundred Guinea Club's dinner and dance, Inn on the Park, London.
	24	Opened and toured the Princess Margaret Haemotology Ward, East Birmingham Hospital.
	29	Presented special awards at the Sony Radio Awards luncheon, Hilton Hotel, London.
June	1	Opened the steel tent, Glenbrook Outdoor Activities Training Centre, Bamford, Derbyshire.
	4	Opened the new Town Hall, Matlock, Derbyshire.
		Opened the new headquarters of Derbyshire Rural Community Council, Wirksworth.
		Visited Matthew Walker (Derby) Ltd, Heanor.
		Visited G.H. Fletcher & Sons Ltd, Heanor.
		Visited the St John Ambulance divisional headquarters, Long Eaton.
	5	Held two audiences, Kensington Palace.
	6	Presented the Queen's Award for Export to Short Brothers Ltd, Belfast, Northern Ireland.
		Attended a reception for the Northern Ireland branch of the NSPCC, Hillsborough Castle.
		Attended the Northern Ireland Secretary of State's dinner, Hillsborough Castle.
	7	Visited the Girl Guides, Ulster Guides' Training Centre, Lorne.
		Visited the 1st Battalion The Royal Highland Fusiliers, Holywood Barracks, Ulster.
		Attended a Government garden party for children's care organisations in Northern Ireland, Hillsborough Castle.
	9	Attended a dinner given by the Queen for Heads of State and delegates attending the London Economic Summit, Buckingham Palace.
	13	Attended a gala performance of the play *David and Jonathan*, Redgrave Theatre, Farnham.
	14	Attended Queensway Ascot Raceday's dinner in aid of the NSPCC, Savoy Hotel, London.
	16	Witnessed the Queen's Birthday Parade, Horse Guards Parade, London.
	23	Attended a ball in aid of the NSPCC, Brighton Centre, Brighton.
	27	Visited the Hospital for Sick Children, Great Ormond Street, London.
		Attended a Royal College of Art gala fashion show, Gulbenkian Hall, Royal College of Art, Kensington.
	29	Represented the Queen Mother at the memorial service for Sir John Betjeman, Westminster Abbey.
		Visited the Haberdashers' Aldersey Church of England Primary School, Banbury, Oxfordshire.
		Attended a ball in aid of the NSPCC, Eaton Hall, Cheshire.
July	2	Attended a Victoria League dinner for seminar delegates, New Zealand House, London.
	3	Toured an exhibition arranged by the Keele Branch of the Royal Commission on Historical Monuments, University of Keele.
		Attended a Keele University degree conferment congregation, King's Hall, Stoke-on-Trent.
	4	Attended a performance of *HMS Pinafore* in aid of the NSPCC, Sadler's Wells Theatre, London.
	6	Attended a Government reception for overseas teachers, Lancaster House, London.
	8	Opened the new headquarters of Itchen South District Scout Centre, Upper Hamble Country Park, Botley, Southampton.
		Visited the Royal Victoria Country Park, Southampton.
		Toured the Tenovus research laboratories, Southampton General Hospital.

10	Attended a gala performance of *The Merchant of Venice* in aid of the NSPCC, Festival Theatre, Chichester.
11	Attended the inauguration of the exhibition *Treasures from the Treasury of St Mark's Cathedral in Venice*, British Museum, London.
12	Attended the Queen's garden party, Buckingham Palace.
14	Opened the 23rd Lakeland Rose Show, Holker Hall, Cumbria.
	Attended a gala evening in aid of the NSPCC, Holker Hall.
17	Opened Whitbread Brewery's new Merseyside headquarters and distribution centre, Liverpool.
	Presented awards in connection with British Week, Liverpool.
	Visited the International Garden Festival, Liverpool.
19	Visited the Bank of England, City of London.
20	Visited the factory of Poll & Withey Windows Ltd, Threxton Industrial Estate, Watton, Norfolk.
23	Attended the centenary service of the Royal Scottish Society for the Prevention of Cruelty to Children, Glasgow Cathedral.
	Attended Glasgow District Council's reception for the RSSPCC, City Chambers, Glasgow.
24	Attended a performance by the Royal Ballet School, Sadler's Wells Theatre, London.
25	Presented London in Bloom awards, National Westminster Banqueting Hall, Bishopsgate, City of London.
26	Represented the Queen Mother at the memorial service for Viscount Astor of Hever, St Martin-in-the-Fields, London.
	Attended a gala night dinner and entertainment in aid of the NSPCC, Grosvenor House, London.
27	Attended the 'After the Races' party in aid of St John Ambulance, Cumberland Lodge, Windsor Great Park.
31	Attended a Zebra Trust reception, Jerome House, Knightsbridge, London.

Engagements of **PRINCESS ALICE**
August 1983-July 1984

September	28	Attended a Friends of St Alban's Abbey Flower Festival Preview, St Alban's Abbey, Hertfordshire.

October	4	Visited the 2nd Battalion, Royal Anglian Regiment, Hyderabad Barracks, Colchester, Essex.
	5	Opened Putney High School's new Assembly Hall, London.
	7	Attended a gala performance of *The Pirates of Penzance*, Key Theatre, Peterborough, Northamptonshire.
	10	Opened and toured the exhibition *Albert, his Life and Work*, Royal College of Art, Kensington, London.
	11	Attended the Multiple Sclerosis Society's 30th anniversary reception, Vintners Hall, London.
	19	Visited 20 Squadron, Royal Corps of Transport, Regent's Park Barracks, London.
	20	Visited the Church of England Children's Society Centres, Milton Keynes, Buckinghamshire.

November	2	Attended the unveiling by the Queen of the statue of Earl Mountbatten, Foreign Office Green, London.
		Attended a reception given by the Prime Minister, Banqueting House, Whitehall, London.
	9	Held two audiences, Kensington Palace, London.
	12	Attended the Royal British Legion Festival of Remembrance, Royal Albert Hall, London.
	13	Attended the Remembrance Day ceremony, Cenotaph, Whitehall, London.
	15	Presented Long Service Badges to members of the Queen's Nursing Institute, Fishmongers Hall, London.
	17	Visited Swavesey Village College, Cambridge.
	22	Attended the East African Women's League General Meeting, Holy Trinity Church House, Brompton Road, London.
		Held an audience, Kensington Palace.

	23	Attended a reception for the Girls of the Realm Guild, Leighton House, Holland Park, London.
December	6	Held two audiences, Kensington Palace. Attended a luncheon given in aid of Physically Handicapped and Able Bodied, Mansion House, London. Attended the annual general meeting of the British Library of Tape Recordings for Hospital Patients, Drapers Hall, London.
	14	Attended a Candlelight Carol Service, St Peter Parish Church, Oundle, Northamptonshire.
January	24	Held an audience, Kensington Palace.
	30	Held an audience, Kensington Palace.
	31	Held an audience, Kensington Palace.
February	2	Held two audiences, Kensington Palace.
	7	Opened a radiotherapy unit, Peterborough District Hospital.
March	1	Visited RAF Swinderby, Lincolnshire.
	8	Held an audience, Kensington Palace.
	14	Opened the Princess Alice Ward, Broughton House, Home for Disabled Ex-Servicemen, Salford, Greater Manchester. Visited the Salford Community Housing Association's Ramsden Fold Development.
	21	Attended a meeting of the Ladies' Guild of the St John Ophthalmic Hospital, Grosvenor Crescent, London.
	23	Attended, and represented the Duke and Duchess of Gloucester at the Memorial Service for the Duke of Beaufort, Gloucester Cathedral.
	28	Attended a concert in aid of the Blackie Foundation Trust, St James's Palace.
April	10	Met the Amir of Bahrain at the beginning of his State Visit, Windsor Castle.
May	12	Visited an exhibition of Chinese watercolour paintings, Stowe School, Buckingham.
	17	Attended a reception given by the Queen, Buckingham Palace.
	21	Visited the Chelsea Flower Show, Royal Hospital, Chelsea.
	24	Left RAF Northolt for West Germany for a two-day visit to the Royal Hussars (Prince of Wales Own) at Fallingbostel, BAOR.
	31	Attended a service of thanksgiving for the dedication of church organs, All Saints Church, Northampton.
June	2	Visited the International Garden Festival, Liverpool.
	7	Opened an International Festival of Embroidery, Clarendon Park, Salisbury, Wiltshire.
	8	Visited the 1st Battalion The King's Own Scottish Borderers, Meanee Barracks, Colchester, Essex.
	12	Visited the Women's Royal Voluntary Service, Swadlincote, Derbyshire. Visited Derbyshire College of Education, Mickleover.
	15	Visited St Clement Dane's Flower Festival, Strand, London.
	16	Witnessed the Queen's Birthday Parade, Horse Guards Parade, London.
	19	Attended the British Limbless Ex-Servicemen's Association tea party, Royal Hospital, Chelsea.
July	2	Visited the Royal Show, National Agricultural Centre, Stoneleigh, Warwickshire.
	3	Attended a dinner party given by the Queen, Palace of Holyroodhouse.
	4	Received the Queen, the Duke of Edinburgh and Princess Anne on their visit to the Scottish Veterans' residence, Whitefoord House, Edinburgh. Attended the Queen's garden party, Palace of Holyroodhouse.
	5	Visited Queen Margaret College, Edinburgh. Attended a service of thanksgiving for the fortieth anniversary of the Thistle Foundation, Robin Chapel, Edinburgh.

	8	Attended the Northamptonshire Regiment's Comrades Association annual reunion church parade, Holy Sepulchre Church, Northampton.
	12	Attended the Queen's garden party, Buckingham Palace.
	17	Visited the East of England Show, Peterborough.
	18	Held an audience, Kensington Palace.
	23	Visited William Goodenough House for overseas graduates, Mecklenburgh Square, London.
	24	Held an audience, Kensington Palace.
		Attended the afternoon performance of the Royal Tournament, Earl's Court, London.

Engagements of **THE DUKE OF GLOUCESTER**
August 1983-July 1984

August	25	Unveiled a Memorial to Airmen, King's Cliffe Airfield, Peterborough, Northamptonshire.
	30	Attended a New York City Ballet gala performance, Royal Opera House, Covent Garden, London.
September	2	Attended celebrations marking the 500th anniversary of Gloucester's Royal Charter, Gloucester.
	8	Visited the Scottish Railway Preservation Society, Bo'ness.
		Visited the public library and rehabilitation works, Bo'ness.
		Visited a factory in Grangemouth.
		Visited Ladysmill Industrial Units, Falkirk.
	13	Opened an exhibition of Canadian landscape painting, Canada House Cultural Centre, London.
	14	Attended the Lord Mayor of Oxford's reception, Oxford Town Hall.
		Opened the *Heritage '84* conference on Tourism and Heritage, Oxford.
		Presented Heritage Awards 1983, at a dinner at Christchurch College, Oxford.
	15	Attended a garden party at the Tunbridge Wells Homeopathic Hospital, Kent.
	16	Visited the National Museum of Wales, Cardiff.
		Attended a reception given by the British Association of Friends of Museums, National Museum of Wales, Cardiff.
	19	Represented the Queen at the St Christopher and Nevis Independence Service, Westminster Abbey, London.
	21	Opened the Medical Oncology Building, Charing Cross Hospital, London.
October	2	Left Heathrow Airport, London, to visit Jordan and the United Arab Emirates.
		Arrived at Queen Alia International Airport, Jordan.
	3	Toured a farm and irrigation projects installations near Amman.
		Toured the Wadi El Yabis Marketing Centre, Amman.
		Visited Tell Deir Alla.
		Entertained to luncheon at the Government guest house, Deir Alla.
		Attended a reception for Commonwealth Ambassadors, British Embassy and British Council staff, Ambassador's residence, Amman.
		Bestowed the Order of St John upon the Queen of Jordan, Royal Palace, Amman.
		Attended a dinner given by the King and Queen of Jordan, Royal Palace, Amman.
	4	Toured desert castles around Amman.
		Attended a reception for benefactors of the Order of St John, Ambassador's residence, Amman.
		Left Amman for Abu Dhabi.
		Arrived Abu Dhabi.
	5	Visited the British Embassy.
		Visited Shaikh Zaid, ruler of Abu Dhabi, Al Khazneh Palace.
		Called on Shaikh Khalifa, Crown Prince of Abu Dhabi, Al Ain.
		Attended a luncheon given by Shaikh Surour, Presidential Court Chamberlain, Intercontinental Hotel, Al Ain.
		Toured buildings of interest in the town of Abu Dhabi.
		Attended a reception at the British Ambassador's Residence.
	6	Left Abu Dhabi airport for Dubai.

6	Arrived at Dubai International Airport.
	Visited the Minister of Defence of the United Arab Emirates.
	Visited the British Embassy to tour offices and meet staff.
	Visited the Dubai International Trade Centre.
	Visited Sheikh Sultan Bin Mohammed, the ruler of Dubai, and attended a luncheon hosted by him.
	Visited the New Sharjah Souq.
	Took tea at the British Embassy, Dubai.
	Toured ports and docks in Dubai Creek.
	Attended a reception given by the British Consul General, British Embassy.
	Attended a dinner at the Hilton Hotel given by the Chief of Protocol.
7	Left Dubai International Airport and arrived at Heathrow Airport, London.
10	Visited the exhibition *Albert, his Life and Work*, Royal College of Art, Kensington, London.
11	Attended a lecture commemorating the 500th Anniversary of the accession of King Richard III, Crosby Hall, London.
12	Opened the Operation Drake Fellowship's Fairbridge Team Centre, Fulham, London.
13	Attended a Pattenmakers Company service, St Margaret Patten's Church, London.
	Presented the Pattenmakers Company Young Enterprise Competition Awards during a luncheon at Cutlers Hall, London.
20	Attended the Butchers' Charitable Institution's annual banquet, Grosvenor House, London.
23	Attended the Victorian Sunday event, Hyde Park, London.
24	Visited the Royal Military School of Music, Kneller Hall, Twickenham.
26	Visited the Marden Fruit Show, Kent.
	Attended the Samuel Pepys Club anniversary dinner, Clothworkers Hall, London.
27	Attended the British Consultants Bureau's Annual General Meeting and luncheon, RAF Club, Piccadilly, London.
31	Attended the Royal Commission on Historical Monuments' 75th anniversary reception, Fishmongers Hall, London.

November	1	Opened the National Road Safety Congress, Eastbourne, Sussex.
	2	Attended the unveiling by the Queen of the statue of Earl Mountbatten, Foreign Office Green, London.
		Attended a reception given by the Prime Minister, Banqueting House, Whitehall, London.
		Attended the Parliamentry Group for Consultancies dinner, House of Lords, London.
	3	Visited Papworth Village Settlement, Cambridgeshire.
	8	Opened Lydney Whitecross Sports Centre, Gloucestershire.
		Visited Dene Forest Railways Norchard Steam Centre, Forest of Dene.
		Visited Formwood Limited, Colford, Gloucestershire.
		Attended the City of London Business in the Community's inaugural dinner, Mansion House, London.
	10	Presented the Structural Steel Design Awards, Savoy Hotel, London.
		Attended a concert marking the 21st anniversary of Jamaican Independence, Town Hall, Kensington.
	11	Opened Thames Tunnel Mills Development, Rotherhithe, London.
	12	Attended the Royal British Legion Festival of Remembrance, Royal Albert Hall, London.
	13	Attended the Remembrance Day ceremony, Cenotaph, Whitehall, London.
	14	Attended a Royal Institute of Chartered Surveyors luncheon, Great George Street, London.
	16	Visited the offices of Laurence Gould and Co, Warwick.
		Visited IBM Midlands Marketing Centre, Warwick.
		Visited Warwick Library, Warwick.
	22	Visited the Royal Army Pay Corps, Worthy Down, Hampshire.
	23	Presented awards at the Brick Development Association luncheon, Berkeley Hotel, London.
		Opened the exhibition *Genius of Venice*, Royal Academy of Arts, London.
		Attended the Italian Ambassador's dinner, Italian Embassy, London.
	24	Visited units of the Royal Pioneer Corps, Northern Ireland.
	29	Visited Edinburgh College of Art.
		Attended a luncheon given by the Association for the Protection of Rural Scotland, Signet

	29	Library, Edinburgh.
	30	Held two audiences, Kensington Palace.
December	1	Attended a Butchers Company luncheon, Butchers Hall, London.
	5	Visited the Royal Smithfield Show, Earl's Court, London.
	7	Attended the Royal Smithfield Club Annual General Meeting, Earl's Court, London.
	15	Visited Westbury and District Hospital, Wiltshire.
		Opened the Laverton almshouses, Westbury.
	20	Attended *The Observer* Victorian Christmas Concert, Royal Albert Hall, London.
January	23	Visited the exhibition *Arab Architecture Past and Present*, Royal Institute of British Architects, London.
	26	Held an audience, Kensington Palace.
February	14	Attended the luncheon and Annual General Meeting of the Parliamentary All-Party Group on Action on Smoking and Health, House of Commons.
		Attended the Chartered Institute of Building's 150th anniversary dinner, Guildhall, London.
	16	Attended a Wax Chandlers' Company reception marking the 500th anniversary of King Richard III's Grant of a Charter, Wax Chandlers' Hall, London.
	23	Attended the Elgar Commemorative Concert, Royal Festival Hall, London.
	24	Attended the Queen's luncheon for the Crown Prince of Saudi-Arabia, Buckingham Palace.
	28	Attended a Grocers Company Court Dinner celebrating the bicentenary of William Pitt the Younger, Grocers Hall, London.
March	7	Held an audience, Kensington Palace.
	12	Opened the *Calligraphy '84* exhibition, Central School of Art and Design, London.
	13	Held an audience, Kensington Palace.
	15	Held two audiences, Kensington Palace.
	21	Attended a reception for winners of the Queen's awards for export and technology in 1983, Buckingham Palace.
	23	Left RAF Northolt and arrived in Luxembourg.
		Toured the fortifications, Luxembourg.
		Visited the European Parliament, the European Courts of Justice and the European Investment Bank, Luxembourg.
		Visited the British Embassy, Luxembourg.
		Opened and toured an exhibition at the Luxembourg State Museum.
		Attended a buffet-dinner at the Royal Palace, Luxembourg.
		Attended a concert at the Eglise St Michel, Luxembourg.
	25	Arrived back at RAF Northolt from Luxembourg.
	27	Visited the Institute of Hydrology, Wallingford, Oxfordshire.
	28	Attended a concert given by the Leicestershire Schools Chamber Orchestra, Stationers' Hall, London.
	29	Attended a ceremony marking the conferment of the Freedom of Northampton on the Royal Pioneer Corps, Guildhall, Northampton.
		Attended the Pestalozzi Children's Village Trust silver jubilee reception, Martini Rossi Centre, Haymarket, London.
April	2	Attended the Prime Minister's reception launching the Historic Buildings and Monuments Commission, 10 Downing Street, London.
	17	Opened King's Heath Careers Centre, Poplar Road, Birmingham.
		Reopened Aston Hall, Birmingham.
		Visited Shard End Boys' Club, Birmingham.
	18	Attended a World Heritage Day reception, Ritz Hotel, Piccadilly, London.
	19	Opened Aldershot Military Museum and Visitors' Centre, Aldershot Garrison.
	25	Left Heathrow Airport, London to attend functions in New York in connection with the English Speaking Union, the American Victorian Society and the Order of St John.

May	9	Visited Sandyford House, Newcastle-upon-Tyne. Inspected restoration work, St Mary's Church and Surtees House, Gateshead. Viewed projects run by the Civic Trust for the North East, on board *The Shieldsman*, River Tyne. Attended a borough reception, Park Hotel, Tyneside.
	10	Inspected Northern Heritage Trust restoration work at Black Bull Inn, Alnwick, Northumberland and at Belford Hall, Belford. Attended a luncheon given by Alnwick District Council, Northumberland Hall, Alnwick. Visited the Burrell Collection and the *Scotstyle* exhibition, Glasgow Art Gallery and Museum. Attended a dinner given by the Royal Incorporation of Architects in Scotland, Albany Hotel, Glasgow.
	11	Opened the Royal Incorporation of Architects in Scotland convention, Albany Hotel, Glasgow.
	14	Opened the exhibition *Peace Through Education*, House of Commons, London.
	15	Visited W.S. Atkins Group Consultants, Epsom, Surrey. Presented awards at a Cancer Research Campaign reception, Carlton House Terrace, London.
	17	Visited Boys' Clubs in Lancashire and Greater Manchester. Attended a reception given by the Queen, Buckingham Palace.
	21	Attended the Society of Authors centenary dinner, Mansion House, London.
	22	Visited Warwickshire College of Agriculture, Moreton Morrell. Reopened Stoneleigh Abbey, Kenilworth, Warwickshire.
	23	Opened an exhibition of Chinese ivories, British Museum, London.
	24	Visited RAF Uxbridge. Attended a gala charity performance of *The Pajama Game* by Theatre West 4, Chiswick Town Hall, London.
	25	Presented the Norah Stucken Trust annual award for horticultural achievement, Stationers Hall, London.
	29	Attended the British Consultants Bureau seminar, British Embassy, The Hague, Holland.
	30	Opened Langley Park House, Slough. Opened the building and construction exhibition *Conex '84*, Derngate Centre, Northampton.
	31	Visited the Royal Bath and West Show, Shepton Mallett, Somerset.
June	6	Attended Epsom Races.
	7	Opened the Civil Aviation Centre headquarters of the St John Ambulance Association and the Feltham Division of the St John Ambulance Brigade, Heathrow, Middlesex.
	12	Invested the Governor-General of Canada as a Dame of Justice, and the Honorable Maurice Sauvé as a Knight of Grace, of the Order of St John, Kensington Palace.
	13	Attended a banquet arranged by the Order of St John, Hampton Court Palace.
	16	Witnessed the Queen's Birthday Parade, Horse Guards Parade, London.
	24	Attended a Son et Lumière pageant, Moor Park, Rickmansworth.
	25	Attended a masque, Royal Academy of Arts, London.
	26	Presented COSIRA Rural Employment Awards, Boughton House, Northamptonshire. Attended Grand Day dinner, Middle Temple, London.
	27	Opened the Spectrum Leisure Complex, Willington, County Durham.
	28	Attended the Association of Building Component Manufacturers' annual luncheon, Savoy Hotel, London.
	29	Attended the memorial service for Sir John Betjeman, Westminster Abbey.
July	3	Held two audiences, Kensington Palace.
	4	Attended the annual general meeting of the Cancer Research Campaign, Royal College of Physicians, London.
	5	Visited the Royal Show, National Agricultural Centre, Stoneleigh, Warwickshire.
	10	Visited the Great Yorkshire Show, Harrogate, Yorkshire.
	12	Attended the Queen's garden party, Buckingham Palace.
	13	Enrolled as Senior Fellow, Royal College of Art, Kensington.
	19	Visited the East of England Show, Peterborough.
	25	Attended a performance of the Royal Tournament, Earl's Court, London.

26 Visited the 1st Battalion The Gloucestershire Regiment on Salamanca Day, Lucknow Barracks, Tidworth.

Engagements of **THE DUCHESS OF GLOUCESTER**
August 1983-July 1984

August	27	Visited the Gloucester Centre's Summer Fete, Orton Longueville, Peterborough, Northamptonshire.
	30	Attended the New York City Ballet Gala Performance, Royal Opera House, Covent Garden, London.
September	5	Opened the 4th World Congress of the International Society for Prosthetics and Orthoptics, Imperial College of Science and Technology, London.
	6	Opened the International Congress of Maxillo-Facial Prosthetics and Technology, Royal College of Surgeons, London.
	16	Attended a Pro Corda Concert, Barbican Centre, London.
	20	Visited the Helen Arkell Dyslexia Centre, Fulham, London.
	27	Opened the John Weston Smith Building, St Christopher's School, Hampstead, London.
	29	Opened Whitley House, Old Swinford School, Stourbridge, Worcestershire. Visited National Children's Homes, Birmingham.
October	1	Attended a gala concert in aid of Birthright, Barbican Centre, London.
	4	Attended a City of London Fashion Show, Mansion House, London. Attended a City of London Banquet, Guildhall, London.
	7	Attended the City of London Solicitors Company's 75th anniversary ball, Guildhall, London.
	10	Visited the exhibition *Albert, his Life and Work*, Royal College of Art, Kensington, London.
	11	Attended the 25th anniversary celebrations of the Jack and Jill Club, South Croydon, Surrey.
	12	Attended a Royal College of Organists dinner, Castle Hotel, Windsor, Berkshire.
	13	Attended a gala concert in aid of speech-impaired children, Guildhall, London.
	20	Attended a charity fashion show, All England Tennis Club, Wimbledon, London.
	23	Attended the Victorian Sunday event, Hyde Park, London.
November	2	Attended the unveiling by the Queen of the statue of Earl Mountbatten, Foreign Office Green, London. Attended a reception given by the Prime Minister, Banqueting House, Whitehall, London.
	3	Left Heathrow Airport, London to attend the Wightman Cup Tennis Tournament, Williamsburg, Virginia, U.S.A.
	7	Returned to Heathrow Airport, London, from the U.S.A.
	9	Visited the Bobath Centre, Netherhall Gardens, London.
	10	Attended a concert given in aid of the deaf, Royal Festival Hall, London.
	11	Attended the opening by the Duke of Gloucester of the Thames Tunnel Mills Development, Rotherhithe, London.
	12	Attended the Royal British Legion Festival of Remembrance, Royal Albert Hall, London.
	13	Attended the Remembrance Day ceremony, Cenotaph, Whitehall, London.
	22	Opened Ad Astra First School, Poole, Dorset. Opened Highfield Flatlets, Southbourne, Dorset. Attended the St Cecilia's Day concert, Royal Festival Hall, London.
	23	Attended the opening by the Duke of Gloucester of the exhibition *Genius of Venice*, Royal Academy of Arts, London. Attended the Italian Ambassador's dinner, Italian Embassy, London.
	24	Opened a new extension at Fleming Fulton School, Ulster. Attended a luncheon given by the Women Caring Trust, Northern Ireland. Visited the new exhibition gallery at the Ulster Folk and Transport Museum.
	29	Visited the Notting Hill Housing Trust Christmas Fair, Town Hall, Kensington.

December	1	Attended a London Home Safety Council luncheon, House of Lords, London.
	8	Attended the Fan Makers' Livery Dinner, Mansion House, London.
	20	Attended *The Observer* Victorian Christmas Concert, Royal Albert Hall, London.
January	19	Attended a meeting of the Medical Research Committee, Cardiothoracic Institute, West London.
February	15	Attended the Asthma Society's *Evening of Fashion and Music*, Drapers' Hall, London.
	23	Attended the Elgar Commemorative Concert, Royal Festival Hall, London.
	24	Attended the Queen's luncheon for the Crown Prince of Saudi-Arabia, Buckingham Palace.
	25	Visited the Merseyside and Wirral branch of the National Association for Gifted Children, Paddington Comprehensive School, Liverpool.
		Opened Thirlmere Green Housing Development and the new Sports Hall, Huyton College, Knowsley, Liverpool.
	26	Attended a charity gala evening *If They Could See Me Now*, Theatre Royal, Drury Lane, London.
	28	Visited the Royal Army Educational Corps headquarters, Eltham, London.
	29	Visited the offices of the Association for All Speech Impaired Children, Smithfield, London.
March	14	Opened the St John Ambulance Museum, Clerkenwell, London.
	18	Presented shamrock to the London Irish Rifles, Duke of York's Headquarters, Chelsea.
	19	Attended the Westminster Spring Festival Daffodil Day rally, Central Hall, Westminster.
	23	Left RAF Northolt and arrived at Luxembourg.
		Toured the fortifications, Luxembourg.
		Visited the European Parliament, the European Courts of Justice and the European Investment Bank, Luxembourg.
		Visited an exhibition opened by the Duke of Gloucester at the Luxembourg State Museum.
		Attended a buffet-dinner at the Royal Palace, Luxembourg.
		Attended a concert at the Eglise St Michel, Luxembourg.
	25	Arrived back at RAF Northolt from Luxembourg.
	26	Attended a concert given by the London College of Music, Great Marlborough Street, London.
	27	Held two audiences, Kensington Palace.
	28	Opened the Clinical Diagnostic Unit, Kidderminster General Hospital, Worcestershire.
		Visited Brintons Limited, Kidderminster.
April	18	Visited Daloon Production (UK) Ltd, Nottinghamshire.
		Visited Newark District Council Offices at Kelham Hall, Nottinghamshire.
	25	Left Heathrow Airport, London to accompany the Duke of Gloucester on his visit to New York in connection with the English-Speaking Union, the American Victorian Society and the Order of St John.
May	3	Returned to Heathrow Airport, London from the U.S.A.
	10	Attended the All Pakistan Women's Association Spring Feast, Intercontinental Hotel, London.
	16	Left RAF Northolt for West Germany to visit the Royal Army Educational Corps and the Royal Air Force Hospital in Rheindahlen.
	17	Left Rheindahlen and arrived at RAF Northolt.
		Attended a reception given by the Queen, Buckingham Palace.
	21	Visited the Chelsea Flower Show, Royal Hospital, Chelsea.
	23	Visited the WRVS *Rags and Riches* exhibition and presented awards, Civic Centre, Hounslow, Middlesex.
	24	Attended the Hospitallers Club of Wales' 80th birthday luncheon, House of Lords.
June	6	Attended Epsom Races.
	7	Presented intensive care equipment to Watford General Hospital, Hertfordshire.
		Opened the Special Care Nursing Wing, Watford General Hospital.
		Opened the Praetorian Halfway Housing Scheme, Shenley Hospital, Radlett, Hertfordshire.

	7	Visited Colnbrook School, South Oxley, Hertfordshire.
	13	Attended a banquet arranged by the Order of St John, Hampton Court Palace.
	16	Witnessed the Queen's Birthday Parade, Horse Guards Parade, London.
	17	Presented the Stella Artois Lawn Tennis Championship prize, Queen's Club, Kensington.
	20	Opened Gloucester Court, Petersfield, Hampshire.
		Opened the Wessex Body Scanner, Southampton General Hospital.
	25	Attended a masque, Royal Academy of Arts, London.
	26	Attended Grand Day dinner, Middle Temple, London.
	29	Presented the Queen Mother Awards for the Keep Britain Tidy Group, Guildhall, London.
	30	Attended the Lawn Tennis Championships, Wimbledon.
		Attended the Lawn Tennis Association's annual ball, London Hilton Hotel.
July	12	Attended the Queen's garden party, Buckingham Palace.
	13	Attended the Royal College of Art Convocation for the enrolment of the Duke of Gloucester as a Senior Fellow, Kensington.
		Attended an Evening of Music and Dance in aid of 'Leukaemia of 365', Eton College.
	17	Visited Ash and Ashwood Family Resource Centre, Woking, Surrey.
	19	Opened the Royal Surgical Aid Society's home for the elderly, High Broom, Crowborough, East Sussex.
		Attended the annual prizegiving at Dorton House School for the Blind, Sevenoaks, Kent.
	25	Attended a performance of the Royal Tournament, Earl's Court, London.

Engagements of **THE DUKE OF KENT**
August 1983-July 1984

September	7	Visited the 5th Battalion, The Royal Regiment of Fusiliers, in training, Dartmoor, Devon.
		Attended a dinner given by the Ambassador of the Korean Republic, Wimbledon, London.
	8	Attended a Civil Service Motoring Association's luncheon, House of Commons, London.
	27	Attended a London Philharmonic Orchestra Concert, Royal Festival Hall, London.
October	1	Left Heathrow Airport, London, with a British trade mission visiting the Republic of Korea.
	9	Visited The Lorne Scots, near Toronto, Canada.
	10	Returned to Heathrow Airport, London from Canada.
	11	Received the Jordanian Ambassador in audience, York House, St James's Palace.
	12	Attended a dinner given for the Wellington Chamber of Commerce, New Zealand, Vintners Hall, London.
	20	Attended the première of *La Traviata*, Odeon Theatre, Haymarket, London.
	26	Chaired the British Computer Society's Annual General Meeting, Royal Institute of British Architects, London.
	27	Visited the Royal Signals and Radar Establishment, Malvern, Worcestershire.
	31	Attended the Royal Geographical Society's presidential dinner, Savoy Hotel, London.
November	2	Attended the unveiling by the Queen of the statue of Earl Mountbatten, Foreign Office Green, London.
		Attended a reception given by the Prime Minister, Banqueting House, Whitehall, London.
		Visited the headquarters of the Simplification of International Trade Procedures Board, Almack House, London.
	3	Visited Plessey Telecommunications Limited, Liverpool.
		Visited the Crawford Arts Centre, Liverpool.
		Attended a Charity Concert, Philharmonic Hall, Liverpool.
	7	Chaired the Committee of Managers Meeting, the Royal Institution, London.
	9	Held an audience at York House, St James's Palace.
		Attended the dedication of the Falkland Islands Campaign Memorial, Guards' Chapel, London.
	10	Presided at the National Electronics Council's Mountbatten lecture, Institute of Electrical Engineers, London.
	11	Attended the Commonwealth War Graves Commission Gardeners' Remembrance Service, St

	11	George's Chapel, Westminster Abbey.
	12	Attended the Royal British Legion Festival of Remembrance, Royal Albert Hall.
	13	Laid a wreath at the Cenotaph, Remembrance Day ceremony, Whitehall, London.
	15	Attended the Army Ski Association's Cocktail Party, London.
	16	Visited the Production Engineering Research Association, Melton Mowbray, Leicestershire.
	17	Attended the Export Group for Constructional Industries luncheon, Savoy Hotel, London.
	21	Chaired the Symposium *Electronics and Information Technology*, International Computers Ltd, Manchester.
	22	Visited the Automobile Association's National Training Centre, Widmerpool.
		Visited Fabrikat Ltd, Sutton in Ashfield, Nottinghamshire.
	23	Visited Mullard Ltd, Durham.
		Visited Electrolux-Flymo Ltd, Newton Aycliffe, County Durham.
	24	Attended a Business and Technician Education Council reception, Reform Club, Pall Mall, London.
	25	Attended the first residential course of the National Electronics Council's Programme *Careers in Information Technology*, Esher, Surrey.
	29	Visited the Imperial War Museum, London.
		Opened the Institute of Occupational Health, Birmingham University.
	30	Chaired the conference *Banking on Exports*, Sutton Coldfield.
December	2	Presided at a degrees ceremony, Surrey University, Guildford.
	7	Attended the 100th Association Football match between Oxford and Cambridge Universities, Wembley, London.
	8	Attended a Royal Agricultural Society of England Council Meeting, Belgrave Square, London.
	13	Visited the 2nd Battalion, Scots Guards, Chelsea Barracks, London.
	14	Chaired a meeting of the United Kingdom Committee of European Music Year 1985, Arts Council, Piccadilly, London.
	15	Attended a meeting of the trustees of the Duke of Edinburgh's Commonwealth Study Conference, Welbeck Way, London.
January	19	Presented Conoco/Jet Motoring Writers and Broadcasters of the Year awards, London Press Centre.
February	6	Attended a meeting of the Oakley Lodge of Freemasons, Basingstoke.
	7	Attended the Royal Agricultural Society of England's Honorary Fellows' Dinner, Boodles's, St James's Street, London.
	14	Attended a luncheon, and visited the *Flanders to the Falklands* exhibition, National Army Museum, London.
	15	Visited the University of Surrey, Guildford.
		Opened the *Treasures from Korea* exhibition, British Museum, London.
	17	Chaired a European Music Year 1985 Committee meeting, Arts Council, Piccadilly, London.
	21	Opened the 20th *British Growers Look Ahead* conference and exhibition, Harrogate.
March	15	Attended the Fellowship of Engineering's annual general meeting, Royal Society of Arts, London.
	16	Attended a dinner of the Norfolk Lieutenancy, Blickling Hall, Aylsham, Norfolk.
	19	Dined with the Mercers' Company, Ironmonger Lane, London.
	21	Visited Davy McKee (Sheffield) Ltd.
		Inspected contingents of the Combined Cadet Force, Endcliffe Hall, Sheffield.
		Attended the annual feast of the Cutlers in Hallamshire, Cutlers' Hall, Sheffield.
	22	Visited H. Clarkson & Co., Camomile Street, London.
		Attended a luncheon at the Baltic Exchange, and opened the London Meat Futures Exchange.
April	2	Held an audience, St James's Palace.
	3	Arrived at Belfast to begin a 24-hour visit to Northern Ireland.
		Attended a reception given by the Northern Ireland Secretary, Hillsborough Castle.
	4	Visited a RNLI lifeboat station, Donaghadee, County Down.

	4	Visited members of the Dorset and Devon Regiment, Bessbrook.
		Visited military bases at Ballykinlar, County Down, and Ballykelly, County Londonderry.
		Visited troops on border duty, South Armagh.
	5	Attended the All England Lawn Tennis Club's Wimbledon Dinner, Institute of Directors, Pall Mall, London.
	6	Held two audiences, York House, St James's Palace.
	10	Met the Amir of Bahrain at the beginning of his State Visit, Windsor Castle.
		Attended a State banquet for the Amir of Bahrain, Windsor Castle.
		Visited the Air Forces Memorial, Runnymede, Surrey.
	11	Attended the Lord Mayor of London's Banquet for the Amir of Bahrain, Guildhall.
		Visited Racal-Comsec Ltd, Salisbury, Wiltshire.
		Visited Membrain Ltd, Wimborne, Dorset.
	12	Attended the Amir of Bahrain's State banquet, Dorchester Hotel, London.
	25	Attended the annual investiture and Grand Festival of the United Grand Lodge of England, Freemasons' Hall, London.
	27	Visited Cooper Roller Bearings Ltd, King's Lynn, Norfolk.
		Visited Bespak plc, King's Lynn.
	29	Attended the Queen's Scouts parade and services, St George's Chapel, Windsor.
May	1	Left Heathrow Airport for Morocco, and arrived at Salé Airport, Rabat.
	2	Called on the Moroccan Minister of Commerce, Rabat.
		Laid a wreath at the tomb of King Mohammed V, Royal Mausoleum, Rabat.
		Visited the Anglo-Moroccan joint venture factory, Chelco, Rabat.
		Attended a Governor's luncheon, Fez.
		Received in audience by King Hassan II, Fez.
		Attended a ministerial and business dinner, British Ambassador's residence, Rabat.
	3	Toured a steel mill, Nador.
		Attended a Governor's luncheon, Nador.
		Attended a Chamber of Commerce dinner, Casablanca.
	4	Visited Thomson CSF, Casablanca.
		Called on the President of CNM/CCI, Casablanca.
		Entertained by the Moroccan Prime Minister at lunch, Casablanca.
		Visited graves of Commonwealth war dead, Ben M'Sik cemetery, Casablanca.
		Left Casablanca and arrived Stansted Airport, Essex.
	10	Visited lifeboat stations at Longhope, Stromness and Kirkwall, Orkney.
		Attended an RNLI musical evening, Blair Castle, Blair Atholl.
	11	Visited the lifeboat station, Arbroath.
	14	Received the Prime Minister of the Cook Islands, St James's Palace.
		Received the Moroccan Minister of Commerce, St James's Palace.
	16	Visited the European Poultry Fair, National Agricultural Centre, Stoneleigh.
		Attended a Government dinner in connection with the Commonwealth War Graves Commission, Marlborough House.
	17	Attended a reception given by the Queen, Buckingham Palace.
	19	Attended the F.A. Cup Final, Wembley.
	20	Unveiled the Fred Perry Gates and statue, All England Lawn Tennis Club, Wimbledon.
	21	Left Heathrow Airport, London for Paris.
	22	Attended a meeting of the European Organising Committee Bureau in connection with European Music Year 1985, Hôtel La Pelouse, Paris.
		Left Paris and returned to London.
	24	Attended the Automobile Association's annual general meeting, Savoy Hotel, London.
		Attended the Piper Champagne National Hunt Awards luncheon, Dorchester Hotel, London.
		Entertained at dinner by the American Ambassador, Winfield House, Regent's Park, London.
	30	Took the chair at a United Kingdom Committee meeting for European Music Year 1985, British Council, London.
	31	Visited Garrett Airesearch Ltd, Blackburn.
		Visited Shorrock Security Systems Ltd, Blackburn.
		Visited the Addison Tool Company Ltd, Bamber Bridge, Preston.

June	1	Attended the French International Tennis Championships, Stade Roland-Garros, Paris.
	4	Held an audience, St James's Palace.
		Visited the Cabinet War Rooms and the exhibition *Resistance*, London.
	6	Attended the Royal Agricultural Society of England President's Day, Chedworth, Gloucestershire.
		Took the Salute at Beating Retreat, Horse Guards Parade, London.
	7	Visited GEC's Hirst Research Centre, Wembley, Middlesex.
		Attended the Prime Minister's reception for the London Economic Summit, St James's Palace.
	16	Attended the Queen's Birthday Parade, Horse Guards Parade, London.
	19	Visited the British Army Equipment Exhibition 1984, Aldershot.
	20	Left London for the United States of America and arrived in Washington.
	21	Visited Annapolis, Maryland.
	22	Visited the Eastern shore, Kent Island and Baltimore.
	23	Attended the 350th anniversary celebrations of St Mary's City, Maryland.
	24	Left Washington for England and arrived back in London.
	25	Attended the opening day of the Wimbledon Tennis Championships.
July	3	Attended the Royal Show, National Agricultural Centre, Stoneleigh, Warwickshire.
	4	Attended the Royal Show, National Agricultural Centre, Stoneleigh, Warwickshire.
	7	Presented challenge trophies at the Wimbledon Tennis Championships.
	8	Presented challenge trophies at the Wimbledon Tennis Championships.
	10	Reopened Lennox House Housing Project, Hackney, London.
	11	Visited Southern United Kingdom groups of the Duke of Edinburgh's Commonwealth Study Conference, Leicester and Stratford-upon-Avon.
	12	Attended the annual service of the Order of St Michael and St George, St Paul's Cathedral, London.
		Attended the Queen's garden party, Buckingham Palace.
		Attended the Royal Regiment of Fusiliers' annual cocktail party, Tower of London.
	13	Presided at a degrees and diplomas conferment ceremony, University of Surrey, Guildford.
	16	Left Heathrow Airport, London to visit New York, Cleveland and Chicago.
	21	Returned to Heathrow Airport, London from the United States.
	23	Attended an evening performance of the Royal Tournament, Earl's Court, London.
	24	Named a new lifeboat, Exmouth, Devon.
	26	Attended, and represented the Duke of Edinburgh at, a memorial service for Viscount Astor of Hever, St Martin-in-the-Fields, London.

Engagements of THE DUCHESS OF KENT
August 1983-July 1984

October	20	Attended the première of *La Traviata*, Odeon Theatre, Haymarket, London.
	24	Attended the Age Concern Vintage Year celebration lunch, Rainbow Rooms, Kensington, London.
November	1	Attended a gala dinner in aid of the Stars' Organisation for Spastics, Europa Hotel, London.
	2	Attended the unveiling by the Queen of the statue of Earl Mountbatten, Foreign Office Green, London.
		Attended a reception given by the Prime Minister, Banqueting House, Whitehall, London.
	9	Attended a reception and concert at Westminster Cathedral, London.
	12	Visited the Lawn Tennis Association's National Training Centre, Bisham Abbey, Berkshire.
		Attended the Royal British Legion Festival of Remembrance, Royal Albert Hall, London.
	13	Attended the Remembrance Day ceremony, Cenotaph, Whitehall, London.
	17	Attended a charity auction, Portland Hotel, Manchester.
	23	Attended a charity gala evening, Lakeside Country Club, Frimley, Surrey.
	25	Visited the University of Leeds.
	26	Opened Worsley Barracks, near York.
		Visited the new almshouses at Ogleforth, York.
	30	Attended an awards ceremony, Royal Northern College of Music, Manchester.

	30	Attended a performance of *Gloriana*, Royal Northern College of Music, Manchester.
December	6	Visited UNICEF UK Committee new headquarters, Lincoln's Inn Fields, London.
	8	Opened the Civic Centre, Ashford, Kent.
		Opened the Royal British Legion Churchill Rehabilitation and Assessment Centre, Maidstone, Kent.
	13	Attended the Not Forgotten Association's Christmas party, Royal Mews, Buckingham Palace.
	14	Held three audiences, York House, St James's Palace.
January	10	Visited Norwich Institution for the Blind, Norwich.
	19	Held four audiences, York House, St James's Palace.
	24	Presented the *Standard* Drama Awards, Savoy Hotel, London.
February	2	Presented the British Forces Broadcasting Service Sporting Personality of 1983 Award, National Army Museum, London.
	3	Attended the Black and White Ball, Harrogate.
	7	Visited the Lord Chancellor's Department, House of Lords, London.
	14	Visited the Civil Defence College, Easingwold, North Yorkshire.
	16	Visited Helen House Hospice, Oxford.
March	14	Attended a gala fashion presentation *Window on Hongkong*, Harrods, Knightsbridge, London.
	16	Attended a dinner of the Norfolk Lieutenancy, Blickling Hall, Aylsham, Norfolk.
	20	Visited Camphill Village Trust, Newnham, Gloucestershire.
		Visited the National Star Centre for Disabled Youth, Cheltenham.
	23	Attended the Memorial Service for the Duke of Beaufort, Guards' Chapel, London.
	27	Presented the annual Composer's Awards, Wedgwood House, Wigmore Street, London.
	28	Attended the Charities Luncheon of the Clothworkers Company, Mincing Lane, London.
	29	Held two audiences, St James's Palace.
April	3	Arrived at Belfast to begin a 24-hour visit to Northern Ireland.
		Attended a reception given by the Northern Ireland Secretary, Hillsborough Castle.
	4	Visited an electronics factory, Coleraine.
		Entertained at luncheon at the Northern Ireland Hotel and Catering College, Portrush, County Antrim.
		Opened a flats complex, County Antrim.
	6	Took the Salute at the Sovereign's Parade, Royal Military Academy, Sandhurst.
	9	Opened the Rosemary Musker High School, Thetford, Norfolk.
	10	Met the Amir of Bahrain at the beginning of his State Visit, Windsor Castle.
		Attended a State banquet for the Amir of Bahrain, Windsor Castle.
	11	Attended the Lord Mayor of London's banquet for the Amir of Bahrain, Guildhall.
	12	Attended the Amir of Bahrain's State banquet, Dorchester Hotel, London.
	25	Attended a dedication service for the Not Forgotten Association's new ambulance coach, Royal Mews, Buckingham Palace.
	26	Opened a new production line, Jameson's Chocolates plc, Tottenham, London.
	27	Attended a dinner for the Variety Club's Sunshine Coach Committee, Garrick Club, London.
	28	Attended the concert finals of the Young Musician of the Year competition, Free Trade Hall, Manchester.
	30	Opened the new Isotope Scanning Unit, City Hospital, St Albans.
May	2	Attended a charity gala concert, Over-Seas House, Park Lane, London.
	3	Attended an anniversary gala concert, Georgian Theatre, Richmond, Yorkshire.
	10	Opened the Clarendon Wing, Leeds General Infirmary.
		Opened British Telecommunications (North East Region) headquarters, Leeds.
	11	Opened the Clothworkers' Textile Structures and Mechanics Laboratory, Leeds University.
		Presided at an honorary degrees conferment ceremony, Leeds University.
		Attended a dinner for honorary graduates, Leeds University.
	12	Attended Open Day, Leeds University.

14	Visited two exhibitions of art at Donnington Priory and Newbury, Berkshire.
	Attended the Newbury Spring Festival concert, St Nicholas' Church, Newbury.
	Left RAF Northolt for West Germany and arrived at Dusseldorf.
16	Visited the Royal Women's Army Corps Command Distribution Centre, Dusseldorf.
	Attended a luncheon, WRAC Officers' Mess, Dusseldorf.
	Visited the Rathaus, Detmold.
	Attended a Royal Dragoon Guards' dinner, Detmold.
17	Visited a regimental kindergarten, Detmold.
	Visited parts of the Royal Dragoon Guards' camp, Detmold.
	Left RAF Gutersloh for London, and arrived at RAF Northolt.
19	Attended the F.A. Cup Final, Wembley.
20	Attended the unveiling by the Duke of Kent of the Fred Perry Gates and statue, Wimbledon.
21	Attended a Royal College of Music appeal reception, St James's Palace.
23	Attended the Yehudi Menuhin Schools 21st anniversary concert, St James's Palace.
24	Entertained at dinner by the American Ambassador, Winfield House, Regent's Park, London.

June	1	Attended the French International Tennis Championships, Stade Roland-Garros, Paris.
	4	Opened an exhibition of work by Bahrain Art Society members, Leighton House, West Kensington.
	5	Opened the new District General Hospital, Stafford.
		Visited Barlaston First School, Staffordshire.
		Visited Josiah Wedgwood & Sons Ltd, Barlaston.
	8	Reviewed the In-Pensioners, Royal Hospital, Chelsea.
	16	Witnessed the Queen's Birthday Parade, Horse Guards Parade, London.
	20	Left London for the United States of America and arrived in Washington.
	21	Visited Annapolis, Maryland.
	22	Visited the Eastern shore, Kent Island and Baltimore.
	23	Attended the 350th anniversary celebrations of St Mary's City, Maryland.
	24	Left Washington for England and arrived back in London.
	25	Attended the opening day of the Wimbledon Tennis Championships.
	28	Opened the new check-in hall, Manchester International Airport.
		Attended a dinner in aid of the Royal Northern College of Music appeal, Manchester.
	29	Visited the Children's Unit of the Christie Hospital and Holt Radium Institute, Manchester.
		Visited the Samaritans' headquarters, Manchester.
		Attended a Royal Northern College of Music Symphony Orchestra concert, Manchester.

July	4	Attended the Royal Show, National Agricultural Centre, Stoneleigh, Warwickshire.
	7	Presented the Women's Singles Championship trophy, All England Tennis Club, Wimbledon.
	8	Attended the final day of the Wimbledon Tennis Championships, and presented trophies.
	10	Attended a concert in aid of the Voice of the Cathedral Appeal, Westminster Cathedral.
	11	Attended a soirée in aid of the Royal College of Music, Winfield House, Regent's Park, London.
	12	Attended the annual service of the Order of St Michael and St George, St Paul's Cathedral, London.
		Attended the Women's Royal Army Corps' 35th anniversary dinner, Guildhall, London.
		Attended the Queen's garden party, Buckingham Palace.
	15	Attended a thanksgiving service, Worth Church, Crawley, Surrey.
		Visited St Catherine's Hospice, Crawley.
	16	Visited York Minster.
	17	Visited St Michael's Cheshire Home, Axbridge, Somerset.
		Visited the factory of Showering plc, Shepton Mallet, Somerset.
	19	Presided at degree conferment ceremonies, Leeds University.
	20	Presided at degree conferment ceremonies, Leeds University.
	24	Attended the naming by the Duke of Kent of a new lifeboat, Exmouth, Devon.
	26	Attended the memorial service for Viscount Astor of Hever, St Martin-in-the-Fields, London.

Engagements of **PRINCESS ALEXANDRA**
August 1983-July 1984

September	3	Attended the Highland Games, Braemar, Deeside.
	7	Visited the Royal Pavilion, Brighton, Sussex.
		Attended a centenary reception of the Institution of Environmental Health Officers, Brighton, Sussex.
	16	Held an audience, Friary Court, St James's Palace.
	19	Attended a Government reception at Lancaster House, London.
	20	Attended the Bob Hope British Classic gala dinner, Grosvenor House, London.
	22	Opened the Enterprise Zone roads, Isle of Dogs, London.
		Opened a new Asda superstore, Beckton, London.
		Attended the European première of the film *We of the Never, Never*, Odeon Cinema, Kensington, London.
	27	Opened St Giles Hospice, Whittington, Staffordshire.
		Attended a thanksgiving service, Lichfield Cathedral, Staffordshire.
		Visited Lichfield Cathedral School and attended a reception.
	29	Visited RAF Binbrook, Lincolnshire.
		Attended the preview of the exhibition *Britain 1923-1983: An American View*, Royal Festival Hall, London.
October	18	Attended a meeting of the British Red Cross Society Council, Grosvenor Crescent, London.
	19	Opened the Burlington House Fair, Royal Academy of Arts, London.
		Attended a reception given by the Prime Minister, 10 Downing Street, London.
	20	Opened a housing scheme for the elderly, Gedling, Nottinghamshire.
		Visited the Arnold Leisure Centre, Gedling.
		Attended a muncipal reception, Bonnington Theatre, Gedling.
	26	Visited the Ilford PDSA Animal Treatment Centre, Redbridge, Essex.
	31	Attended a Hallowe'en Ball, Intercontinental Hotel, London.
November	2	Attended the unveiling by the Queen of the statue of Earl Mountbatten, Foreign Office Green, London.
		Attended a reception given by the Prime Minister, Banqueting House, Whitehall, London.
	4	Opened the Holbeach Community Centre, Lincolnshire.
		Opened Geest Industries houseplant complex, and distribution centre, Spalding, Lincolnshire.
	7	Attended the Cliff Richard Silver Jubilee Concert, Apollo Victoria Theatre, London.
	9	Left Heathrow Airport, London to visit Vienna.
		Attended a performance of opera, Vienna Opera House.
	10	Attended a reception at the Palace Schwarzenburg Hotel, Vienna.
		Attended an official luncheon given by the British Ambassador in Vienna.
		Visited the Albertina Museum, Vienna.
		Attended a gala performance by the English Theatre Company, Vienna.
		Attended an official supper party given by the Mayor of Vienna, at the Rathaus, Vienna.
	11	Visited the Augarten Porcelain workshops, near Vienna.
		Attended a luncheon given by the Federal President.
		Attended a choral performance given by the Vienna Boys Choir, Palais Augarten.
	12	Attended a Church of England Remembrance Day Service, Vienna.
		Attended a reception for staff at the British Embassy, Vienna.
	13	Arrived at Heathrow Airport, London from Vienna.
	16	Switched on the Christmas lights, Regent Street, London.
		Attended a charity dinner-dance given by the Anglo-Peruvian Society, Porchester Hall, London.
	17	Attended a charity exhibition *The Art of Living*, Alpine Gallery, London.
	20	Visited the Ditchley Foundation, Oxfordshire and attended part of a conservation conference.
	22	Presented the Design Council's Schools Design Prize, Institution of Civil Engineers,

	22	London.
		Attended the New Bridge lecture, Ironmongers' Hall, London.
	23	Visited the Whitechapel Bell Foundry, London.
		Attended the Printers' Charitable Corps banquet, Grosvenor House, London.
	30	Attended the City of London Red Cross Christmas Market reception, Old Library, Guildhall, London.
December	2	Presided at a degrees ceremony, University of Lancaster.
	14	Presented the 1983 Children of Courage Awards, Westminster Abbey, London.
		Held an audience, St James's Palace.
	15	Visited St Christopher's Hospice, Sydenham, London.
		Attended the Olympia International Showjumping Championships, London.
January	17	Visited Chadwick House, the headquarters of the Institute of Environmental Health Officers, Rushworth Street, London.
	18	Visited the Haywards Heath headquarters of the Royal Commonwealth Society for the Blind, Sussex.
		Attended a luncheon in honour of Sir John and Lady Wilson, Balcombe Place, West Sussex.
	23	Attended a reception marking the beginning of restoration work on the organ of the Royal Albert Hall, London.
February	8	Attended the funeral of the Duke of Beaufort, Badminton.
	9	Visited the BBC External Services, Bush House, London.
		Visited the Mental Health Foundation's offices, Hallam St, London.
	10	Attended the *Kids 'n' Cops* charity concert, Old Town Hall, Fulham.
	14	Opened Park Lodge hostel for men, Hackney, London.
		Attended a Watermen's Company reception, St Mary-at-Hill, London.
	16	Held two audiences, St James's Palace.
		Attended the Mountbatten Festival of Music, Royal Albert Hall, London.
	23	Named the RNLI lifeboat *Sir Max Aitken II*, Cowes, Isle of Wight.
March	29	Attended a Furniture Makers' Company anniversary reception, Guildhall, London.
		Attended the United Kingdom première of the film *Yentl*, Leicester Square Theatre, London.
	30	Attended the Royal Air Force anniversary concert, Royal Festival Hall, London.
April	4	Attended the 'Spring Celebration' health festival, in aid of Birthright, Savoy Hotel, London.
	10	Welcomed the Amir of Bahrain at the beginning of his State Visit, Heathrow Airport, London, and accompanied him to Windsor.
		Attended a State banquet for the Amir of Bahrain, Windsor Castle.
	12	Presented the Ross McWhirter Young Citizens' Awards, Goldsmiths Hall, London.
		Attended the Amir of Bahrain's State banquet, Dorchester Hotel, London.
	14	Attended the memorial service for the Dowager Countess of Airlie, Cortachy, Angus.
	17	Attended the Television and Radio Industry Club luncheon and presented the 1984 Celebrity Awards, Grosvenor House, London.
	26	Visited *HMS Broadsword*, Devonport Naval Base.
		Visited the Highbury Mencap Centre, Plymouth.
	28	Attended the 38th Burma Star Reunion, Royal Albert Hall, London.
May	2	Attended a Children's County Holiday Fund thanksgiving service, Guards' Chapel, London and a reception at St James's Palace.
		Attended the Sir John Keswick Memorial Lecture, Royal Institution of Great Britain, London.
	3	Held two audiences, Friary Court, St James's Palace.
		Attended a recital by the Boston Symphony Chamber Players, Merchant Taylors' Hall, London.
	4	Opened the Friends Dental Unit for handicapped people, Chichester Hospital.
		Visited the CARE West Sussex Village, Burton Rough.
		Visited Seaford College, Petworth, Sussex.

	5	Attended a performance of *Great Expectations*, Royal Theatre and Opera House, Northampton.
	8	Inaugurated Wessex Water Authority's drainage and marine treatment schemes, Wyke Regis, Dorset.
		Attended celebrations marking the 700th anniversary of the granting of a Royal Charter, Lyme Regis, Dorset.
	10	Attended the dedication of the Diplomatic Gates, Grosvenor Square, and a reception at the American Embassy, London.
	11	Attended the general court of the Royal Humane Society, Mansion House, London.
	14	Visited North Ayrshire District Hospital, Kilmarnock.
		Visited Culzean Park Centre, Maybole, Ayrshire.
	21	Visited the Chelsea Flower Show, Royal Hospital, Chelsea.
	23	Opened the Retirement Homes Association's village, Elmbridge, Cranleigh, Surrey.
		Attended Queen Alexandra's House centenary concert, Kensington Gore, London.
	24	Opened Unigate's new St Ivel creamery, Wootton Bassett, Wiltshire.
		Attended a dinner in honour of Dr Luis Palau, Tallow Chandlers Hall, London.
	31	Attended the UK première of *The Terry Fox Story*, Leicester Square Theatre, London.

June	1	Attended the opening of the exhibition *From Borso to Cesare d'Este 1450-1628* Matthieson Gallery, London.
	4	Opened the Maidstone Hospital, Kent.
		Attended the preview of *On Your Toes*, Palace Theatre, London.
	6	Attended Epsom Races.
	7	Visited the Tavistock Clinic, Belsize Park, London.
	12	Met delegates to the 9th Cystic Fibrosis Congress, Metropole Hotel, Brighton.
		Visited the 2nd Cystic Fibrosis Adults Conference, Norfolk Continental Hotel, Brighton.
	14	Left Gatwick Airport, London for the U.S.A. and arrived at Houston, Texas.
	15	Attended an English National Opera reception, River Oaks County Club, Houston, Texas.
		Attended a reception on board *HMS Active*, New Orleans, Louisiana.
	16	Visited the 1984 Louisiana World Exposition, New Orleans.
		Attended the English National Opera's performance of *Gloriana*, Theatre of Performing Arts, New Orleans.
		Attended a buffet dinner, Windsor Court Hotel, New Orleans.
	17	Toured the French Quarter, New Orleans, and visited Brennan's Restaurant.
		Attended a reception for the Central City Opera, Platte River Rowing Club, Denver, Colorado.
	18	Visited Central City Opera House, Denver.
		Toured the Rockies, Colorado.
		Attended the English-Speaking Union's reception for the Queen's Birthday, University Club, Denver.
	20	Attended an English-Speaking Union reception and luncheon, Waldorf Astoria Hotel, New York.
		Attended the English National Opera's performance of *Rigoletto*, Metropolitan Opera House, New York.
		Attended a dinner, Avery Fisher Hall, New York.
	21	Visited premises run by the Richmond Fellowship, New York.
		Attended a British Olympic Association reception and lunch, St Regis Hotel, New York.
		Attended a reception for the Leeds Castle Foundation, New York.

July	2	Returned to Heathrow Airport, London from the United States of America.
	4	Visited BBC Radio for celebrations of the diamond jubilee of Schools Broadcasting, Pebble Mill, Birmingham.
		Attended the Anglo-American ball *Les Retrouvailles*, Royal Academy of Arts, London.
	5	Visited Elizabeth Garrett Anderson Hospital, Euston Road, London.
		Held two audiences, St James's Palace.
	6	Attended the Wimbledon Tennis Championships.
	9	Presided at congregations for the conferment of degrees, University of Lancaster.
	10	Presided at congregations for the conferment of degrees, University of Lancaster.
	11	Presided at degree conferment congregations, University of Lancaster.

16   Attended a reception for delegates to the Richmond Fellowship international conference, Goldsmiths Hall, London.

17   Attended the Queen's garden party, Buckingham Palace.

18   Attended a reception given by *Ognisko Polskie*, Princes Gate, London.

19   Opened the Cyclotron, Neutron Therapy Research Unit, Clatterbridge Hospital, Merseyside.
Visited St John's Hospice, Clatterbridge.
Attended the Billy Graham Mission England meeting, Anfield Football Stadium, Liverpool.

22   Visited the Forres Fair, Morayshire.
Visited the Royal Findhorn Yacht Club, Morayshire.

23   Visited Leanchoil Hospital, Forres.
Visited local industries, West Morayshire.

25   Held three audiences, Friary Court, St James's Palace.

26   Attended the memorial service for Viscount Astor of Hever, St Martin-in-the-Fields, London.
Presented prizes at the Carl Flesch International Violin Competition, Barbican Hall, London.

27   Attended the annual horse show and Metropolitan Police Tournament, Mounted Training Establishment, Imber Court, East Molesey, Surrey.

Engagements of **PRINCE MICHAEL OF KENT**
August 1983-July 1984

September

8   Attended a Son et Lumière display, Horse Guards Parade, London.

9   Left London for a five-day visit to the United States in connection with the America's Cup.

20   Attended a luncheon, Old Bailey, London.

22   Presented *A Taste of Britain* awards, RAC Club, Pall Mall, London.
Began a two-day visit to RAF Waddington, Lincolnshire.

24   Visited the Transport Trust exhibition, Donington Park Motor Race Circuit.

October

4   Visited Vauxhall Motors and Gordon Coachworks Ltd.

7   Attended the presentation of prizes, Chosen Hill School, Churchdown, Gloucester.

14   Attended the Royal British Legion Poppy Ball, Intercontinental Hotel, London.

15   Left London for Texas, in connection with the English National Opera's 1984 Tour.

21   Visited Avon Tyres Ltd, Melksham, Wiltshire.
Visited Morgan Motors, Malvern Link.

26   Attended the Royal Life-Saving Society luncheon, and presented the 1983 *Water Watch* competition prizes, London.
Attended the British Bobsleigh Association's Olympic Evening, Haslemere, Surrey.

November

2   Attended the unveiling by the Queen of the statue of Earl Mountbatten, Foreign Office Green, London.
Attended a reception given by the Prime Minister, Banqueting House, Whitehall.

3   Opened the Automotive Studies Buildings at West Bromwich College of Commerce and Technology, Birmingham.

11   Attended a Defence Electronics Industry luncheon, Ironmongers' Hall, London.

12   Attended the Royal British Legion Festival of Remembrance, Royal Albert Hall, London.

13   Laid a wreath at the Service of Remembrance, Cenotaph, Whitehall, London.

20   Attended a charity concert, Royal Opera House, London.

22   Presented the 1983 Torch Trophy Trust Awards, Simpson's, Piccadilly, London.

24   Presented RAC Rally prizes, Bath.
Attended the annual dinner of the British Society of Magazine Editors, Royal Lancaster Hotel, London.

25   Visited the Royal Hospital School, Holbrook, Suffolk.

28   Attended a Kennel Club Committee Dinner, London.

December

1   Attended the Motor Industry Research Association's annual luncheon, London.
Attended a reception commemorating the 70th anniversary of the Anglo-Hellenic League,

	1	Belgrave Square, London.
	6	Attended the Burmah Castrol/IMI 1983 awards ceremony, Savoy Hotel, London.
		Attended the annual prizegiving at the Springfield Boys Club, East London.
	7	Attended the presentation of the Ferodo Trophy, Dorchester Hotel, London.
	13	Attended the annual dinner of the Institute of Chartered Secretaries and Administrators, Guildhall, London.
	19	Attended a charity carol service, St George's Church, Hanover Square, London.
	21	Attended the London Fire Brigade's carol service, Central Hall, Westminster.
February	8	Attended the funeral of the Duke of Beaufort, Badminton.
	9	Presented the Diamond Jubilee Trophy, Royal Automobile Club, London.
	10	Visited Cruft's Dog Show, London.
	14	Visited the National Leathersellers Centre and Spencers Tannery, Northampton.
		Attended a Women on the Move against Cancer reception, National Geological Museum, London.
	16	Left London to spend three days with the British Olympic bobsleigh team at Sarajevo, Yugoslavia.
	22	Left London for Canada, and arrived at Shearwater, Nova Scotia.
		Welcomed at Province House, Halifax.
		Visited and took tea with the Lieutenant Governor, Government House, Halifax.
		Attended a dinner given by the Premier of Nova Scotia, Nova Scotian Hotel, Halifax.
	23	Flew to Sydney, Nova Scotia and attended a reception given by the *Silver Dart* anniversary committee, Telegraph House, Baddeck.
		Unveiled a plaque commemorating the 75th anniversary of the first powered flight in the British Empire, St Mark's Lodge, Baddeck.
		Presented prizes to winners of a schools' poster competition, St Mark's Lodge.
		Visited Alderwood Rest Home, Baddeck.
		Toured the Alexander Graham Bell National Historic Park, Baddeck.
		Attended a dinner at the Baddeck Consolidated and Rural High School.
		Visited Cape Breton Adult Vocational Training Centre, Sydney.
	24	Unveiled a plaque commemorating the opening of the Town Hall, Louisbourg.
		Visited the Fortress of Louisbourg Museum.
		Attended a luncheon at the Hotel de la Marine, Louisbourg.
		Toured and dined at the Canadian Coast Guard College, Sydney.
	25	Left Sydney, Nova Scotia for New York and London.
March	12	Attended a gala performance of *Gloriana*, London Coliseum.
	15	Attended the County Safety Officers annual general meeting, RAC Club, London.
	16	Attended the Ponies of Britain Ball, Assembly Rooms, Stamford, Lincolnshire.
	23	Attended the memorial service for the Duke of Beaufort, Guards' Chapel, Wellington Barracks, London.
	29	Attended a reception given by the Prime Minister to honour the British Olympic team, 10 Downing Street.
April	2	Attended a Victoria and Albert Museum reception, Apsley House, London.
	3	Attended the 64th anniversary dinner of A.P. Bank Ltd, Savoy Hotel, London.
	4	Attended a reception marking General Motors' 75th anniversary, Merchant Taylors Hall, London.
	10	Attended the State banquet for the Amir of Bahrain, Windsor Castle.
	12	Attended the Amir of Bahrain's State banquet, Dorchester Hotel, London.
May	3	Opened Standard Telephone and Cables' new submarine cable facility, Southampton.
	9	Attended the opening of the Abbeyfield Housing Project, Rushmoor, Aldershot.
	14	Opened the British Car Auctions premises, Watton Summit, Preston, Lancashire.
		Attended the première of *Memed, My Hawk* in aid of UNICEF, ABC Cinema, Shaftesbury Avenue, London.
	15	Visited the British Motor Industry's Heritage Trust, Studley, Warwickshire.
		Attended an Institute of the Motor Industry's dinner, Penta Hotel, Heathrow, London.

	16	Opened the Institute of the Motor Industry's conference, Penta Hotel, Heathrow.
		Attended a Grand Day dinner, Inner Temple Hall, London.
	17	Attended a reception given by the Queen, Buckingham Palace.
	21	Visited the Chelsea Flower Show, Royal Hospital, Chelsea.
	22	Attended a gala performance of *Onegin,* London Coliseum.
	31	Visited the Royal Alexandra and Albert School, Reigate, Surrey.

June	2	Presented Royal Life Saving Society awards, Guildhall, London.
	5	Opened the International Vehicle Noise and Vibration Conference, Birdcage Walk, London.
		Visited Amberley Chalk Pits Museum, Gloucestershire.
		Opened Amberley Narrow Gauge Railway, Gloucestershire.
	7	Opened the Beardwood Centre for Arts and Lectures, Colfe's School, Lewisham.
	10	Attended Air Day, Church Fenton, Yorkshire.
	15	Visited the Le Mans International Motor Race, France.
	20	Visited the Army Equipment Exhibition 1984, Aldershot.
	24	Attended the Anton Dolin International Gala, Royal Opera House, London.
	26	Visited the Hunterstone Nuclear Power Station, Firth of Clyde.
	28	Attended the Society of Genealogists' annual general meeting, Royal Overseas League, London.

July	3	Opened Prince Michael Court for the Royal British Legion, Crayford, Kent.
	7	Visited the Army Air Corps air show and inaugurated the Museum, Middle Wallop, Hampshire.
	10	Attended the Queen's garden party, Buckingham Palace.
	11	Took the Salute at the Royal Tournament, Earl's Court, London.
	12	Attended the Claremont Garden Festival, Esher, Surrey.
	14	Started the 1984 Round Britain Offshore Powerboat Race, Portsmouth.
	16	Attended the Berkeley Square Ball, London.
	17	Visited Rediffusion Simulators Ltd, Gatwick, Surrey.
	18	Attended the Royal Patriotic Fund's annual general meeting, Royal Hospital, Chelsea.
	19	Attended the film première of *Supergirl,* in aid of the Muscular Dystrophy Group of Great Britain, ABC Cinema, Shaftesbury Avenue, London.
	22	Attended the British Grand Prix, Brands Hatch, Kent.

Engagements of **PRINCESS MICHAEL OF KENT**
August 1983-July 1984

August	22	Opened the *Woman's Hour* Painting Competition, Tate Gallery, London.

September	8	Attended a Son et Lumière display, Horse Guards Parade, London.
	9	Left London for a five-day visit to the United States of America to attend the America's Cup.

October	3	Presented the *Beautiful Britain in Bloom* awards, Café Royal, London.
	5	Visited Berisfords Ltd, Congleton, Cheshire.
	6	Attended the gala performance of *Little Shop of Horrors,* Comedy Theatre, London.
	12	Attended the British Fashion Council's Ball, Grosvenor House, London.
	14	Attended the Royal British Legion Poppy Ball, Intercontinental Hotel, London.
	15	Left London for Texas, in connection with the English National Opera's 1984 Tour.
	31	Attended the *Browns for Birthright* Fashion show and dinner, City of London.

November	1	Attended the Metropolitan Police charity dinner and concert, Cunard International Hotel, London.
	2	Attended the unveiling by the Queen of the statue of Earl Mountbatten, Foreign Office Green, London.
		Attended a reception given by the Prime Minister, Banqueting House, Whitehall.
	4	Attended the opening of the Beaufort School pool, Tuffley, Gloucestershire.